THE GAY JEW
IN THE
TRAILER PARK

MILTON STERN

Herndon, VA

Published in the United States by

STARbooks Press

PO Box 711612

Herndon VA 20171

Printed in the United States

Many thanks to graphic artist John Nail for the cover design. Mr. Nail
may be reached at: tojonail@bellsouth.net.

Titles by Milton Stern

The Girls (1985)

America's Bachelor President and the First Lady (2004)

Harriet Lane, America's First Lady (2005)

On Tuesdays, They Played Mah Jongg (2006)

Michael's Secrets (2009)

Men, Muscle & Mayhem (2011)

The Gay Jew in the Trailer Park (2012)

WHERE TO FIND ME

My blog "Have You Heard the One about the Gay Jew in the Trailer Park" can be found here: http://Gayjewmobilehome.blogspot.com/.

Please, do not share this book!

I once got a twenty-minute, oral, in-person, scathing review from a woman who borrowed a copy of one of my books from a friend of mine.

Make your friends buy their own copies, and then, I will listen to their criticism with pleasure.

I need the royalties.

I live in a trailer park, dammit!

Dedication

For Esmeralda, the Amazing Rescue Beagle, who was always there for me.

I started off my two novels with "none of this ever happened, but it could have." Well, on the following pages, "all of it happened, and maybe some of it shouldn't have!"

.

Contents

INTRODUCTION: HAVE YOU HEARD THE ONE ABOUT …

The Gay Jew in the Trailer Park?
The what?

I had been an apartment dweller for more than a quarter century, and I did not pursue home ownership until the market went nuts. I have lived in bad neighbors and neighborhoods that were worse. From Newport News, Virginia, to Hampton, Virginia, to Lake Worth, Florida, to West Palm Beach, to Washington, DC, and finally to "luxury living" in Rockville, Maryland.

My family would always call me impulsive, but that is because I don't share every detail of my life. I investigate before I plunge into something, and then I tell them what is going on. But let me be clear, if my parents were still alive, my moving into a mobile home would have killed them.

I have always been an oddball. My mother never heard me say, "But everyone else is doing it." She would always say, "Why can't you be like everyone else." I knew this about myself ever since I brought the green crayon to first grade class after reading *Harold and the Purple Crayon*, and everyone else brought red or purple crayons. All day, I heard, "Why did you bring a green crayon? Everyone else brought orange and red."

My longest apartment stay was more than twelve years in the sometimes gang-infested neighborhood of Mount Pleasant in Northwest Washington, DC. I had neighbors upstairs who fought constantly, and my friends urged me to move before one of them eventually shot a bullet through their floor into my bedroom. The rent was dirt cheap, and the location was convenient.

But even I got sick of it, so I moved to what they call luxury living in a multiuse development called Rockville Town Square in Rockville, Maryland. Unfortunately, this became the straw. If you have never lived in a multiuse development, don't. Every *feshtungina* weekend was a *facockta* festival or parade. There was constant noise from the rooftop nightclub or "Mommy on the Square" night, or concerts, etc. And in luxury living, no one, and I mean *no one*, looks at you or says hello. I knew three of my neighbors.

In Mount Pleasant and in Florida, even Newport News and Hampton, I knew everyone.

With home prices soaring out the roof, and my exhaustion with living in spaces previously occupied by someone else, while my neighbors were just on the other side of all my walls, I wanted new construction, no attachment to anyone else's home, and peace and quiet. A mobile home emerged as the answer. I had considered this for a long time, since 2002, and after much investigation, I took the steps to owning my own home. On July 1, 2011, I became Poor Gay Jewish Trash (PGJT). I grew up PGJT, so this wasn't a stretch.

What I shared over the course of my first year in a home on wheels were my adventures as a Gay Jew in a Trailer Park.

First lesson: Mobile Home Community is the preferred term, and I was determined not to move into a Trailer Park. If you were to see what I found, you would be surprised — and somewhat curious — and maybe a little appalled.

But, I have never cared what other people think about me.

Have you heard the one about the Gay Jew in the Trailer Park?

"Two Jews meet on the street."

"Why are all your jokes about Jews? Don't you know I find that offensive?"

"OK. Two Chinese men meet on the street, and one says, 'What are you doing for Yom Kippur?'"

Some may find my observations of Jews, Gays, Straights and Goyim offensive as I glorify or reinforce certain stereotypes. As a humorist and comedy writer, I wouldn't be doing my job if I didn't offend somebody, or at times, everybody.

And speaking of humor, what I share with you is all in fun. I don't take myself seriously, so why should anyone else?

So, *have* you heard the one about the Gay Jew in the Trailer Park?

REFLECTIONS ON A QUARTER CENTURY OF APARTMENTS

When did other people's marital problems become mine?

I marvel at the fact that I have been able put up with just about anything from my neighbors for longer than most people ... until...

For twenty-six years, I lived with people next to, above, or below me at any given time, usually two of the three, as I have either lived on the bottom floor or top with neighbors on both sides.

My first experience was a townhouse in Dutch Village in Newport News, Virginia. I managed to rent a home with a Lesbian couple next door and a Gay couple next door to them. Every morning, I would hear "Honey, what do you want for breakfast?" "Just oatmeal, Dear!" loud and clear through the paper-thin walls. They never fought, and I am still friends with one of them to this day (they broke up in the 1990s). Unfortunately, the guys whom I also befriended and enjoyed having as neighbors died of AIDS as many of my friends did during the height of the epidemic. They are all missed very much.

On the other side was an obsessive cleaner who I swear would pick up her furniture with one hand, vacuum under it then drop it from a height of three feet. She vacuumed night and day. But she was pleasant. Also, she had the greenest apartment I ever saw, and I am not talking about environmentally. Lime green shag carpet, green wallpaper, green sofa, green drapes. Green is my favorite color, but even I wouldn't go that far.

I also had a long-haired Dachshund-Yorkshire terrier mix named Daisy. My neighbors loved her, and she liked it there.

The experience of living in Dutch Village was a pleasant one until I decided to move into a smaller apartment in the same complex when my brother moved out and my car was stolen — the two events were not related. I then had people above me. The couple was pleasant enough, but I swear they had a pet elephant that used to run back and forth in their apartment night and day. The stairs to their apartment were next to mine, so I heard their comings and goings all the time. This also was the apartment that was robbed while I was at work. The manager's son was pulling up to apartments with a moving truck and using the master key to rob people. Fortunately, my parents were babysitting Daisy at the time. Long after I moved from there, they caught him. We don't know what took them so long because all of us suspected him.

However, all that did not deter me from renting my next apartment in what was called a "luxury complex" in Hampton, Virginia. This time, I was on the top floor. The couple below me screamed at each other and threw things all the time, and the couple next door? Oh my God. They would beat each other up daily. The irony is they were the last people you would expect to exhibit such behavior. They were a young, attractive, well-to-do couple who were always holding hands and friendly when you ran into them on the landing (all entrances were outside), yet once the door was closed. Take cover!

I could never figure out if they were having rough sex or just trying to kill each other. I would have called the police, but what do you do when the battering is equal opportunity, and from the sounds of it, you had an inkling this was something they enjoyed? I'll never forget the morning I greeted them, and they both had shiners. Neither of them batted an eye (pardon the pun) as they said good morning.

This is the time that I began to realize when you live in an apartment, other people's marital problems become yours whether you like it or not, no matter if you live in a dump or a luxury complex.

Nana, my mother's mother, lived below Aunt Anita and Uncle Walter during the 1950s (just so you know, you are going to meet a lot of my dead family members). She used to tell us how they would fight every night, so she would grab a cigarette, sit in the dark and listen until she got bored. Then she would bang a broom handle on the ceiling for them to shut up. When you only got one TV station in town, entertainment was listening to your relatives argue about money. Anita and Walter stayed married till death did them part. They were two of the nicest people I ever knew, but their marital problems became Nana's without her requesting permission to take ownership.

If you read *On Tuesdays, They Played Mah Jongg* and *Michael's Secrets*, there are two characters based on Anita and Walter, and one in the first book based on Nana (shameless plug www.miltonstern.com).

What followed was my five-year stint in Florida. First, I rented a cottage in Lake Worth that was attached to a house. What I soon learned was the house was a brothel. My friends and family are learning of this for the first time here. Halloween was always interesting — think about it.

If you think couples arguing is annoying, you should live attached to a brothel. I cannot begin to describe what I heard at all hours of the night — and day. And why is it that hookers in real life are nowhere near as pretty as the ones on TV? This place had the skank market cornered.

I then rented a converted butler's quarters built in the 1920s (my favorite decade of the twentieth century) that sat above a matching studio apartment that was once the nanny's quarters in Flamingo Park in West Palm Beach, Florida. Of all my apartments, this was my favorite and ironically, the smallest. It had one ten-by-eighteen living room/bedroom area and the other ten-by-eighteen half was divided into a kitchen and bathroom with a half wall dividing them. For once, I had windows all around (apartments usually have windows on one, or if you are lucky, two walls). It was in a great location and neighborhood.

My downstairs neighbor was a Muslim drag queen, who also had a side gig as a drama queen.

One day, he went to retrieve his mail out front, wearing a dress but with no wig, make-up or jewelry. I said hello then, "You really need to accessorize."

We were located behind a large home, and there were motion lights that came on when you walked down the driveway to get to our apartments. He used to complain that when I got up in the morning, I set off the motion lights and woke him up, so I was asked to walk on the other side of the house. The newspaper I had delivered would also disturb him, so I was asked to have it delivered to the front yard. If I came in late at night, I was to walk on the dark side as well. However, he *never* abided by these rules.

One night, he and his boyfriend were having a fight, and the motion lights kept going on and off, as each threatened to leave the other, and they were going back and forth at 2:00 am. So, I got up, walked downstairs, knocked on their door and said, "If you are going to practice your high drama to make a point, do it on the other side of the house, so the lights don't wake me up."

That drama drag queen had the nerve to complain to the landlord the next morning that I had embarrassed him, and they were having a problem and could not help setting the lights on and off because he was afraid to walk on the other side of the house since he thought he saw a snake. She tried to get angry with me, but I soon shut her up with how I had put up with his demands that I not set off the lights and how I had a wet paper every morning because I was not allowed to have it delivered to my own door and how I had to walk on the dark side of the house so as not to disturb him.

Again, someone's marital problems became mine. And this was the time I realized I will put up with just about anything for longer than most people.

In January 1997, I packed up Serena, my one-year-old toy parti-poodle, and everything that would fit into my 1992 Plymouth Colt — after having sold everything else — and moved to Washington, DC. My friend Christian, whom I had known since the early 1980s, told me to stay with him until I found an apartment.

A funny story. In all the time I knew Christian, I always wanted to say something after he introduced himself, but the situation never materialized until we went to a Christmas party in DC. We walked in, and he introduced himself to the host, "Hi, I'm Christian." Then I walked over and said, "Hi, I'm Jewish." We laughed until we pee'd then we laughed at that.

But I digress ...

Christian was renting an apartment in the Mount Pleasant neighborhood of Washington, DC, a garage-level, one-bedroom with a back patio we nicknamed the graveyard and no laundry hook-up but a dishwasher and central air. This was during the height of "Coffee Talk" on *SNL*, so we were doing all the "The peanut is neither a pea nor a nut, discuss ..." "A basketball is neither a basket nor a ball, discuss ..." when I said, "Mount Pleasant is neither a mount nor pleasant, discuss ..." and we laughed until we ... you get the idea.

The "Mount Pleasant is neither a mount nor pleasant" line has become a running joke with several of my friends to this day because guess who moved out of that apartment and guess who permanently moved in within a week of his arrival? Christian moved in with his drunk, pathological liar, sexually addicted boyfriend, and I took over the apartment and stayed there for twelve and a half years.

Where do I begin? I had to get a portable washing machine and wheel it to the sink the entire time I was there. I did not have a driveway or garage, so my car looked as if it had been in the demolition derby because of street parking and the non-English speaking *alta cocker* across the street who would move his car every hour and hit all the other cars. One morning, he parked in front of my car with his still in gear, and I couldn't move my car because his kept rolling into it.

I couldn't go out to the patio/graveyard because of the rats, and there was a crack in the foundation, so moisture was a problem. But as I keep stating, I'll put up with anything.

If you knew the dump I grew up in, you would understand my tolerance.

Talk about a dump.

The sad part is that when I was living at home in Newport News we were always under threat of foreclosure — as if any bank would want to be saddled with that crappy house. We also never were allowed to answer the phone because it might be a bill collector.

When I first moved out on my own, my phone rang in my new apartment, and I didn't know what to do. I picked it up, and I just breathed. I think it was the first time someone phoned an obscene caller.

My father used to say we had to do $10,000 worth of repairs on the house before they would condemn it. Thank you. I'll be here all week. Tip your waitress. Don't order the fish.

Anyway, where was I? Oh yes, the neighbors.

The first two were a Gay man and his straight woman roommate who wore spike heels along with their two barking dogs. The dogs never wore heels, nor did the Gay guy who weighed in at three-hundred pounds. She weighed three-hundred pounds as well. Not that there is anything wrong with that, but it gives you an idea how heavily they walked across their hardwood floors.

They never fought, just made a lot of noise. She eventually moved out, and he would get twinks to watch his place and walk his dogs when he traveled. They would never show up, and the dogs would whine all day and night, so I ended up taking care of them again and again when he would go out of town. I kept suggesting kennels, but he kept hiring no-show twinks. He did eventually have two responsible house sitters — a woman and her young daughter, but they would scream and fight all the time when they stayed over. They also had a habit of dropping everything on the floor.

Six years later, he moved out, and the landlord said she found new tenants he recommended, a woman and her daughter. You guessed it. And they brought their small dog — their ninety-pound small dog who barked more than the other two combined.

They would yell, scream, crash and bang. They dropped everything on the floor (didn't I just say that?), and just when things couldn't get worse, her estranged, drunk, self absorbed, loud British

7

husband moved in. He had one of those deep British voices you could hear in the next county. Now all I heard was screaming, yelling, crashing, banging, cars banging into garage doors (they had use of the driveway and garage, which backed up to my bedroom closet), more screaming, hitting, yelling, and what I suspect was the occasional gun shot, and I put up with it until ....

One day, I lost it. I marched upstairs, knocked on their door and told them one more sound and I was calling the police. And I yelled, "Get fucking counseling!" She had the nerve to complain she could hear me laugh and sneeze. Really, laugh and sneeze!?! I think those two things are more tolerable than yelling, screaming, shooting, hitting and the occasional bad sex.

They were so loud that all the neighbors on the street could hear them, and everyone asked me how I put up with it. As I said, for a low enough rent, I'll tolerate anything.

Again, someone else's marital problems became mine.

Then, the pompous queen next door rented out to a bunch of twenty year olds who threw a party every weekend. I complained because no one could get any sleep and called the pompous queen to have him talk to his tenants. They got mad at me for complaining and kept on throwing parties.

They complained about me, the quiet one. The one who never threw parties, or yelled, or for that matter, shot someone. I don't even own a stereo. I hate noise. I hate screaming and yelling. I don't even like loud music. I grew up in a house full of screaming and yelling, and I don't like to be around it. I often think of Anne Bancroft's line in *Torch Song Trilogy* about how she grew up in a house full of screaming and yelling, so she never screamed and yelled ... or something like that.

After the longest time at one address, and ironically the worst place I ever lived, I moved to Rockville. When I moved, my friends never said, "Where?" they said, "Thank God!" No one wanted to visit my apartment in Mount Pleasant because of all the noise ... and the occasional shooting victim on the sidewalk. Seriously, the first night there in 1997, someone was shot out front. The last week I was there in 2009, someone was shot out front.

I forgot to tell you about the guy screwing a hooker on my patio one night. He parked his AMC Hornet out front, took her up to my patio and screwed her right there. I came home to find them mid-coitus. Did they stop? No. Did I stop them? No. The guy was driving an AMC Hornet, so I figured he must not get laid often (I drive an

AMC as well), so I stepped over them and went inside. By the time I had opened the door again to walk Serena, they were gone.

So, I moved to Rockville Town Square, a multi-use development that allows dogs and has parking. As I mentioned before, living in a multi-use development is like living in the middle of a goddamn parade. Every weekend there is a festival or marathon or some other crap catering to unhappy couples and their rotten kids.

Serena lasted six months before she gave up and died at age fourteen. Four months later, I adopted an eight-year-old rescue beagle, I named Esmeralda, who was so frightened by all the noise outside that I had to walk her in one of the adjacent neighborhoods before she would go to the bathroom. I felt the same way.

Did I tell you there was a fire station next door? You guessed it. I could not open the windows because every ten minutes the sirens would go off.

And I managed to end up with fighting neighbors again. These two argued, hit, threatened and screamed and yelled and threw each other against the wall that abutted my bedroom. They were a combination of every couple I had the pleasure of sharing walls with for more than a quarter century. One morning, the missus came home at 5:30 am, carrying her shoes and wearing last night's dress. I counted the minutes before she started calling her husband racist names and begging him to hit her. "Go ahead, hit me. I dare you. Hit me!" She would say that all the time.

Once, I screamed, "Hit her goddamnit; I need to get to sleep."

I think she hit him, but he didn't hit her. He did choke her during sex. I know because I heard everything. I also heard her say she was going out and was surprised he wasn't going to stop her. From what I heard every night, I am guessing he gave her cash to tip the go-go boys just for some peace and quiet.

And now you see why I moved away to a quiet little town near a prison and a Walmart, into a small home that wasn't attached to anyone.

JESSUP? WHERE IN THE HELL IS JESSUP?

I have learned so much about mobile home shopping, but the most important lesson is that it is less about the home and more about where you park — I mean place it.

You may find a fantastic doublewide, but there may be only one community with an open lot, and then you find out the difference between a "trailer park" and a "mobile home community." And if you don't know the difference, drive around and visit some. You will learn very quickly. If you see cars on blocks, old school busses parked next to trailers, homes made of aluminum, honey, you just drove into a trailer park. If you see manicured lawns, modern manufactured homes, landscaped community areas and no junk cars or cars parked on the street, you just drove into a mobile home community.

Keep in mind that there are strict zoning rules about where to put a mobile home park ... I mean community, so chances are you will be off the beaten path a bit and near some industrial storage sites. Oh, and don't forget that all mobile home communities and trailer parks are in the direct path of tornados. So if you are a storm watcher, just follow the tornado to your new home.

I needed to get the tornado myth out there and move forward. Every time I mentioned my buying a mobile home, someone said, "What about tornados?" I lived in Florida for five years and never saw a hurricane. I lived in Rockville for two years, and we had an earthquake. If you live your life in fear, you are missing out on so much.

Back to the communities ...

I was out looking at various parks and communities one day, and I was a bit disappointed. I decided to take a break and go to the PW's Gay sports bar in Laurel (yes, one exists) for lunch when I passed by a well-manicured community with trees lining the entrance, so I doubled back and pulled in to drive around. There were no junk cars, and the place was immaculate. There were new cars parked in the two-car driveways, and they had sidewalks, and all the homes looked to be younger than ten years old.

That was when I decided to drive over to the sales office.

I indicated I wanted to see any homes for sale, and I preferred a new one because I have spent a lifetime living in someone else's former space. The park manager then drove me down the main street to look at the only new home they had left, and it was a model. My first impression was a good one. It had a deck and a shed, and a two-car driveway that was only big enough for compact cars (note to self: put the 1979 Lincoln Continental on eBay).

Once inside, I kind of liked it, but I wasn't thrilled. It was eight-hundred-twenty square feet, but I have to say they were the most efficiently laid out square feet I had ever seen. I remarked that there was little closet space, but the manager pointed out the Amish-built shed that came with it, and there was a true laundry room — not just a closet with a stackable. It also had something apartment dwellers rarely have, a back door! I also marveled at windows on every wall, not just one wall as apartments often have.

There were ceiling fans in every room, a kitchen island with pendant lights, a dishwasher, central air, and being the model, all the windows had tasteful drapes and window treatments. I expected to feel like a giant in a doll house, but surprisingly, I didn't.

I did ask to see a larger home, and he showed me one, but I was also informed that the only community that had an open space for that one was located in another park, and I had seen that park … and it was a trailer park not a community.

I thanked him for his time and asked him to send me the brochure on the model home since it had just been set up and they did not have printed brochures yet with the layout and dimensions. He did inform me that it had six to seven inches of insulation in the walls, floors and ceiling, and triple-pane windows and was Energy Star rated. From my research, I learned that any manufactured home built after 1996 had to meet stricter government codes than stick-built homes. That is what the rest of you live in — stick-built homes.

I then drove home, thinking about what it would be like to live in Jessup … JESSUP?!? Was that where I was? According to the GPS, I was in Jessup. I had been driving around so much that I thought I was in either Columbia or Elkridge. How in the hell did I end up in Jessup? Oh well, who cares?

When I got home, I did what anyone in the 21st Century does. I Googled Jessup. Well, there seemed to be, or had been, or still was a prison there. No problem, the criminals were locked up — I hoped.

And if not, "rough trade" could be fun. At least I knew there would be a tattoo parlor nearby, and once I Googled, I found one.

However, who knew such a place could be so convenient. There was a brand new gym only one mile away, along with an organic market, a "Chinese Take-Away" — as Hyacinth Bucket on *Keeping Up Appearances* calls it, and every Jew needs to be near a Chinese Take Away on Sunday. There was a barber right down the street. And the biggest plus was a Super Walmart right around the corner. I could become one of those "people of Walmart"! I also found I would be five minutes from two MARC train stations and only twenty minutes from a Metro Station. How convenient.

Then my phone rang. The manager called to tell me if I made an offer on the model, he would give me six months free lot rental. I asked why, and he said singlewides don't sell quickly, and it was the last one in the community. He also said they don't like riff raff and I was "good people," and they wanted good people in the community.

Had I stumbled upon a restricted community? I did see a black man pulling into the driveway of one of the homes. What would they do when they found out this "good people" was a Gay Jew?

I called the next day and made an offer.

BUYING A CAR WOULD HAVE BEEN EASIER

A few years ago during the housing boom, a real estate agent friend of mine (all Gay people have at least one friend who is a real estate agent) tried to convince me to buy a condo — a six-hundred-square-foot condo for $285,000. I even went so far as to get pre-approved for a mortgage. I was pre-approved for $400,000. I thought that was ridiculous. But banks were ridiculous then. For me to make payments on a $400,000 mortgage, I would have to forego food, car, utilities, retirement, drag wear, massages with happy endings, etc.

I come from the old school where your housing expense is no more than twenty-five-percent of your take home pay. Not the other way around! Needless to say, I did not make an offer on that sixty-year-old, former apartment, fixer-upper condo in North Fairfax, which did not have a washer/dryer hook-up, AC or a dishwasher. It also only had one window and street parking.

So, I sat on the sidelines while I watched idiot after idiot buy these expensive homes they had no business even visiting during an open house. I worked a couple of open houses for my real estate agent friend, and I found the buyers amusing. "Mmm, only $585,000 for this one bedroom condo sounds reasonable. I can get used to the trains going by at all hours of the night at these prices."

I kept saying to myself, "These homes are not going to appreciate. How high can these ridiculous prices go? This is all going to crash." And I am not even psychic. Am I the only one who saw that?

Now, if you are reading this from a part of the country where housing prices have seriously fallen, you are wondering why I went the mobile home route. Here in the DC region, prices were still ridiculous, and thanks to all those people who bought homes they had no business buying and banks lending to people whom they knew could not make the payments, to buy a home was now almost impossible without having at least twenty-percent down and a seven-figure income as well as a kidney to sell or a side gig as a hooker.

When I first looked at a mobile a few years ago, I was told you needed good credit and ten percent down. That was still the case when I finally made up my mind to do this, and ten percent of $60,000-

$90,000 is a lot easier than twenty-percent of $585,000. So, I thought this would be easier to settle as well. Hell, I could buy a $50,000 car in an hour by filling out a few forms (and I have no business buying a $50,000 car), so how hard could buying a mobile home be?

Boy, was I in for a surprise!

The first thing you need to know is that buying a mobile home is like buying a car, renting an apartment, and getting approval to buy into a co-op on the same day. Your new home will be titled through the DMV or in Maryland's case, MVA. However, a mortgage is a mortgage, and the park, excuse me, community, is another story entirely.

First comes the Mobile Home Community or Trailer Park depending on where you decide to go. You may have cash to buy the home, but the park has to approve you. They need the last two year's tax returns, W-2s, and 1099s; then they need the last two month's paystubs from all your jobs (I have two); then they need bank statements proving you have the security deposit, which is equal to one month's lot rental and first month's lot rental; a form filled out by your present landlord or managing company stating you are a good tenant; a letter from your veterinarian stating your dog is of good temperament and under thirty-five pounds and not one of five (yes, five) prohibited biting breeds; a list of your vehicles, year, model and condition (my youngest car was twenty-nine years old) — this is a trick question because you only get your two-car driveway and can have no more than two cars; a letter from all employers proving you are still employed; and permission for them to run a credit check. Then you must sign a form and give them a $25 check to process all this and receive the "Mobile Home Park Rules."

There are forty pages of Mobile Home Park Rules! And you better read them. You must mow your grass. You must get approval to landscape. You must get approval to paint your home exterior in an approved color. You must get approval to add an awning. You cannot let your kids under eighteen out after 10:00 pm or before 6:00 am. You must clean up after your dog. You must not throw loud parties. Your pipes must be "heat-taped" in winter (I had to ask about that one). You cannot do car repairs. You cannot have a non-titled car on the premises. You cannot have any trash on your property. You cannot have overnight guests for more than four days without registering them with the management office. You cannot sublet your home (my favorite rule). And so on and so on.

At least I knew it would be a quiet clean community. I also knew that everyone who said to me, "You can always rent it out," didn't know a thing about mobile home living. See above; not allowed!

Then comes the home mortgage. For the bank, you need all of the above, and don't say make copies of what I gave the community. You need to do it all over again because they are separate entities. In addition, you need to give a $1,000 deposit to hold the home and show you are serious and not a tire kicker. Yes, they call them tire kickers in the mobile home business, too. I couldn't find the tires. The axles are removed and sold back to the manufacturer once the home is parked. I wish I still had them because they fetch $700 — $1,000.

The best part is that every time they run a credit check, your credit score goes down a few points due to people running credit checks on you. How ironic. At least four times, credit checks will be run on you. So you better hope your score is a good range above seven-hundred (thank God mine was). They will sell to someone with as low as six-hundred-thirty but reluctantly and not without a bunch of other hoops to jump through.

Just when you think you have given them every piece of information you can, they call you up and say they need one more thing. I finally did say to the guy that I could go to the car dealer down the street and buy a car worth the same as the mobile home in an hour and with none of this information.

And finally, you must obtain mobile home insurance and have proof you did!

I never realized becoming Gay Jewish Trailer Park Trash was going to be so difficult and at times, expensive.

IMAGINE IF YOU WILL ...

While I awaited approval from the park and the bank, so many things were running through my head due to issues, which as a friend of mine says, "that are between me and my pharmacist."

When you grow up in a home on the brink of foreclosure and are trained not to answer the phone — when Ma Bell has actually been paid, you tend to think you are always on the brink of disaster. My brother kept asking when I was going to discuss living on Dresden Drive in Newport News, Virginia. My answer was that just about any financial decision I have made in my life was about Dresden Drive. Did I really want to dredge up all that childhood drek, too? Again, that is between my therapist and me.

However, to keep my only living relative happy, here goes — and this is it.

Our parents treated things and money as disposable. You have heard of disposable income, of course. For those who haven't or those who have come of age during the last two decades, disposable income is the money you have for fun after you have paid all your bills, put gas in the car, bought groceries and put some aside for your retirement and your kids' education. Believe it or not, there was a time you could do these things on a regular basis. As anyone my age — except me — can remember.

For my parents, you first spent your money on stuff or vacations you did not need, then you paid your bills, put gas in the car, bought groceries and did not put aside some for retirement and your kids' education.

My father, may he rest in peace, ended up in "Section 8 Housing for the Elderly" because my parents never planned ahead. Ironically, this staunch conservative, anti-New Deal Republican used to expound on how Franklin Delano Roosevelt ruined this country. Of course, I would remind him that if it were not for Franklin Delano Roosevelt, he would be living on the street with no home and no Social Security.

It is funny how one hates a program ... until he needs it.

Now, when you grow up in a situation where your parents are constantly trying to keep up with the Jeffersons while living like the Bunkers, you can go in two different directions. You can continue the pattern, or in the case of yours truly, you can do a complete one-eighty.

I don't try to impress anyone. I don't care what anyone thinks about what I drive or where I live or what I wear. Those that have seen how I dress can attest to this. I dress like Charlie Brown. A blind man can go into my closet and get dressed without worrying about what matches what. All of my clothes look alike — oxford shirt and kakis (and no jeans). I had to dress down for work last week, and no one noticed.

I have already told you about where I've lived, and I drive an AMC. As Rose Nylund once said, "I am the battered consumer; I drive a Gremlin!" In Mexico, the AMC was still a Rambler. Whenever I go to the car wash, the workers from Mexico always call me the man with the Rambler (incidentally, I have a Rambler American, too).

And most of all, I am going to live in a trailer park for God's sake! Point made.

As I have told you, Mother never heard me say, "Everyone else is doing it." What she would say was, "Why can't you be like everyone else?" I proudly march to my own beat, not even to that of a different drummer.

Now, has my oddness been a hindrance? You be the judge. I have been on a few dates where the guy came over to pick me up, took one look at the neighborhood and the apartment I lived in (especially in Mount Pleasant), and given me the look. You know the look. It is the one you get when you buy a new sofa, which requires an acquired tasted to appreciate, and when your friends see it, they say hesitantly, "Nice sofa," then look at someone else in the room and either drop their jaws or roll their eyes. Has this bothered me? No. If you don't like where I live, you have two options: either buy me a new house or don't see me again.

No one ever bought me a house, and I am still single.

My late partner used to say when someone would worry about what others thought, "Are they paying my rent?" I still use that expression. Now I will say, "Are they paying my mortgage?"

Here is a bit of wisdom: If you go through life worrying about what other people think about you, you will never be happy.

I am happy.

I do want to make one thing clear though. I am talking about worrying about what other people think about the material things you have, where you live, what you drive, what you wear, or even the job you have. If you like being a sanitation worker and it makes you happy, be a goddamn sanitation worker and go to work every morning with a smile on your face!

Here is an example: Every morning when I exit the Metro, there is a gentleman there whose job it is to empty the recycling bins. Instead of just emptying the bins, he parks his master bin (I don't know the technical term) near the recycling bins and collects everyone's used papers by hand and says "good morning" and "thank you" with a smile on his face. Do you know how many people walk by him, throw their papers into the master bin and don't say a word? I wonder if they are worried a colleague will see them say hello to a janitor. I walk right up to him, hand him my paper, and I say, "Good morning, how are you today? Thank you."

Grandma, my paternal grandmother, once told me, "Never make fun of a person's job. Anyone who does an honest day's work for an honest day's wage deserves respect." Good advice. Grandma worked retail until she was seventy-two. She also didn't care what others thought and pretty much said what was on her mind all the time. I miss her.

I have always worked two jobs (and still do) because I am afraid I'll end up homeless — again between my pharmacist and me. I waited on tables every weekend (and at times full time) until I was thirty-seven. I have worked retail, washed dishes, scooped ice cream, handed out towels in a gym (no jokes), mopped floors, cleaned houses (I tried to start my own maid business), and I even worked in a funeral home. I went to every one of those jobs with a smile on my face. And I still managed to put in at least eight hours of volunteer work a week and still do.

My parents were embarrassed that I was still waiting on tables on the weekends while managing a publishing unit full-time during the week. I wasn't. I did an honest day's work for an honest day's pay.

In spite of my work ethic, there will always be that voice in the back of my head telling me that I am only one paycheck away from sitting with Esmeralda on a blanket on 14th and H Streets with a sign that says, "My dog and I are homeless, please help us. Will work for Milk Bones."

I love Suzy Orman, and I especially love when she says, "Denied!" But I don't dare write a letter to her show asking approval to buy anything because I fear she will tell me, "Denied!"

I know it is silly. I have two incomes, no debt and savings for retirement. Why am I so worried?

With all that said, however, I think I may have finally reached a point where for once I just might be a little concerned about what other people think.

Imagine if you will ...

I didn't get approved by the park or the bank. Imagine I couldn't even get approved to move into a trailer! Now that would be humiliating. Even I, the one who doesn't give a shit, would have to change his identity and move to an undisclosed location.

I could see all those pretentious queens right now: "Oh her! She's the one who was turned away by a trailer park. She couldn't even afford a singlewide. Stay clear of that one."

NOW THE FUN BEGINS

The nail biting was over. I was approved. I was on my way to becoming Gay-Jewish Trailer Park Trash! My parents rolled over in their graves. Some of my friends (read acquaintances) disowned me.

But from what my home-owing friends told me, there is always something. Remember when I told you this was like renting an apartment, buying a car, and moving into a co-op at the same time? I wasn't kidding. For my fellow renters, what follows will very helpful for you when you decided to live single in a doublewide ... or in my case, a singlewide.

First came the insurance company. I have paid my own renter's insurance since I first rented an apartment, but this was weird. No one told me that the insurance company coordinates with the bank, and after writing a check for the first-year's homeowner's insurance, my insurance would be included in my mortgage payment (I almost typed rent there — bad habits are hard to break), and I will never write a check for home-owner's insurance again. I took care of this right away. I don't like to share explicit financial information, but let's just say it averages about sixty-percent of stick-built homeowner's insurance.

I was then asked to call the electric company — for once, not Pepco! Yay! For those who don't live here, Pepco is not the company you want during a terrorist attack. One summer, we had a fifteen-minute thunderstorm, and the power was out for ten days. The acronym stands for "Potomac Electric and Power *Outage* Company." I am now with Baltimore Gas & Electric.

I also had to set up the water, which apparently was already set up but needed to be put in my name although mine is a new home on a previously unoccupied lot. This was most apartment-like. All we had to do was turn a knob, and I would be happy and moist — that works every time.

However, the fun part was something that in all my research into making the mobile home plunge, I never knew or missed completely. There are no gas lines for a mobile home. I had to set up a propane account. Yes, those same tanks you have for your $1,500 Weber Grill are used for my new home for hot water, cooking and heat. This reminded me of one of my favorite movies, *The Long Long Trailer*, starring Lucille Ball and Desi Arnaz and directed by Vincent Minnelli.

Remember that yellow trailer, which by the way was Minnelli Yellow, a special color created by MGM for Mr. Minnelli as yellow was his favorite color. Watch *Til the Clouds Roll By* and fast forward to the Judy Garland number, "Who Stole My Heart Away," and she holds a scarf that is Minnelli Yellow. Great number, too. Mr. Minnelli only directed Miss Garland's scenes in that movie. That is why I told you to fast forward.

Where the hell was I? Oh yes.

In *The Long Long Trailer*, the second night they decide not to stay in a trailer park, and they get stuck on an old logging road, and one of the things Nicky (Desi) has to do is hook up the gas. So I wondered if my first cooking experience will be like Tracy's (Lucy's)? And is it illegal to cook in a mobile home when it is mobile? I do have windows up front with blinds and curtains like hers. Let's hook it onto a 1953 Mercury Monterey convertible and see!

So if you decide to go the mobile route, be prepared to sign an agreement with a propane gas company, which is more comprehensive than a new car lease or anything I needed for the other utility companies.

What I also forgot about since it had been so long since I changed jurisdictions — or even states — was that each of these new companies had to run a credit check. With each credit check, your score drops a point or two because people keep running credit checks. I would not be surprised to find mine had dropped by one-hundred points since everyone within a twenty-mile radius of Jessup, MD, had run a credit check on me.

I never realized it takes an excellent credit rating to become trailer park trash. Dolly Parton was right, "It takes a lot of money to look this cheap."

Then came my favorite part, dealing with the cable company. This actually went smoothly, until I got a call two days later telling me that I scheduled my appointment too far in advance and I must do the process all over again. So much for being punctual. Pepco also told me I scheduled my cancellation too far in advance. How does one cancel too far in advance? Your computers don't have calendars on them?

And last, I called the movers!

But there is always something, and in my case — two somethings.

First, after scheduling the movers, I looked at my calendar and realized the National AMC Rambler Convention in Annapolis was the same day as my move-in date, so I had to push it ahead one week. This also meant rescheduling the other utilities, even the ones I scheduled too far in advance, so I started the process all over again.

Then came the other something. Two days after approval, I got a letter in the mail from the Mobile Home Finance Corporation telling me I had been denied! I am usually not one to panic or worry, but my stomach went into my throat, I began to sweat in a very unlady-like manner, and I think I farted, too. I flailed my arms, and I screamed in a high-pitched tone that even Esmeralda couldn't hear.

DENIED — that Suzy Orman word I fear the most — my only fear in life. I thought I was approved. Now denied!?! Immediately, I called the trailer park sales office — I mean mobile home community showroom — and told them about the letter.

They laughed.

I was fine because my financing was through a local bank not this Mobile Home Finance Corporation. What happened was we went to them first because they used to have great terms and rates, but somehow in the last few months, mobile homes began to follow the same rules as stick-built homes. One now needed twenty-percent down. My offer was ten-percent down and a fifteen-year mortgage. They immediately sent my application to a local bank, and it was approved. The Mobile Home Finance Corporation had to inform me that I was denied even though we withdrew my application.

By the way, I had received a letter from them two months prior telling me I was approved. I guess it's like those credit card offers — "You have already been approved." Then you apply, and you get "Denied." Much like having someone tease you for a week before your first date, then denying you sex when you actually go on the date. Not that this ever happened to me ... recently.

Fine or not, I really didn't need to get a letter like that this late in the process, and I'll never be able to replace the wine glasses that broke when I screamed. No, it wasn't Memorex.

Now, if you are reading this because you are considering the move to a mobile home, you heard it here first that the rules have changed and ALL mortgages are being treated the same. Use a local bank or credit union as I did.

If you are one of those people paying a thirty-year mortgage on an upside-down house, yes, you read the above correctly — ten-percent down and a fifteen-year mortgage. Also, my payments will be twenty-five-percent of the national average for a house payment, and I get to live with like-minded people. Jealous?

The Gay Jew in the Trailer Park

CLOSING DAY

I knew this day was coming. On January 1, I made it a goal to own a mobile home by August 1. Little did I know how nervous I would be the morning of the big day.

I have not thrown up since March 1997. I remember it, too. Out of curiosity, I had eaten a can of fruit cocktail in heavy syrup. I do not like fruit cocktail in heavy syrup, but for some reason, I bought a can. It was like the time Mary Richards bought asparagus even though she hated asparagus. She hoped to someday like it, and she wanted a change. That was the episode when she moved out of that fabulous studio apartment. Ironically, when she moved, she said after everyone left her new place, "I ... hate it."

Why am I telling you this? I don't know. Oh yeah. The morning of the closing, I thought I was going to throw up for the first time since 1997, and I hadn't even eaten fruit cocktail in heavy syrup. I don't know why I was nervous. After all, I had spoken to the salesman every day for the prior week. I had all my ducks in a row. I think I was staring all those years of debt in the face and making myself sick.

What if I, like Mary, hated it? I can't just break the lease. I will own the goddamn place. I could always pick it up and move it. I could always change my mind. No, I told myself I was going to do this, and do this I was.

I had a few moments to kill, so I decided to go to the car wash. My phone rang, and it was the sales office. They wanted to know if I had this form and that form. Of course I did, but when I saw his number on the caller ID, I panicked, and I thought I would throw up all over my original upholstery.

I arrived at the sales office fifteen minutes early, and I was told they had to redo one form because it was off by $32.46. Then, I sat in the room and waited.

Now, here is more advice or wisdom or shared experience if you will for those considering the manufactured plunge. Although no lawyers are involved and there are no exorbitant settlement fees (I only had to pay $45 for a settlement fee), you still have to initial this and sign that and have your license and passport photocopied (I guess to make sure you aren't using your home for a terrorist cell). This process takes one hour and three checks — settlement fee, down payment, and appraisal fee (which they took out of my deposit, but they wanted a separate check for the appraisal anyway to keep it kosher).

I did learn something. Because of the bad economy, all home sales — manufactured, modular, condo, mcmansion, what have you — are down, so I got a sweet deal. My home appraised for thirty-eight-percent more than I was paying. Built-in equity, they tell me. As a lifelong apartment dweller, I have no idea what that means, but I was told it is a good thing.

Remember when I said this was like buying a car, renting an apartment and moving into a co-op at the same time? For one hour after the settlement, I sat with the park manager who went over the rules, which I had already read quite thoroughly, line by line. Two violations, you get a warning. Three, and you are asked to pack up your house and leave. I love rules!

Try that in your gated community or condo! "Excuse me, you need to take your home and leave, NOW!"

I think if all residents could do this, the world would be a happier place. Do you know how hard it is to evict people from an apartment? We tried to do that in one of my former residences (I won't tell you which, but you can probably guess because the experience was neither a mount nor pleasant, discuss), and it was a disaster. We even had the cooperation of those living in the buildings on either side, yet they are still living there today.

I, again, initialed and signed, and initialed and signed the park rules and park lease.

Then, they handed me the keys.

Did I cry? Did I smile from ear to ear? All I could think was, "I have to buy my own trash cans, a weed eater, rake, garden hose …"

When I was back in my car, I did call my brother and make a sound into his voicemail we have made since we were little kids that indicates extreme happiness — a sound rarely made. My father used to call it the pig noise and would threaten to beat us every time he heard us doing it. I won't share the sound because it has been known to cause cats to commit suicide.

After closing, I had to go to the Post Office to pick up my mailbox key because that is yet another thing that is handled separately. Jessup has the most quaint post office in the country — just two guys and a small counter, and oh so friendly!

Then, I went to the nearest grocery store. Again, everyone was oh so friendly. "Welcome to Jessup. You are going to love it here. Did you move here to be closer to the women's prison and visit your sister?"

I don't have a sister.

After living in the city and then in a luxury apartment, I forgot how friendly people can actually be. I think I am going to ... like it.

Esmeralda, we were not going to be living in Rockville anymore!

RUNAWAY DOG

Since the weekend before the actual move was a holiday weekend, I took advantage of the time to bring over all my stuff for the shed, which before had been in my bedroom closet, and get the bathrooms set up and decorated thanks to Jaclyn Smith and her coordinated accessories. I also thought it would be a good idea to bring Esmeralda out one day to see our new home.

This isn't the first time I have moved with a dog. Serena moved twice with me. When she was one, we moved from eighty degrees in West Palm Beach to thirteen degrees in Washington over Martin Luther King Day weekend in 1997. She adjusted quite well after two days in my Plymouth Colt with all our remaining belongings. Sure, she shivered, but once inside, she was cozy and warm, especially with Christian's pug, Yoshi, who fell in love with her immediately. Whenever I was in the room with them, I felt as if I was intruding. Thank God, they were both spayed and neutered.

The second move with Serena was to Rockville. By then, she was thirteen, deaf, blind in one eye and losing what little sight she had in the other eye. I brought her up after the furniture arrived. She didn't care once she found her food, but she did sleep in the closet the first couple of nights with her head on one of my shoes. She did adjust well, but six months later, she died. She hated Rockville more than I did, do, still do, done, did. Whatever.

I guess for Serena it was easy because I had held her when she was one day old. I babysat her mother, Venus, while she was still nursing Serena and Muchy (pronounced mooocheee), her brother. She had no abandonment issues.

Serena was a toy parti-poodle (two color poodle) and as such a rescue, since up until recently, breeders would kill them because they could not be registered and were considered part of a bad gene (ironically all breeding poodles give birth to one parti-poodle at some point). Venus was pregnant when my friend John rescued her. When Serena was born, he saw she was two colored and said I could have her if I didn't say who gave her to me. I kept my word until the AKC recognized parti-poodles as a breed. Serena was a tuxedo parti-poodle with black face and back, white feet and a bow-tie pattern on her chest in white, perfectly symmetrical. She would have been a champion show dog. She was beautiful, and she knew it. I never saw a dog pose for the camera the way she did.

Esmeralda is a different story. Four months after Serena died, I was delivering items to the Washington Animal Rescue League our car club, the Straight Eights (yes, even with a name like that, it is a Gay car club), collected. I was feeling a bit lonely, so I strolled down the hallway of this fantastic no-kill facility and spotted a Jack Russell Terrier who looked as if he would make a good pet, but he was a bit needy. Sharing the room with him was an aloof beagle, who looked as if she had given birth non-stop for years. She was a bit skinny and did not make any effort to get my attention. She had given up. The sign said she was eight years old, and the name they gave her was Lulabell.

Always the guy who likes the special needs and underdogs (Serena had luxating patella, canine IBS, and an alpha personality that scared pit bulls), I asked for more information on Lulabell. It turned out she spent her first seven or so years in a puppy mill as the "breeding bitch," in a cage and possibly gave birth three times a year for her entire life there. Her front teeth wore worn down from chewing on the cage. From the puppy mill, she was rescued by a well intentioned but psychologically challenged women in Mississippi who had a bit of a hoarding situation. She had more than three-hundred dogs living on her property and in her — brace yourselves — mobile home.

The Washington Animal Rescue League along with several other rescue organizations rescued her and the other dogs. Lulabell, who was very beta, had been attacked (a very small piece of one ear is missing, and she has bite marks on her snout), and she was food shy. She would only eat if no other dog was around for fear of being bitten again. She was and still is scared of any barking dogs, except other beagles.

Lulabell was also considered a challenge because of her appearance. She is a beautiful tri-color beagle, but her nipples and belly are distended due to multiple births. This apparently grossed out some potential parents. What did I care? At close to fifty, you should see my nipples.

She also sneezed a lot due to her allergies.

I couldn't help myself. I adopted her, and because she sneezed as much as I do, I named her Esmeralda, after Alice Ghostley's character on *Bewitched*, who would sneeze and the thought nearest to her cerebellum would materialize. Or was it her cerebral cortex?

Esmeralda was her first real name (Lulabell was a rescue league designation), and I was her first human. I often say, Serena thought she was a person, and Esmeralda thinks I am a dog with cash and a car.

For six months, Esmeralda would not eat until I went to sleep. For the first few weeks, she lived under the premise that I would take her back at any time. She had been fostered a few times before I got her. We were like strangers in the same home. Slowly she came around, and the first real sign was at the Straight Eights annual meeting when she insisted on sitting on a chair next to mine. She is not one to snuggle, but she showed her loyalty in other ways.

The reason I am telling you all this is because I should have known better than to take Esmeralda to my new home before the furniture and the rest of our stuff arrived. I thought it would be good for her to see where we would be moving.

What is amazing is that I am the self proclaimed expert on everything, so how could I be so dumb?

When we arrived at the house, I took her inside, and she freaked. I went out to the car to get a load of stuff, and when I opened the front door, she bolted out and ran under the car. I called her, and she came out, then I grabbed her quickly and took her back inside.

It was obvious she thought I was going to leave her in this house, especially since it was a mobile home (how could she tell?). I stayed inside with her and acted as if all was normal, putting this and that away and even doing a load of laundry. But, she continued to whine and follow me everywhere as if I were going to leave her.

Then, I wanted to try the keys I had copied for the back door. So I slowly opened the door and blocked it, so she couldn't get out ... or so I thought.

She leaped over my leg onto the back porch and into the woods. I hollered after her and dropped my keys. I screamed, "Esmeralda, come here! Come here now!" She took one look, and off she went. I chased after her until I could no longer hear movement. I screamed her name over and over.

I then looked around. I was in the woods. I never go into the woods. I am a Gay Jew, I don't even hike. I was scratched and bitten, and I thought I was covered in spiders. I was wondering if I now had Lyme Disease. I tripped on vines and my shoes were filthy. I am known for my clean Chuck Taylors, and my white Chucks were covered in dirt. What was I doing?

33

I exited the woods realizing it was getting me nowhere. A lady drove by and asked if I lost my cat since she heard me yelling. I told her about Esmeralda, and she was so nice (as everyone is in these parts) and looked to see if Esmeralda was wandering the neighborhood. I called my brother who assured me she would come back because this is what beagles do. He has one named Charlie.

I got in my car and drove around to see where the woods ended. Fortunately, there was a fence on the other side some two or three acres away, so I returned home in case she decided to come home. By now, forty minutes had gone by with no sign or sound from Esmeralda.

Then, I did something I rarely do. I prayed. The last time I prayed was during a violent allergy attack when I prayed for death. This time I asked God to bring back my dog. I mean how stupid could I be? I buy a house and lose my dog in the same week. I needed God's help.

Surprisingly, I was not in a panic. When I am in a panic, I get diarrhea. I did have to pee, but I always have to pee.

I sat down on the back porch and waited. I had never had this happen before, so I didn't know how long one should wait before calling the … whom do you call when your dog runs away? I felt assured someone would find her. She has a microchip and her tag has my number on it (that reminded me, I needed to order a new tag). But what if she never showed up and ended up spending the night in the woods? What if I never saw her again?

By now, it had been an hour, and I then started to panic even though in the back of my mind, I knew she would come back. But when?

I had one trick left up my sleeve, so I thought I would give it a try. In my loudest but calmest voice, I yelled, "Bye Esmeralda. I'm leaving now. Want to go for a ride in the car?"

Less than a minute later, I heard a jingling behind me. I looked around front to the driveway, and guess who was sitting by the passenger side of the car as if nothing had happened?

I slowly walked up to her and said quietly, "Come here, Esmeralda." She wagged her tail and walked over to me, and I scooped her up. She was wet, muddy, dirty, and covered in sand. Sand? Where in the hell did she find a beach in Jessup?

I called my brother, and he jokingly asked if I was going to beat her. I didn't even yell at her. I was so glad to see her. All I said was, "Where have you been? As soon as we get back to the apartment, you are getting a bath!"

I carried her inside, and she drank some water and ate a Milk Bone as if the prior hour had not even occurred.

Let this be a lesson to anyone. Don't take your dog to your new home until it looks like your new home with all your old furniture ... unless all your old furniture is crap.

I still want to know where the beach is in Jessup.

MELT DOWN

Moving days are always loads of fun.

For those who don't know me, let me tell you something about myself. I don't accept help easily. Having learned at an early age that I would need to take care of myself, I have become fiercely independent where all aspects of my life are concerned. I had a boyfriend once who told me the most frustrating thing about me was the fact that I wouldn't let anyone help me. The most frustrating thing about him was he would get drunk and leave his toupee in the bushes.

When I moved to Rockville, the only help I needed was for my friend, Mindy, to watch Serena on the day the movers arrived. By 4:00 pm that day, I was all moved in, and every box was emptied. I couldn't ask her to watch Esmeralda because they don't like each other.

However, something told me this move would be different. My brother, Alex, offered to help me on the Friday before the movers came, and I accepted his offer. He was really going out of his way, driving up to Rockville — a three-hour drive from Newport News — to spend about three hours, helping me cart my electronics and clothes in his truck to Jessup. This was a huge help because the one thing that takes the most time during a move is emptying the wardrobe boxes while the movers wait and charge by the hour. I decided with Esmeralda with me, it would be a nightmare if I waited until the official move day to do this.

Also, for those who don't know me, my clothes are big and my shoes bigger — size fourteen. When I travel, I cannot take more than two pairs of shoes or I will need another suitcase. After helping me, Alex drove home in a series of thunderstorms, making a three-hour drive a four-and-a-half-hour drive! I cannot express my appreciation for what he did. He said it was fun. It takes so little I guess.

I cannot imagine spending a few hours with me, ordering you around to put this there and that over there fun! I annoy *myself*!

Did I also tell you I like being in charge and giving orders? They say every eleventh person born is a leader. I consider myself a number eleven. Actually, "they" didn't say it; Lucy said this to Charlie Brown. The crap I remember.

My friend, Frank, or as I refer to him, the "Martha Stewart of McLean" (he doesn't know I refer to him this way because I just thought this up), called me on Friday night and asked if I needed help. I said, "Oh, I'm fine; everything is packed. My brother helped me move all my clothes and electronics today. He was a huge help. The movers will be here in the morning, and they are the best." He decided he better help and would be at my apartment at 8:00 am. I accepted his offer. Wow, was I maturing?

There is also something else I must share. I like things to happen on time. Not early, never late, but always on time! I can be a real pain in the ass about this. I also had a boyfriend say he couldn't point out my faults because I would beat him to the punch. He was a nose candy freak who couldn't achieve an orgasm.

There is an entire list of adjectives to describe me, and I add to it more than anyone. For the purposes of this story: obsessive, overbearing, controlling, irritating — just to name a few.

Saturday morning came, and the movers and Frank both arrived five minutes early. I was not ready! I needed five minutes to get the apartment concierge to open the loading dock and lock the elevator. She was late! Frank came up, and I started barking, "Take the laundry basket and granny cart to the car!" I have a granny cart because my apartment was two blocks (no kidding) from the parking garage. Frank didn't say a word and did what I told him. He was so calm.

In ninety minutes, the movers were all loaded up. I used the same company that moved me to Rockville, Great Scott Moving, and one of the same guys also helped with that move. They are the best movers, so I have to give them a plug!

Now, all I had to do was lock up and get in the car and go, so I could arrive before they did. As I was pulling away with Frank behind me, I saw the moving truck ahead of us.

They arrived at the house five minutes before we did. Oh no. Not early, never late, always on time!

Now, the nervous wreckedness began. I immediately opened the house and showed them where everything was to go.

The problem with an empty space and a space with furniture is one looks so much bigger than the other! Seriously, I didn't know this? Apparently, other people do.

Here is something else you may not know about me. I am a bit claustrophobic. I don't panic in elevators, but I don't handle tight rooms, especially full of people, very well. The front bedroom, if you can call it that, is seven-by-twelve. My original plan for setting up that room was not working, and suddenly, I was in the middle of this little room with a bunch of boxes, two book cabinets that did not fit and a desk that was in the way.

I don't know if you have witnessed a meltdown, but you have not lived until you have seen one of mine.

First, I started spinning around — kind of like Linda Carter turning into Wonder Woman, except without the blur or the magic bracelets. Then, I started flailing my hands. Then, I started a combination of whining and kvetching accompanied by high-pitched sounds that can be heard miles away by rodents and birds of prey. I kept repeating, "Nothing fits! Nothing fits! This isn't going to work! This isn't going to work!"

Can you picture all of this?

While Frank was considering calling a shuttle from Saint Elizabeth's, my phone rang. It was the cable guy. He was fifteen minutes early! They are never early. I told him, "I am not ready for you! Give me fifteen minutes! We just arrived!" He said no problem; he would go get a bite to eat.

Then I melted even more. Thank God for Frank. He said, "Just step out of the room. Come over to the kitchen, and let's tackle something else first. Breathe. Breathe. Count to ten."

I stepped out of the office. In about fifteen minutes, I was fine.

We unpacked everything else in about three hours. Then, we took the oversized book cabinets out to the curb, put a "FREE" sign on them, and they were gone in less than an hour.

Problem solved.

Ironically, the appeal of this house was finally having a real office space. Who knew such a gift would send me over the edge?

FOUR-LEGGED WRECKING CREW

Forget everything you've ever read about moving with your pets. It is all bull shit!

You remember a week ago my lovely rescue beagle, Esmeralda, ran away for an hour? That was nothing compared to the first few days in our new mobile home.

Surprisingly, the one thing all the advice columns said not to do, I did, and it went well. They said (and I really wish I knew who "they" were) have someone watch your dog on moving day, then slowly introduce your dog to your new home. I took her with me. I also purchased a fifteen-foot chain, so she could be outside watching while the movers brought everything in.

Before you call the Humane Society, the chain is only for when I am outside, so she won't go nuts while inside watching me. Esmeralda has this incredible need to be where I am, although she refuses to sit next to me.

As you know, I only have a general history of her first eight years of life, but apparently, she had been hooked to a chain before because she wasn't even bothered by it. She watched patiently as my things were unloaded from the truck and taken inside and wagged her tail the whole time.

I thought, "Wow, this is going quite well. She is really adjusting." Once everything was in, I unhooked her, walked her around a bit then took her into our new home. I set up her water dish and some food, just as I was advised by "they." She drank some water then followed me around. She also witnessed my meltdown. Finally, she found a spot in the corner behind my bistro table to curl up and nap or observe.

I was so pleased.

Now, I must make one clarification. Mindy does not dislike Esmeralda. She just doesn't want her in her home again. The reason is because Esmeralda decided to damage an expensive custom-made window blind five minutes after being left alone. I take the blame because I knew Esmeralda hates blinds. She damaged them in my apartment the first week she was there, and the trick was to roll them half way up ... or so I thought.

Frank, who was still with me, and I decided to run an errand to Lowe's and get some dinner on moving day. I rolled all the blinds halfway up, closed all the doors to the bedrooms and bathrooms, and fed Esmeralda before leaving the house.

Before I go on, I have to share one more thing about my sweet little beagle. The Washington Animal Rescue League evaluated her and declared her a "purple" dog, meaning laid back, docile, just needing a quiet place to rest and be comfortable. I wonder what quack evaluated her, Dr. Phil?

That first week in my apartment, she removed a door frame, took down the blinds, knocked over a lamp, and pretty much drove herself crazy. OK, it was the first few weeks in a new home. But understand — the bitch has only six teeth and can chew through a wall!

Silly me, I figured by now, she was done with her need to tear down a home piece by piece. Was I a fool!

When Frank and I returned two hours later, she had removed the blinds from both windows in the living room and dining room, and she had destroyed them in the process. She also left a vengeance poop on the living room floor by the front door.

OK, she was adjusting. I didn't even yell at her. I just cleaned up the mess, and we went back to our business. Besides, they were just $4 mini-blinds. She didn't touch the window treatments. She only hates blinds. I did put scratch guards on the door, door frame and window sills before moving day, so I was safe there.

And, she never damages furniture or curtains! Or so I thought.

The next day, I left to go and clean the old apartment and run a few more errands, mainly to get new blinds. When I returned …

My lovely little Esmeralda removed all the curtains and left another vengeance poop on the floor by the front door. I yelled. I know I shouldn't have, but jeez, she had chew toys, food, a Kong filled with treats, and more than anything, a lovely new home with no screaming neighbors, sirens, or loud fire alarms going off every time Five Guys burned an order of fries! She just wagged her tail because she thought it was all a game.

Did I mention I also take her on *four* forty-five-minute walks a day! How much energy can an old "purple" dog have?

I put in the new blinds on and rolled them all the way up, winding the cords around the valances, which she generously left in place, probably because she couldn't reach them … or so I thought.

On Monday, I returned to work, and I called a dog walking service to come over that evening to interview because I thought that having a mid-afternoon break from her new career, razing mobile homes, would be entertaining for her.

I came home a couple of hours early and discovered something very odd. Two of my dining room chairs were on their sides and pictures I had on a side counter were knocked over. Had someone broken in? And yes, there was another pile of vengeance poop near the front door.

That little dog had managed to walk on top of the dining room table, knocking over the chairs either on the way up or down. She also left nose prints on the windows, paw prints on the table and teeth marks on the chairs. I was planning on replacing the table anyway because it was a tad too big for the space — but not so soon!

In addition to all the above, she had howled, whined and barked herself hoarse. When she tried to bray, she sounded like Brenda Vaccaro. I looked at her and said, "You need to quit smoking menthols."

I was at my wits' end! I was also becoming quite religious asking God to help me not to kill this poor helpless creature I decided to rescue, who was destroying my new home piece by piece.

I considered getting a crate and putting a sign on it that said, "Beagle Jail. You do the crime; you do the time." But after spending the first eight years of her life in a cage, she would probably hang herself in her cell or shank me with a Milkbone carved into a knife when I returned home.

As I was taking all the damaged goods to the curb for the garbage men to pick up, my neighbor across the street, a nice retired lady, came over and said, "Are you throwing all the window treatments away? They're new."

I told her the story and how I was interviewing dog walkers, and she said, "I'll walk your dog twice a day while you're gone. My husband says I am too old to get another dog, so I would love to watch yours."

And she agreed to give her two walks for $2 less a day than I was going to pay the dog walker for one. Also, since she had two beagles at one time, she knew the craziness of the breed. I invited her in, and she took Esmeralda on a test walk. Esmeralda, who usually doesn't like anyone but me, was not upset in the least (I did walk with them to be sure).

We made a deal, I gave her the keys, and as I opened the door to say goodbye to her, I noticed that the wood was completely scratched away from the legs of an antique telephone table by my front door that was Nana's. There were also bite marks on the top of it. I rolled my eyes at Esmeralda, who was lying on the couch looking all innocent and wagging her tail.

The next day, I called Mrs. M around noon to see how the walk went. She said everything was fine, and she stayed with Esmeralda for a while and watched some television if that was all right. I had no problem with that.

When I returned home, everything was fine. My dog was tired, and I walked her as usual before dinner and again before bedtime, and that night she slept and snored peacefully in a new space she claimed in the corner of my bedroom closet. I put a pillow in there for her to be comfortable.

Is she spoiled? Yes. Shut up.

There is an old Jewish joke, or story if you will, that goes like this:

An old man is on the roof of his home during a flood. A helicopter flies overhead, and the pilot says, "Grab the ladder and climb up."

The man says, "Don't worry; God will save me."

A woman in a boat rows by and says, "Hop in!"

The old man says, "Don't worry; God will save me."

A talking whale swims by and says, "Hop on my back."

And the old man says, "Don't worry; God will save me."

The old man drowns as the flood waters rise and upon arriving in heaven says to God, "Why didn't you save me?

And God says, "Are you *meshugina*? I sent you a man in a helicopter, a woman in a row boat and a *Mydamn* talking whale for *My* sakes?"

When I looked for a mobile home, this park — I mean community — was not on my list, but I pulled in anyway upon seeing the manicured lawns. They had one new home left. I bought it. If Esmeralda had not removed the curtains and blinds, I would not have thrown them out. If I had not thrown them out, Mrs. M would not have come over to talk to me and offer to be her dog walker — and occasional babysitter if I go out of town, which is a better prospect than a stranger.

Someone at work said I had a guardian angel. Miracles happen all the time; you just need to know how to recognize them when they do.

Another good thing about Mrs. M is that she is the neighborhood busybody. She watches out her window all day to see what is going on, so I don't have to buy an alarm system. However, I think she is using my home as a base operation for her spy game because my kitchen blinds, which Esmeralda cannot reach without a trampoline, are always turned up when I return home, indicating she is watching someone. She also said she would use the dog walking money for Bingo. I don't know. The TV is always tuned to QVC when I return home.

But who am I to question God ... Oh yes, I'm Jewish; we always question God.

THE BIG MAN
IN THE LITTLE HOUSE

Now that Esmeralda had settled in, I could start to enjoy my new home, and she could, too. Esmeralda discovered that having a long house with an open floor plan makes a great beagle race track. During sudden bursts of energy, she runs from one end of the house to the other while barking at me when she passes by. This lasts about five minutes and is funny to watch because she is a little clumsy and has a big *tuchus*, like mine. I think she is also Jewish. Do you know what they call a Jewish ballerina? A klutz.

But enough about her. I'm the one paying the bills, and I can operate the can opener!

As I settled in, there were some subtle differences I was beginning to notice.

In a luxury building, you have a concierge who accepts your packages for you. This is a major convenience. Here they leave packages on your porch. However, if you are as fortunate as I am to have the community spy living across the street, who is also your dog walker, she will sign for them and bring them in for you. Or as I did for Mrs. J, the chain smoker next door, I signed for hers and gave it to her when she arrived home on Saturday.

In a luxury apartment building, you have garage parking. This is lovely until you go grocery shopping and realize you live two city blocks from the garage. This is not a joke. I lived two city blocks from the garage. I had to go through three security doors before entering the hallway, then walk to the other end of the building while carrying bags. As I told you, I ended up buying a granny cart and a dolly.

My mobile home has a small driveway, and it is a pleasure to walk from my car to the front door in just a few steps. It is also a pleasure to walk the dog without having to wait for an elevator that may or may not be in service ... or have a vicious Bijon waiting inside the elevator to attack your dog because her alcoholic owner never trained her.

But, here is where size matters. My driveway, although a two-car affair, can only accommodate two subcompacts, side-by-side. Before I moved, I had to sell my 1979 Lincoln Towne Car because her ass stuck out in the street.

In a luxury building, the crazy people are outside and cannot get access without a fob — unless they move in next door. I never told you about the woman who would search the online sex offender registry every time a new tenant moved in. She was convinced everyone was on the registry (the same way Suzanne Sugarbaker reported Charlene's nanny to *America's Most Wanted*). This former neighbor of mine thought everyone wanted to rape her.

I heard she was attacked by three Gay men right outside the building. Two held her down, and one gave her a makeover.

Here, the crazies have their own homes, and guess who is the world's foremost crazy magnet? Me. That's right. I have a witness.

My friend, Ed, and I were at the DC Auto Show, and the only crazy in the place found me and started a conversation. Ed couldn't get over how I am a crazy magnet. Sometimes I end up dating them — it cuts out the middleman.

We have one here who knocks on your door asking if you need yard work. Yard work? I have a yard that is no bigger than my driveway. I can mow my grass with an old fashioned reel mower in ten minutes. He always seems to knock on my door just as I'm getting ready to take a piss, too. How curious.

A luxury building is noisy. Seriously, I have never lived in or visited a luxury apartment building that was not noisy. Someone is always throwing a party, or the location is next to a busy street. The hallways are filled with people having loud conversations as they try to impress their neighbors with where they are going and what they are going to spend when they arrive there. I think they are purposely designed to allow hallway conversations to travel into your apartment by pretentious people and those that love them.

Mobile home communities are quiet. That's right, quiet. People stay in their homes. I usually sleep through the night. Sometimes, the quiet keeps me awake. If your neighbors are outside, they are usually sitting on their decks having a conversation with some friends, but nothing loud. I have walked Esmeralda at all hours of the day and night, and I have yet to hear any noise.

However, there is one aspect of mobile home living that is cause for adjustment. The size of things. Although I gained one-hundred-twenty square feet of living space — efficiently laid out I must add — there are certain things that are smaller — especially the bathtub. You can get a "glamour bath" installed, but I opted out.

I think that if they let everyone take a shower in their new home before purchasing it, no one would buy a new home. Getting used to a new shower is the hardest thing to do. We have all stayed in hotels with little water pressure or tiny tubs or shower heads that are set too low. My brother calls them penis showers. We are both over six-feet tall, so hotel showers aim right for our "members-only section." To wash my hair in a hotel shower, I have to do my Cirque du Soleil moves. Some might find that alluring.

In my luxury apartment, I had what they called a "deep soak tub." I had to step way over the edge then down into the tub. It was huge and a pleasure to take a shower. However, giving the dog a bath required me to get into the tub with her (Serena, too, when I first moved in). I got totally used to stepping up and then down. Sometimes in a hotel, I would find myself stepping way up before getting into a tub.

My new tub is the exact opposite. It has a low rim, and it is set higher than the floor. It is also set against the side of the house. The first time I stepped in, I slammed my foot on the bottom thinking I had three more inches of tub. Once in, I realized that because of the slant of the roof, my head was two inches from the ceiling. Fortunately, I put in a hand-held showerhead. The tub is also six inches narrower than my old one. It is a good thing I lost weight, or I would have to step out to wash my ass.

When I was done with my first shower, I stepped out of the tub expecting to step up. When there was no floor where I thought it would be, I tumbled and almost slammed into the opposite wall (my master bathroom is as wide as the house as most mobile home bathrooms are). Fortunately, I recovered before leaving an imprint of my naked body on the exterior wall of the house, or worse, falling through the vinyl siding. Now that would have been something for the evening news.

Even without a deep soak tub, living here is so much better than where I was. They may have called it luxury living, but I was never champagne and caviar.

THE HAPPY HOMEMAKER

If I had my wish, I would have become a housewife. I love cleaning, laundry, cooking (and making reservations), and driving car pools.

I would live in a split-level raised-ranch style home with my husband, two kids and a dog in a cozy Southern town. I would drive a 1960 Rambler Ambassador Cross Country Station Wagon. It would be pink and white with a matching interior and have Weather-Eye All Season Air Conditioning and a push button Flash-O-Matic transmission.

I would play Mah Jongg with the girls on Tuesday evenings and Thursday afternoons just like the girls in *On Tuesdays, They Played Mah Jongg* and *Michael's Secrets* by Milton Stern (shameless plug). The Tuesday evening group would gossip about the Thursday afternoon group and vice versa, and I would be the only one to play in both groups. On Wednesday nights, my husband and I would play bridge with the Weinsteins. On Saturday nights, we would go for cocktails and dinner at the Huntington Club with the Flickdenfelds or the Salkens.

Our kids would go to the Jewish day school, and we would belong to a Conservative Synagogue — Bet Midler or Bet Davis or something like that. While the kids were at school, I would volunteer to help with Soviet Jewry even after realizing it had nothing to do with earrings. I would serve as Synagogue Sisterhood President for at least three years, perform in our synagogue's annual cabaret and organize the annual rummage sale to benefit Jewish refugees. I would also go around the neighborhood and collect donations for the Heart Fund and American Lung Association even though I was a social smoker.

On Fridays, I would get my hair done in the morning with all the other Jewish women at Nachman's Hair Salon, so I could look good for Shabbat services that night. And my clothes would be tastefully tailored in a style similar to my favorite First Lady, Jacqueline Kennedy.

I would have a home cooked meal on the table every night, pot roast, meatloaf, baked fish, or baked chicken. All meals would include overly boiled, tasteless vegetables and a starch, rolls and iced tea — I am Southern after all. If I were feeling lazy, I would make spaghetti and a salad, and if I were angry, I would make tuna casserole.

At least once a week, my husband would come home and find me in a bad mood. He would ask why I was in a bad mood, and I would reply, "If you don't know, I'm not going to tell you." Then I would storm out to the back porch and sneak a cigarette. A good housewife has to be dramatic on occasion.

My husband and I would have relations on Thursday nights since I was getting my hair done on Fridays. All other nights, my hair would be wrapped in toilet paper to maintain my bouffant while I slept on a satin pillowcase. If I didn't play Mah Jongg on a Thursday in the summer, I would be at the Jewish Community Center Pool and go down the slide and make a big deal out of it because normally I would swim with my head above water to protect my coiffure. I wouldn't slide down until everyone was watching because I must always be the center of attention (some things would remain a constant).

With very few exceptions, I just described a woman I knew named Harryette — my mother.

Alas, my dream of becoming a housewife is just a faded hope for three reasons:

1. I was born in 1962.
2. I was born with a penis.
3. I was born in 1962.

Being single at my age diminishes my chances of finding a sugar daddy. I asked my friend Danny what was the stage between daddy and troll. He said, "Last week." I love this joke so much that I will repeat it later.

However, I may work two jobs and bring home the bacon — kosher of course, but I still love and find time for housework. Yes, I love it all, vacuuming, laundry, dusting, scrubbing, etc. I have been doing my own laundry (and my family's) since I was thirteen. I make my bed every morning even though I live alone. I have three vacuum cleaners and a carpet steamer. Why three? The upright is for the carpets, the canister for the linoleum and hardwood floors and getting under furniture, and the stick vac for quick clean ups. I don't use a mop. I clean floors on my hands and knees. I make a big bucket of suds with ammonia and detergent and go at it — none of those goofy contraption duster thingamabobs for me. My broom isn't outside my window serenading me; he is in the broom closet waiting to be used on a daily basis.

I found a store in Jessup called Ollie's Surplus, and they had vintage Top Job for $1 a bottle; I bought five bottles! I was so thrilled.

I sometimes clean in heels because it is good for the calf muscles. And I always wear a do-rag to keep the dust out of my hair.

Now, why am I sharing all this? Well, who knew moving into a mobile home would make cleaning even more fun! Joan Crawford, whom I admire and love, would be so happy here. But first, a story.

Back in the day in the Ivy Farms neighborhood of Newport News, Virginia, there was one empty lot at the end of one of the streets (I won't say which one to protect the present occupants, but it rhymed with mumby and started with a G). One day, an eighteen wheeler with half a house came in followed by another with the other half, and construction workers put the two sections of a house on the lot, connected them, then laid brick on all sides to make it look like a stick-built house. But I knew what it was, and so did all the women in the neighborhood, especially Harryette.

I remember her saying, "They can brick up that piece of shit, but once you go inside, you know it's a goddamn trailer because it's one long hallway with rooms on either side. They aren't fooling anyone."

When I heard her say that, I stopped playing Donna Reed — or was it June Cleaver or Our Miss Brooks? — in my bedroom and ran outside and down the street to see the "open house." I was eight years old, but I knew perfection when I saw it.

Yes, it was one long hallway with rooms on either side. It was also fabulous! Even at that young age, I appreciated the efficient use of space. One could so entertain in there ... and clean in a breeze!

And it had the one thing I have always wanted in a home, a bathroom that does not back up to the dining room. There is nothing worse than having your only bathroom on the other side of your dining room wall. Someone goes to the toilet, and everyone hears it while they are eating. Every apartment I have rented had that awful feature because apartments are usually squares not rectangles.

Years of working in restaurants taught me how to clean a space efficiently with little to no time. At the end of the evening shift, a waiter has thirty minutes to vacuum, clean and set tables for breakfast, scrub down the serving area of the kitchen, clean the bathrooms, and put everything away. It is a great training ground of people who like to clean.

I could clean my apartments in about two hours from top to bottom, but it was a bit of a cluster-fuck at times because I was always going in circles in one room then out the other and back and forth, knocking over the bucket of suds on many an occasion and getting tangled up in vacuum cords more often than I care to admit. My dogs would get nauseated watching me act like a whirling dervish or a Tasmanian devil, depending on how much time I had.

Enter my new mobile home with its long layout and a series of rooms in a row. Oh my God, the first time I did my weekly top to bottom cleaning, I was in heaven. All I had to do was start at one end with the vacuum, then the other vacuum, then go back with the Windex, then back with the Endust and two dusters (yes, two), then back with the sudsy ammonia water, and before I knew it, ninety minutes had elapsed, and I was done! Four laps were all it took, and I didn't knock anything over or get tangled in cords. Even Esmeralda loved it because she followed me back and forth without vomiting.

My mother may not have appreciated the efficiency of a mobile home because she did not like to do housework. She thought the best way to keep a room clean was not to use it. We never sat in our living room, and we had four inches of dust to prove it. Nana, on one of her visits, said to my mother, "There is a cob web over there." My mother replied, "Don't look at it, and it won't bother you."

During that same visit, Nana was standing in the kitchen holding a broom, and my father said to her, "Leaving so soon?"

Nana once told me a story about visiting a friend when she was a little girl whose house was a mess with potato peels in the corner of the kitchen, just to name one atrocity. Her mother prohibited her from visiting that girl again. Nana then told me if you keep a messy house, you won't have friends. I will never forget that.

There is only one thing about being a clean person that I find curious. They have all kinds of psychiatric terms to describe clean people. My favorite is anal retentive — "my mother rushed my potty training, and you are paying the price for it." And until the shows *Hoarders* and *Clean House* became popular, sloppy people were admired for their ability not to care. Sloppy people were always fun ... until you had a sleepover and had to take a *Silkwood* shower upon your return home.

I don't spend my time wearing latex gloves and dusting envelopes like the woman I saw on *20/20* in the 1980s, but I do appreciate a clean home, so here's to all the people who like to do housework.

One more piece of advice. The secret to keeping a clean house is not to let it get dirty! And to all you slobs, clean your goddamn houses!

BE CAREFUL OR IT WILL TILT!

The one thing about living in an apartment that bothered me the most was the difficulty in getting someone evicted. I know that sounds cruel. Those people who lived above me in Mount Pleasant needed to be put out on the street five minutes after they arrived.

The one thing I love about living in a mobile home community, especially one with forty pages of rules, is the ease at which you can evict someone. And the best part is when they leave, they take their home with them.

"Get out, and take your goddamn trailer with you!"

You poor condo dwellers. I guess you can only evict those who live in corner units.

A couple of weeks ago, what was once a doublewide across the street from me became a vacant lot in a matter of hours. I felt like Gladys Kravitz in that episode of *Bewitched* when Endora and Uncle Arthur kept arguing about her living in Samantha and Darrin's neighborhood. They made Endora's house appear and disappear over and over again. Gladys called the police and said, "I swear, officer, there was a house here a minute ago."

Over the course of the next week, after Trailer Park Endora's doublewide disappeared, I finally witnessed the process for mounting a mobile home. Actually, the term is anchoring, but mounting sounds like so much more fun. Well, to be totally technical, the house has to be placed and leveled first.

First, they clear the lot of debris then level the land. Next they place cinderblocks on top of each other in strategic locations to hold the frame of the house. Yes, mobile homes have steel frames. They are also unitized like a Nash.

With the precision of a Swiss watchmaker, an eighteen wheeler backs the sections of the home onto the cinderblock pilings, one at a time. Once the house is leveled and the two halves are attached, the axles are removed. The owner can get a $700–$1,000 credit for the axles if the home is purchased before mounting … I mean anchoring. I missed out on that monetary benefit.

Then comes the scary part. The house sits on the cinderblocks, some stacked five high, while the home is being leveled and remains that way for a week! This looks most precarious. It is as if you could walk by and push the house, and it would fall over. Of course, the laws of physics are on the house's side (as a matter of theory ... not actually painted onto the side of the house) because the weight of the house keeps it in place unless there is a violent storm, which there wasn't, even though all mobile homes have a tornado magnet built in. There, I said it again, so you don't have to.

Actually, Walmarts seem to have a tornado magnet. Have you ever noticed how tornadoes always rip the roofs off Walmarts? As a rule, I never shop in a Walmart during any weather event.

I worked construction for a summer after college graduation during the Reagan trickle-down economy when unemployment was quite high, and homes that were not set directly on a cement foundation were held up by similar means, so I don't know why I had concern for this house.

But for the week the house remained that way, I began to wonder: If I had more than twenty people over to my home and they all stood on one side of the house, would it tilt over? Would we reenact the *Poseidon Adventure*? Would I have to put on fifty pounds, a la Shelley Winters, and swim through my house to search for survivors? Would Gene Hackman make a guest appearance?

I then asked my neighbors about the cinderblocks, but they assured me mine was anchored because they watched them anchor it ... as they watch everything else that goes on in our neighborhood!

My fears were allayed by the next step — the actual anchoring. Steel poles are placed at all four corners and depending on the house's size, mid-way down each side. The poles are anchored six feet into the ground. Then steel bars are attached diagonally from ground to the frame. These poles and bars are what keep the house from blowing away. Each state has different rules for how a home is anchored, but all require it of mobile homes now. There was a time when they didn't, and if you buy a used mobile home (pre-1985 in some states, pre-1996 in others), you need to be sure it is anchored and not just sitting on cinderblocks.

In earthquake zones, mobile homes sit directly on a cement foundation. I did my research.

Another interesting aspect of the anchoring process is the concern all the neighbors have for it being done properly.

I was the first to learn which house was going into the recently vacated lot. The property manager told me they sold the green doublewide with the wraparound porch. I told Mrs. M across the street, and she asked which side the entryway would face, where would the air conditioning unit go, where would they put the shed. I would have to learn that if I am to be a neighborhood busybody, I need to get more information!

As the home was awaiting anchoring, it seemed as if everyone in the community drove or walked by to check out the home. All were wondering who bought it and were scrutinizing the anchoring and skirting technique. Yes, our mobile homes have skirts! This is most reassuring because in my neighborhood, you better know how to mount or you will get an earful!

In addition, I now know that half my neighbors came over and checked out my home after it was anchored ... and skirted, which explains the dirty carpet I had to steam clean!

I still want to know who used the nonfunctioning toilet before I bought it.

SHHHH, YOU'LL WAKE
THE NEIGHBORS

Old habits die hard. Ask any public nose picker.

I was the perfect apartment tenant. I was respectful of my neighbors, didn't play loud music, didn't throw loud parties, and in the throes of orgasm, always buried my face in the pillow ... or an armpit.

I never wanted to be the guy hearing broom handles banging on his floor. Yet, I always ended up being the guy with the worst neighbors — no need to rehash that.

There are also those who move into an apartment for the first time and do not realize how much their neighbors can hear. For the first few months, they have intimate conversations using their loudest outdoor voices. I have heard it all! Do I really need to know that the Preparation H burns when you apply it? Or that your husband likes it when you dress up as a sheep?

I especially enjoy the ones who move into a luxury condo and are appalled at how much they hear from next door ... or below ... or above. A friend of mine once said, "For what I am paying, I shouldn't hear my neighbor flushing his toilet." To myself I said, "You may call it a condo, but it is nothing but an apartment with a mortgage. Unless the walls are made of lead, you are going to hear your neighbors!" This was another reason I never seriously considered a condo.

Now, I live in a mobile home with my own four walls and no one on the other side, but I still find myself tiptoeing around and whispering. I never wear shoes inside. I quietly go about my business, and I still don't own a stereo. I even sing quietly. And before you say "Thank God," Esmeralda likes my singing. Serena didn't like it, but she liked my dancing. Esmeralda finds my dancing disturbing. I guess the pole is a bit much for some dogs to appreciate.

There are times when I turn on the TV, and the sound will be very loud for no known reason, so I immediately turn it down and apologize to no one in particular. I was watching porn — I mean an educational documentary — on my computer, and all of a sudden one of the characters started screaming, and I immediately muted it. No one needs to hear that ... not even me.

Some mornings, Esmeralda doesn't want to get out of bed, and I end up standing by the front door, saying quietly, "Esmeralda, come here. We're going for a walk. Don't make me yell. I don't want to wake the neighbors." She just looks at me as if I am an idiot. Come to think of it, she looks at me like that a lot. Then I whisper loudly for her to get up. We have all done the loud whisper, which isn't quite a whisper. You sound like a three-pack-a-day smoker trying to get a waiter's attention.

Why do I keep doing the apartment dweller thing?

One of my friends, upon hearing about my descent into trailer park trashdom, remarked that you can hear your neighbors fart when living in a trailer. I actually believed him. For the first week I lived in my new home, I made sure all my farts were silent, and when a loud one slipped out, I cringed, knowing my next door neighbor heard it. I was so embarrassed. What if he could smell it, too?

I guess after spending more than half my life with people on the other side of my walls, it would be a while before I broke old habits.

I have grown accustomed to the quiet. I rather enjoy not having my neighbors' marital problems becoming mine. Life is so drama-free. I do admit that sleeping the first night was odd since there was nothing but silence. I kept waking up anticipating someone's head hitting a wall after hearing, "Go ahead, hit me ... I dare you ... hit me .... <THUD!>"

If you are wondering about the neighbor fart thing, my home is fully insulated, so I have not heard a fart from next door. My friend Frank has knocked on the door, and I have yelled "Come in," and he has never heard me. Good luck hearing any bodily functions. And if you do hear a neighbor fart, call the *Guinness Book of World Records*, or look up because someone is headed for low-earth orbit.

Esmeralda doesn't even hear my car pull up when I come home from work, and I drive a thirty-year-old AMC!

However, there is one habit I needed to break very quickly. My apartment in Mount Pleasant was ground level (I'll never admit it was a basement) with one hidden window, hence calling it "The Patty Hearst Memorial." In Rockville, I lived on the fifth floor with no buildings facing me. I could walk around naked in both, and no one could see me. My blinds were open all the time to let in natural light and be free.

So much for natural light. It was a few days before I realized I was putting on a show every time I walked from one end of my home to the other, giving anyone looking in something very natural to see or at my age, something very unnatural one should not be forced to see.

As Joan Rivers said, "A peeping Tom reached in and pulled down my shades."

That habit is now broken but not before a couple of near misses.

I cannot wait to be comfortable enough to sing my favorite American standards as loudly as I want. Esmeralda will be thrilled when that day comes. She especially likes "Zing Went the Strings of My Heart." That one makes her poop outside.

LIFTING THE
MARY RICHARDS CURSE

I cannot begin to tell you how many wedding, baby shower, engagement and other "special" occasion gifts I have bought over the years. My favorite line from *Sex and the City* is when Carrie asks when she gets to have a "Congratulations You Didn't Marry the Wrong Guy Shower" as she laments having to buy an expensive gift from a registry for someone's baby shower.

I don't mean to sound bitter — but you are bitter, Blanche!

However, there comes a point in a single man's (and I am sure woman's) life when he gets sick of having to celebrate other people's milestones by spending inordinate amounts of money because they want the pleasure of his company and lots of free stuff when no one celebrates the single man's life.

Personally, I think the whole registering for presents thing is the most selfish act in the world. There, I said it. You were thinking it, but I said it.

I'll give you some examples. I knew a couple who lived together for seven years. Then, they got married and registered at the most expensive store they could find. Seriously? All I could think was you've been screwing each other for seven years, and now you decide to get married, so we have to help you fill your home with necessities? What did you use all those years? Paper plates and plastic sheets?

My favorite was the friend of mine (and I say friend loosely) who got married on July 4th weekend in Newport, Rhode Island. The trip would have cost me more than $4,000 not including the present from their registry I would be obligated to buy. I sent my regrets. And he had the nerve to get pissed at me. All I did was RSVP that I could not make it. I actually was going to send a present, but when he got pissed, I changed my mind. He hasn't spoken to me since. That saved me from having to buy a baby present for their unfortunately ugly child.

Seriously, did I ask him to spend $2 to celebrate my latest trick? I should have. Actually, I should have made him fly in and watch!

And don't get me started on baby showers. All of a sudden, we have them at work. I thought these were just for your girlfriends to attend. Now, if you are going to have children, shouldn't you wait until you can afford to buy your own diapers?

I refused to participate at a work-related one, and I was made out to be a pariah. I didn't fuck her, so why should I celebrate? I didn't even get a kiss or a cigarette.

Ucccchhhhh.

I have never held a housewarming party, or more exactly, apartment warming party, either. I just think that if I am going to move into a new home, it is my responsibility to furnish it. If I cannot afford to furnish it, I have no right moving in. Also, as you can gather from the above, I never have been comfortable asking for presents. I don't throw myself birthday parties or any other parties to try and get presents.

Before I continue, I must offer a clarification. No one enjoys buying presents more than I do. I love giving gifts. However, I especially like giving them on my own terms. If I know your birthday is coming up, I would rather surprise you than be told to buy you something. There is no joy in obligated gift buying. The irony is I rarely celebrate my own birthday, but I love celebrating other people's birthdays.

A couple I know recently got married but could not afford a large wedding, so they just invited family. They were so low key that few people even knew they were getting married in the first place because they didn't want it to be a big deal. Not only did I buy them a present, I hooked them up with a free meal during their honeymoon since I knew one of the restaurant owners in the town they were visiting. And, they were a straight couple. I am not telling you this to make myself out to be special. It is just that it was a pleasure to give a gift that wasn't requested or expected or registered.

If you move into a new home, I will be the first to give you something to celebrate the occasion, unless you throw your own housewarming party. If you have a baby, I will buy you a present, but don't invite me to the shower. Besides, there was a time when Jews didn't throw baby showers. One always waited until after the baby was born.

Another note on birthdays. What is up with Gay men celebrating every goddamn birthday? Seriously? "I am going to be thirty-seven, and I am throwing myself a party!" Thirty-seven, who cares? We know what you are doing. You just want gifts! And the ones who do this never write a fucking thank you note either!

I *always* write thank you notes. I guess it is because I get so few presents ... said the old bitter queen.

I also expect people to do the right thing. When I moved to Rockville after twelve and half years in Mount Pleasant, I didn't get one housewarming present. That is OK. I didn't ask for any, but you would think all those people I bought presents for over the years to celebrate their life-changing events would have sent me a goddamn card or something. I think that was the point where I said enough is enough.

There was the couple who bought a new home, and I bought them a Mezuzah complete with rabbinically blessed parchment, too. The couple who got married, and I bought them a complete set of China. The couple who bought their first new car, and I bought them a complete car care set. None of these gifts were solicited. I just bought them.

Do you know what those couples bought me? If you said nothing, you win the magic duck.

So, when I bought my first home, I was asked if I would throw a housewarming party. The thought never occurred to me. Have we met? I don't ask for presents, nor do I register.

Now, there is something else I don't do well either — throw parties. I have the Mary Richards curse. Any child of the 1970s knows all about the Mary Richards curse. Some of my parties in the past have been absolute disasters.

When I was in the seventh grade, my best friend, Scott, and I decided to throw a party. We went to different schools. We invited our friends to his house, so everyone could mix it up. They didn't. The ones from my school would be in one room and those from his in another. And they kept switching rooms all evening, never wavering from their schoolmates. I heard about this for a year. This was strange to me because when we would go to United Synagogue Youth (USY) conventions, I was the one who would always sit with new people. Isn't one of life's great joys, meeting new people? My fellow Newport News USYers didn't understand this as they sat together like snobs. I would always hear "Why are you sitting with them?"

I threw my next party when I was in ninth grade, and one of my guests proceeded to try to convince everyone in the room to accept Jesus. The rest of my guests were Jewish, and all but one still are.

I didn't throw another party until I moved into my first apartment. This time, I invited a cross-section of guests, and it was the first time I encountered cliquedom. Apparently, some people there felt we should all be grateful for their presence. Not only that, everyone left before ten. My cousin Carole-Sue told me they left because I had the lights on too bright.

However, I never gave up. Over the years, I threw a party where all forty-two people I invited to my studio apartment in West Palm Beach showed up, and one guest monopolized the room by telling everyone how she wanted her twenty-three-year-old daughter to get her tubes tied but no doctor would do it. There was the party where two drag queens got into a fist fight in the parking lot. There was the party where it turned out there was a feud between two groups of guests, and the room went silent for almost an hour until everyone left. There was the party where I said BYOB and no one did, so I had a bunch of boring sober people in my house until three in the morning.

And the *pies de resistance* was the party where my then-boyfriend was caught screwing a passed out guest on the coats in the bedroom while a former one was doing another's boyfriend in my walk-in closet. Some would say that party was a success, but they didn't have to clean up the mess!

So you can understand my resistance at throwing another party. Dinner parties didn't seem to be a problem as long as I kept the guest count to no more than four.

Well, I decided maybe I should give it one more try. And here is where living in a mobile home has its advantages. You have an open layout that is perfect for entertaining, ample parking for your guests, and no codes for guests to punch in to be buzzed up.

However, the biggest advantage is the "Yoko Ono Factor." What is that you ask? In the movie *Jeffery*, the question is asked, "Why did the Gay man date Yoko Ono?" and the answer: "To see the apartment of course!"

I knew most guests would come just to see the "trailer"!

I decided to celebrate Lucille Ball's 100th Birthday (August 5, 2011), and I planned the party with very short notice. I also did not call it a housewarming. I just said let's celebrate the Queen of Comedy and come see my new home. I invited a cross section of guests and did what my mother taught me about always inviting those who have invited you. This was easy because the single Gay man over forty rarely gets invited anywhere. Apparently, even Lesbians consider me a threat. It must be my AMC — a total Lesbian magnet of a car.

Well, was I surprised. For the first time, I threw a party where people actually enjoyed themselves. No drag queens tore each other's wigs off. No cliques were there to look down at the other guests. There were no mass migrations from room to room. No one got laid in the bedroom — was this a plus? There was just enough booze. The lights were adjusted perfectly, and the music at just the right level. The best part was everyone was talking to people they were meeting for the first time rather than just to people they already knew.

You should have seen the looks on the guests' faces as they entered my home. All of them looked up and down as if to say, "So this is what a trailer looks like inside."

I think that the secret to my success was the fact that when one attends a party in a mobile home, he doesn't feel a need to impress the others in the room or act like an ass. Mobile home living allows you to be yourself and enjoy life! After all, the host can't possibly put on airs when his house was brought in on a semi! And how often do you go to a party hosted by a Gay Jew in a Trailer Park?

I FEEL THE EARTH MOVE
UNDER MY FEET

Brace yourself, there's a storm coming. Of course, when you live in a mobile home, you are aware of every tornado watch. It's not out of fear that you stay informed; you do it so that you can say, "I told you so," to your friends.

For some reason, your friends are almost disappointed when your home doesn't go airborne and land on your sister. Dorothy may have lived in Kansas, but she did not live in a trailer park, bitches!

I don't know how many of my friends are obsessed with the impending natural disaster I am to experience in my new home. "Aren't you afraid of high winds? Aren't you afraid of flooding? Aren't you afraid of tornadoes?" I watch the news. The tsunami in Japan didn't take away only mobile homes; it took away ALL the homes! A hurricane flooded New Orleans, not just the trailer park in the West End.

I saw a comedian on Logo the other night who said tornadoes are God's away of erasing trailer parks with a sweep of her hand, saying, "No, no; don't live there!" So now, even Gay comedians are getting in on the act.

Who the fuck cares! As I said before, tornadoes don't destroy mobile homes; they destroy Walmarts.

I had lived in my new home for more than a month. Anyone who lives on the East Coast knows about all the violent thunderstorms we get in the summer months. We had quite a few big ones since I moved in, and let me tell you the house did not shake, the roof did not peel off, the windows did not shatter, and the house did not go floating down the street — although that would have been cool!

My home is built to higher standards than stick-built homes, and it had to withstand traveling by semi from Pennsylvania over potholed highways in the middle of February to its final destination in Jessup. Some of your luxury cars could not survive that!

And here is something else you might want to consider. Since I bought a brand new home, I have a fifteen-year warranty on it. That is better than what Chrysler offers.

This comes in very handy.

Being a new home, there were a few items that needed to be addressed, so a carpenter from the factory came down to do work on my home on August 23, 2011 (I include the date for a reason). I also worked from home that day.

I needed to have a wall panel replaced in my office as it was slightly off color, a small crack in the ceiling patched up and a squeak in the floor fixed. If you buy a mobile home, buy the brand I did. I visited the factory a few years ago, and they do great work.

The gentleman patched the ceiling and then went into my office to replace the panel. Did I mention I have three bookshelves with over 500 titles on them and that I edit Gay erotica part-time and handle sales distribution of such materials from our web site? That inventory is what is in my office! I didn't mention it to the factory guy either. I had to empty the shelf that was blocking the panel, so he could have access. The books were stacked neatly on the floor, books with titles like *Homo Thugs*, *Boys Hard at Work*, *Kidnapped by a Sex Maniac*, *Men, Muscle & Mayhem*, *Who's Your Daddy?* ... you get the idea. When he went into the office, I took that opportunity to take Esmeralda for a walk.

Upon our return, I checked on his progress, and he asked me, "Do you make money selling these?" We then had a very interesting conversation about how he and his wife are friends with a Gay couple, and his wife likes to read Gay erotica, and if his co-worker had come down, it would have been awkward since he is a big homophobe ... or as I like to refer to them, "closet cases." It wasn't exactly the reaction I expected, and I was pleasantly surprised.

I wondered if his co-worker had tattoos?

Anyway, the last thing he needed to fix was the squeak. The squeaks are actually caused by pipes rubbing against the floor. The floors are first built upside down in the factory with the pipes pre-fitted and fastened, then flipped.

He asked me to stand on the spot and rock back and forth while he went under the house and to stop rocking when he shouted that he had located the squeak. So I rocked back and forth. Now, I had not been out dancing in a long time, and I started humming Michael Jackson's "I Want to Rock with You."

Remember that song and the dance we did to it in 1979? You would bend your arms at the elbow and swing them back and forth while rocking your hips. And if you were stylin' you rocked forward then backward. I was stylin'.

So there I was, humming and rocking. He had already found the squeak and fixed it, but I couldn't stop. Next thing I knew, he was standing there watching me. He cleared his throat.

All I said was, "Cool, you stopped the squeak."

He then had me sign the work order, shook my hand and was on his way. He was good, clean and efficient. And before you ask, no he wasn't "doable." I never get the hot ones. My friend Ed gets the hot ones. I get the efficient ones.

When he left, it was 1:40 pm. I had not eaten anything, so I decided to change out of my shorts and T-shirt, go out and get some lunch. No sooner had I changed and was applying Chapstick, when I heard a thumping that sounded as if Esmeralda was really scratching herself and hitting the floor with her rear paw.

I then smeared my Chapstick all over my face. The thumping got louder and more rapid. I thought that Mr. Fix It had done something to mess up my pipes, and the house was now making a very loud noise as a result. Then the house began to rock slightly, and the floor was moving.

We were having a fucking earthquake! An earthquake? In Jessup? No one made trailer park earthquake jokes! I stood in the middle of the great room and started spinning in circles the way I normally do in these situations, except I didn't turn into Wonder Woman (someday I will), and I thought, "Am I supposed to be under something or in something?" Obviously, I am not from earthquake country.

After thirty seconds, it stopped. Then Esmeralda came out from under the bed and looked at me as if I moved the house. I stepped outside, and some of my neighbors were outside as well. We all asked each other if we felt that.

And to all you trailer haters, no house was toppled over. Another fact — being mobile in nature, our houses are built to withstand earthquakes! They flex. Esmeralda and I went back inside and checked every room. No cracks, nothing broken. There was only a cabinet door in my office that was open.

Upon further investigation, I noticed the sofa was now six inches from the wall. My menorah collection had rearranged itself. And the weirdest thing was my flower arrangement in the guest bathroom. It had spun around one-hundred-eighty degrees.

I called Ed, who recently moved to California and had yet to experience an earthquake to announce two things: I was first to get an earthquake, and I was going looting!

That is what one is supposed to do after an earthquake, right? Look for a Radio Shack and start looting?

My brother asked me to get a flat screen. Another friend told me to steal jewelry. Too bad we don't have a Frederick's of Hollywood in Jessup; I could have used some new lingerie.

Of course, looting in Jessup means throwing a brick through the front window of Wing's Liquor, Bar & BBQ and stealing a bag of Doritos. However, this did not make the rednecks inside very happy.

Oh well. The next day, the news reporters talked about how folks have to wait sixty days after an earthquake to get earthquake insurance. Ha! I already had earthquake insurance, bitches!

If that weren't enough, at the end of that same week, we had to prepare for Hurricane Irene, the largest hurricane to hit the East Coast in seventy years.

Did I ever tell you I am the "Queen of Bad Timing"?

So, then I got an email from my friend … I'll just call her Bev because that is her real name. I love Bev, but Bev does not like where I live — ever.

When I lived in Mount Pleasant, she worried I would get caught in the crossfire of MS-13 Gang violence. Puhleeze. I went to the same barbershop the gang members used. I even had my "tag" shaved into my hair. I was known as "Poodle Walking Faggo." Whassup Homos?!?

Well, the email from Bev was a link to an article about how those living in mobile homes needed to evacuate immediately and commit suicide because their lives were not worth living. What those who read it neglected to do was finish the article. They were referring to mobile homes that were not anchored and were built more than twenty years ago.

This brought back memories of my days in Newport News and Williamsburg whenever the rare snow storm approached. My parents would call me where I worked every ten minutes telling me to go home immediately. I didn't even live with them, and I am not making this up.

They would call and call and call. One storm hit on a weekend, and I was working at Marino's Italian Restaurant in Williamsburg. We were slammed since we were the only restaurant on the street with power. And the owner would come to me every ten minutes and say, "Your mother is on the phone." "Your father is on the phone." I finally threatened to call the police and get a restraining order. That didn't stop them.

I was nearly thirty years old at the time, and they were still doing this. I am also the only one in my family that would have to drive home in snow storms, and I managed to do it without incident every time.

My parents are dead now, and I am nearly fifty, so I can now enjoy the occasional natural disaster in peace ... or so I thought. Bev called me to tell me to come stay at her house and bring Esmeralda. She sent me emails, contacted me on Facebook. You get it. I finally asked her to stop. Her wife, Marlene, separated herself from the situation. "It wasn't I who called you!"

There is something I also don't do. I don't panic, and I don't deal very well with people who do panic.

My neighbor asked, "Are you ready for the hurricane?"

I answered, "If I am not, will they cancel it?"

It will be what it will be.

The Friday before the big hurricane weekend (which was only four days after the earthquake), I went out to do my regular grocery shopping. I could not get over the people with their big run on groceries. And all of them were buying bottled water. Seriously? Don't hurricanes come with rain? Just put a goddamn bucket outside, and you can have all the water you want.

I just got my usual stuff, rolled my eyes and left.

Hurricane Irene blew through as expected. Esmeralda and I survived. The power never went out. There was no damage to my home.

I heard a tree fell on the house next door to Bev's. Bev also predicted I would tell everyone.

For once, Bev was right!

IT WAS BOUND TO HAPPEN

I had a date. Have you picked yourself up off the floor yet? Yes, the man who invented the "Milton-Date" keeps getting on that horse in the hope of finally being able to ride it at least once around the stable. Some say I'll write a book about all my bad dates.

But before you hear about the big date, some observations of late. I don't know if this is true where you live, but in the DC Metro area, the first things people ask are "what do you do for a living?" and "where do you live?" Then you are asked, "Do you own or rent?" You know what my answer has been over the years, which explains my lack of viable life-partners.

However, whenever I invited people over, I never felt the need to say, "Come to my apartment, and here is the address." I would just give the address and let them figure it out. Of course, upon arrival, I would get asked, "Do you own or rent?"

I always wanted to say, "Here is a copy of my lease. Now fuck me and leave."

I never did have the nerve to say that, but wouldn't it have been cool if I did? And convenient?

One guy many years ago complimented a couch I recently purchased when living in Dutch Village in Newport News and then said, "I bought one just like it, but I had to 'Jew the guy down'." I just told him to leave. I didn't even give him a handshake or a cigarette.

But now, I live in what some consider a curiosity. Think about it. How many people, beside me, do you know who live in a mobile home? Do people only come over just to see it and not me? They do look up and down and all around with that look on their faces that says, "I always wondered what these look like inside. I wonder if it will tip when all of us stand on one side?"

I have to admit that I have had to mention my type of home in situations where I didn't have to in my life as a rent-boy ... I mean renter.

For instance, when living in Mount Pleasant, my apartment had a door at street level, so when I took a cab, I would say the second door from the corner. A week ago, I had to leave my car at the shop, so I took a cab home — no cheap trip in Howard County.

When the cab driver pulled onto my street, he said, "Oh, I must have made a wrong turn."

I said, "You're right. This is where I live."

Should I have said, "The mobile home park up on the right" or "Look for the guy in the wife-beater walking his Bijon Frise"?

Do we have to point out what kind home we live in when either taking a cab or giving someone directions?

"Yes, it's the cheaply constructed McMansion at the end of the block." "After you make the first left, look for the house with the upside-down mortgage and blue shutters." "My building is the one up there with the tiny condos, paper thin walls, and Nazi-like condo board."

Actually, I think people should do the above from now on. It would save all of us a bunch of trouble.

Upon pulling up to my house he said, "Do you like living in one of these?"

I knew it was bound to happen. Someone would refer to my home as "one of these." Seriously, you'd think I live in a tree house. I should get a sign that says "no girls allowed."

So I said, "Sure, as long as you get a good set of Michelins, these houses are quite comfortable."

He didn't laugh.

I knew that wouldn't be the last time I heard "one of these," but it gets better.

I left work a half hour early the evening of my big date. My first date of 2011. A lot of good that did me. There was an accident that shut down I-95 and diverted all the traffic onto Route 1. I found this out while stuck on Route 1 by asking the Lesbian in the car next to me. I knew she was a Lesbian because she had short hair, looked like an attractive version of Bruce Jenner, and was driving a Chrysler PT Cruiser. Two things I know about Lesbians. They are the only people who buy PT Cruisers, and they all either owned, learned how to drive in, or lost their Lesbian virginity in an AMC, which I drive — another reason I go dateless. After telling me what was going on, she said, "Nice car. I used to own one."

"No kidding?" Then, my genitalia performed their own sex-change.

I finally made it home two hours later. That's right. It took me more than two hours to drive ten miles. I thought I was back in Rockville. Thank God that wasn't an everyday occurrence.

Getting home this late meant I had little time to walk Esmeralda, feed her, take a shower and wait for my Viagra to kick in. While walking her, my phone rang. It was my date.

He said, "I must have made a wrong turn. I'm in a trailer park."

"The preferred term is mobile home community, and mine is the second one on the right after the mail boxes."

Esmeralda and I rounded the corner and saw him sitting out front in his F-150. I thought, "*You drive a pick-up, so you better not judge.*"

Once inside, he looked around, up and down, the way everyone does when they first enter my home, and he asked, "Do you like living in one of these?"

WHERE ARE MY GAYS?

Kathy Griffin asks that all the time. Where are my Gays? A few of my friends have also asked if there are any Gays in the park. Funny thing is no one ever asks if there are any Jews. I guess once we finally finished that forty-year trek through the desert in search of Chinese take-out, we decided no more nomadic living for us.

I somehow missed that memo.

I have also noticed I am the only one with a Mezuzah on his door. There are Crucifixes a plenty.

However, there are a couple of cars with HRC stickers. Could they have bought those cars used?

The good thing about having a dog, especially one like Esmeralda, who must walk miles before finding just the right spot to go potty then do the potty-dance, which consists of going back and forth and doing circles before finally going, is that I get to see the entire neighborhood at least four times a day.

In every one of my past neighborhoods, I have been known as the guy who was always walking his dog. I am also the guy who has the dogs who take forever to go. Want a picture? Imagine a six-four queen, wearing Chuck Taylors while walking a long-haired Dachshund-Yorkshire terrier mix, named Daisy; now imagine him walking a toy parti-poodle, named Serena; and now a beagle, named Esmeralda. Yes, you would give him a nickname as well.

"His dog is so Gay it's a fog."

As you know, I don't give a flying fuck what anyone thinks, and back in the day, I used to wear some really short shorts that were so tight you could guess my religion.

While Esmeralda and I are out on one of our regular walks, I always observe my neighbors, and they are all so friendly. It is very easy to engage in conversation in a mobile home community. After all, you can't be a snob. Seriously, what would you say? "Oh her, she lives in a singlewide."

However, you want to know where the Gays are. Well, let me tell you what I have observed.

There is the woman who has a Jamie Leigh Curtis haircut, lives on a corner lot, drives a compact pick-up and has a large bag of kitty litter in the truck bed at all times — sometimes several bags. Is she preparing for snow, or does she have lots of pussy? You do the math. She also wears jeans morning, noon and night. And yes, the truck is a stick shift.

There is the guy with the barbed-wire tattoo on the bicep, a Gay comb-over (shaved head), a yellow Hummer, and a yappy Pomeranian, who always does yard work shirtless (him, not the Pomeranian). His body isn't all that; I'm just saying. His lawn furniture would make Martha Stewart jealous. He also decorates for every holiday; I repeat, *every* holiday. You should see his house on Armistice Day. You come to your own conclusion.

There is my next-door neighbor. His yard is immaculate. He drives a spotless pick-up, and he apparently has a work-out room in his home. I have never seen a woman come or go. However, he once had a career as an auto restorer, specializing in body work. He is very friendly, kind of shy, but a really nice guy. His nails are immaculate as if he gets a manicure weekly. I cannot figure him out. I am usually wrong when it comes to these types, so I dare not ask. I bet if I ever get to see the inside of his home, I would know immediately. And no, I am not about to shit where I eat. Nothing good comes of doing the neighbors … believe me.

My favorites are the three men who live together around the corner. One is around eighty, one around sixty, and the other is about thirty. I have never had a conversation with the eighty-year-old. Although a little chunky and always shirtless, the three of them don't look alike. They have decorated their windows and their shed with butterflies, yet they are always working on their cars, which also have butterfly stickers. I observed their shed when the door was open, and it is more organized than a labor union. It turns out the middle one was an American Motors mechanic — not a Gay thing, but cool nonetheless, and the younger one drives a vintage Jeep — also not necessarily Gay but cool as well. Get this: the middle one refers to the older one as his uncle and the younger one as his nephew. So, that is what the kids are calling them these days. The jury is out, but I think deliberations will be just a few short hours.

They remind me of the time we took a trip to Felton, Pennsylvania, to look at a Chrysler New Yorker. The guy selling the car was a redneck, living with another redneck, and their overly friendly and gentle Rottweiler, named Onyx. Their house had a gondola and a lighthouse, and all their antique cars in this muddy place in a town riddled with McCain-Palin posters were just a little too pristine. Boy did they have us fooled. The entire town was Gay. Not a woman in sight!

So, your Gays are everywhere. You just need to know where to look!

SHE DOESN'T DO THAT
IN MY HOUSE

Has this happened to you? You go away for a few days, and you leave your dog with a friend. Upon returning, you are told what a great house guest she was. She didn't destroy anything. She didn't poop or pee in the house. She was the perfect angel. She slept in their bed. Then the first night you are back, she takes a shit in the middle of the living room to get back at you for leaving her for three days.

I rarely travel, and when I do, it is usually for just a couple of days and only once or twice a year. With Esmeralda, the problem has been what to do with her. I tried one of those doggy daycare places where they let the dogs run around like idiots all day. I don't know, but Montessori for mutts just isn't her idea of fun.

When she returned home, she was a neurotic mess for a couple of weeks. Or maybe I was.

She doesn't like barking dogs. If we encounter a barking dog while out on a walk, she just ignores the dog completely and picks up the pace to get as far away as possible. A lot of this has to do with her past encounters with aggressive dogs. But I can identify with her because I don't like yappy dogs either ... or their owners. We have one with two Yorkies who yap and growl and foam at the mouth — the dogs, too. I wonder if they had their shots?

Also, have you ever noticed that women with male dogs, no matter the size of the dog, always have the most aggressive dogs? Are they protecting their masters? If I see a woman walking a male dog while I am out with Esmeralda, I immediately cross the street. I always get from the woman, "Oh, he is so friendly." And I answer, "Oh, my dog isn't, so this makes it easier." I figure by using "I" statements I can avoid a discussion about how friendly her Cujo is while trying to remove its jaws from my dog's throat.

When I lived in Rockville, there were these two women with very aggressive dogs, and they would let them wrestle and play in the hallway right outside the elevators. I stepped off with Esmeralda one day, and they immediately attacked (the dogs, not the women). I scooped Esmeralda up immediately, and one of them said in her best Yuppie voice, "Oh, she doesn't like puppy play time?" I answered,

"No, she doesn't like dumb ass owners and their ill-behaved mongrels attacking her when they should do their puppy play time in a park rather than an apartment hallway. Are the two of you retarded?"

I'll bet when one of those Yuppies has her first child, she'll be one of those mothers who insist on bringing her screaming brat everywhere and complaining when a restaurant doesn't cater to children. You know the type. They usually have a $3,000 carriage and take the child on the Metro and read a book to the child in a very loud voice, so you will know what great parents they are. Meanwhile, they beat their children with wire hangers when no one is around.

Speaking of children, my late Serena hated children. She was very smart. We had this blonde woman in the neighborhood I used to call "mother of the year." She would jog with her horrible offspring in one of those jogging carriages and expound life lessons in the loudest voice possible, so we would all be impressed with her mothering skills. She would also steal furniture while people were moving in or out. I am not making that up. She assumed that if the movers put a chair or other item on the street for a few moments while they made room or gathered more items, that item was free for the taking. I guess this was her five-second rule. She used to get into arguments all the time with people. I heard more than once, "Oh I thought you were throwing it away." Who throws away a Queen Anne desk in museum quality condition?

When the landlords redid my kitchen, she actually stepped into my apartment and asked one of the workers to move the stove outside, so she could take it home. This was the goddamn new stove they were getting ready to install! I walked into the kitchen and ordered her off the property and to take her blond pet chimpanzee with her.

Anyway, before that incident, her future serial killer son wanted to pet Serena one day, and I said, "I am sorry, but she is afraid of children, so I would prefer he didn't." From that day on, she would always say as she passed me on the street, "That is the dog that hates children." And I would say, "Oh look. It's mother of the year."

Speaking of touching my dog. I don't like children I don't know touching my dog. My dog is clean, and children have hands full of food and God knows what else. Kids also grab and poke. With Serena, I would scoop her up whenever a kid came near, and one mother got really upset, insisting I let her child touch my dog, and I said no, and she just insisted, so I said in my creepiest voice, "Can I touch your child?" She ran off and never asked me again.

Then there was the hippy who said to his kids, "Go get that dog." The kids came running, and I scooped Serena up. I turned around and … I cannot write what I said to him, but most of the words sounded like fuck and motherfucker.

Esmeralda is OK with kids. Her dog walker, Mrs. M, has two grandchildren who go with her when she walks Esmeralda. As a matter of fact, Esmeralda likes children more than I do. Since Mrs. M is so good with her, and Esmeralda likes her and Mr. M, they were the logical choice to babysit while I was gone for only three days.

I returned, and Mrs. M told me she was no trouble at all. They loved having her. So sweet and well behaved and perfectly housebroken. She even napped with Mr. M while Mrs. M went shopping. They want to babysit her again.

I'll have to think about that while I clean the shit stain off my new carpet.

MAKE IT STOP

Funny how quickly one learns he can no longer call maintenance or apartment management every time he has a problem. Well, not ha ha funny, but whimsical. No wait. Whimsical isn't the word. The word is frustrating.

Although I am very good at putting together furniture (if I do say so myself), when it comes to home repairs, I am like George of the Jungle. Any time I have attempted to fix something around one of my apartments, the situation usually ended up with me calling a repairman to come fix what I had "fixed," and the landlord paying triple the initial cost of the repair. I became very good at saying things like, "I don't know how that pipe came loose and flooded the kitchen?" "I looked up, and the next thing I knew, the light fixture came crashing down."

I should have earned an Academy Award years ago.

While in college, I was hired part-time as a construction worker. After watching me hammer nails in a fashion that either split the wood, bent the nail or missed the target completely, I was relegated to perform menial tasks that I was assured were vital to the construction of the house. "Hey, Stern, move those two-by-fours from the front yard to the back." Needless to say, I became a very good *nuch-schlepper*.

I still wonder if any of those houses with my split wood or bent nails are still standing. By now, some have to have been remodeled, and somewhere there is a happy homeowner, who is pulling up his carpet and saying, "What the fuck kind of moron framed this house?"

This is where I feign surprise and say, "I don't know how that floorboard split in half?"

Now, I am a happy homeowner. Silly me. I thought I could prance around in an apron, pearls and sensible heels, and all would be well.

I do have a warranty on the structure and the appliances being that this house is brand new, and I have managed to get a few things fixed without admitting I am the one who broke them.

When I first tried out my Weedeater, a lawn care tool I despise, not only did I weedeat my shin (is weedeat a verb?), but also, I managed to poke a few holes in the skirting around my house. A few days later, I called Bubba, head of the management office (yes that is his name) and said, "There are a lot of cracks and holes in my skirting, can you guys replace them? I think the lawn care guys did that when this house was the model." Two days later, I had new skirting.

I would like to thank the Academy, my agent and Moses.

But even I knew that a day would come when my Claudette Colbert routine would no longer get things fixed for free. I am a homeowner now, so there is no longer a naïve landlord or apartment manager to call, which brings us to Global Warming.

Huh?

Stick with me here. When I taught school (and I was really a lousy teacher), I used to say to my students, "It is a fast-paced world, so you need to keep up with me!"

Global Warming has brought us extremely hot summers with violent storms and bitter cold winters with lots of snow according to Al Gore, who is now single, which has nothing to do with the price of eggs at Weis.

I grew up in Newport News, Virginia, and like much of the Eastern Seaboard (is that supposed to be capitalized?), we rarely had spring or fall. One day, the temperature would be eighty degrees, and the next day, the fifties. Anyone from this part of the country is used to that.

A consequence of having these extreme temperature changes is that on Monday you are running your air conditioning and on Tuesday, you turn on the heat. We called it life; now they call it Global Warming.

That is what happened one week. On Friday, the temperature was beautiful and in the eighties. On Saturday, it dipped into the fifties, so I turned on my heat for the first time.

Propane heat, like gas heat, is a little foreign to me. I am used to electric heat, which comes on immediately. Gas heat seems to do something that makes odd sounds for a few minutes before the fan comes on. See how technologically advanced I am?

My heater kept doing the odd sound thing for a bit too long, and the fan would not come on. Any normal homeowner would have done one of two things: either fixed it or called a repairman. I am not normal.

I opened up the furnace and looked around. Remember the episode of *The Dick Van Dyke Show* where they had a flashback to Rob and Laura's wedding? His Jeep broke down, so he opened the hood and said, "Well, that's a motor." I pretty much did the same thing.

I looked for a pilot light or a fan switch and couldn't find one. So, I called Bubba. He told me to look for the gas control switch and tell him what direction it was pointing. I said, "Up and down."

He said, "That's correct. Now look for the primer switch." And of course, he could have been talking Chinese to me. After ten minutes describing every switch and wire on the furnace, I found it. It, of course, was not in the "on" position.

He then told me to flick the on/off switch on and off a few times until the flame took. Yes, I did find that switch, too. He said once the flame took, the heat would come on, but he also warned me that since this was the first time it would be running, there would be a lot of smoke, so don't be alarmed.

Before I continue, let me tell you that propane cooking makes the smoke alarms, and I have four, go off every time you preheat the oven. I plan to switch to electric at some point because this is driving Esmeralda crazy even if I hit the button on the alarms almost immediately. She is running out of places to hide.

Well, the heat came on, and I didn't see any smoke, but within seconds, all the smoke alarms went nuts. Esmeralda went running and hid in the bedroom closet. I then proceeded to run from one end of the house to the other pushing the buttons on the alarms in an attempt to make them stop.

This, of course, proved futile. I even opened the living room windows, but the alarms kept sounding, and I was on my fifth lap around the house, when I finally screamed in frustration, "MAKE IT STOP!"

And they did!

I didn't know whether to be happy or a little scared.

Did my years of watching *Bewitched* and studying Endora finally pay off?

I didn't know.

I did turn the heat on and off a few more times, and the alarms never sounded again.

Now, only one questions remains. Will I use my powers for good or for evil?

FOR TWO EASY PAYMENTS
OF $19.95

I admit it. I have bought my share of drek over the years, and apparently I have not learned my lesson. Even though I have banned myself from watching QVC — except when Joan Rivers is selling her jewelry, I still manage to buy the occasional piece of crap for only two easy payments of $19.95. And, have you ever noticed the only time you buy that crap is when you least can afford it? You said yes, didn't you?

Remember that thing you plugged into your wall and it used the wiring in your house to get you free cable? I bought one. The only station I got was the Fidel Castro Channel directly from Havana. Remember Deal-a-Meal from Richard Simmons? I dealt all my meals for the week by Tuesday at 10:15 am. There was this cream that was supposed to knock ten years off your face. Oh it knocked them off all right, along with seven layers of skin. I looked like a burn victim for a month.

I bought the wallet for organizing all your cards and IDs, etc. Everyone asked me why I was carrying a lady's billfold. I bought that glove for grooming the dog. All it did was annoy her. There was the cup holder you attached to your car door that knocked the can of soda in your lap every time you hit a bump. There were those things for hanging pictures on the wall that could easily be removed by pulling a tab. They removed half the wall.

In my defense, I learned these buying habits from my father. He was the king of buying drek. Ironically, whenever you bought something, he would always say, "How much did they get you for that?" He thought the whole world was getting ripped off. I bought a new car and rather than congratulation me, he said, "How much did they get you for that?" This was a man who bought a Desoto and a Corvair ... and don't get me started on his long string of crappy Fords.

He once bought this vegetable protein powder you were supposed to add to food to make it last longer or be more filling or as filler or as a supplement. I never did figure it out. He bought a case of it. I think it was the same soy protein additive that was popular in the 1970s that school cafeteria's added to their hamburger meat. Well, we poured it on our meat, and let's just say the only thing it added was more time on the bowl.

My dad bought my brother and me ten-speed bikes, and he never let us forget it (to this day whenever someone buys me a gift, I expect to hear about it for twenty years). The bikes, which were orange and called Fiorellis, were from Italy, complete with Italian directions. But, that wasn't Italian he was screaming while trying to assemble them. I think he bought them from one of his shady friends, of which there were a few. Apparently, they fell off the back of the truck.

We had a friend whose parents completely furnished their house with stuff that fell off the back of the truck. His father always had ten watches up his sleeve and three around his ankle he would sell you for the right price.

According to my father, Uncle Stanley, his brother, was worse. If a man was standing in back of a truck on a street corner and said, "Psst, come here." Uncle Stanley was sure to buy whatever he was selling. When he would tell me this story, I would always think of Lucy Ricardo in the butcher shop trying to sell that side of beef.

My most recent purchase worthy of the "Drek Hall of Fame" was an item that was supposed to make water sealing my deck a breeze. I had been looking forward to sealing my deck for a while. When I moved in, it was "green," and I was instructed to wait eight to ten weeks before sealing it.

However, by week ten, we were in the middle of two hurricanes and a five-day stretch of rain that dumped twenty inches on us. My deck was becoming a sponge, and I was desperate. We then endured another month of rain until the few days before Yom Kippur. According to the Thompson's Water Seal directions, I needed three days before and three days after for proper application and drying. I read that while standing in Lowe's and deciding which product to buy.

Next to the cans of water seal was this plastic device for spraying on the water seal for even coverage and less mess, and it sold for $19.95! I looked it over, and it resembled a pesticide dispenser. Rather than scrutinize its construction, I was mesmerized by that magic price: $19.95. I bought it. But knowing my history and just in case I had done it once again, I bought an extra can of water seal, a cheap roller, a brush and a paint tray.

The older, wiser me always has a backup plan.

The time had come for me to water proof my first deck! I was excited. I put the dispenser together and filled it with Thompson's

Water Seal. Then I pumped it as the instructions said to get the sealant to flow throw the hose.

I pumped and I pumped, but no sealant was making its way through the hose. I didn't understand this. I have been told I have magic hands and can get any hose to fill then spill. Had I lost my touch?

Apparently, I had not lost my touch, but I did manage to do something else. I water sealed my walkway. That lovely little dispenser had split in half along the bottom and let out a full can of sealant. I didn't even get mad. I rolled my eyes, hosed off the walkway, pulled out the paint tray, roller and brush and proceeded to do the deck the old fashioned way.

My projects always seem to end up this way. The easy way ends up being a disaster, and the old fashioned way saves the day.

I should never buy anything with a price tag of $19.95.

Will I ever learn?

HALLOWEEN IN THE HOOD

If there is one holiday that really gives you a feel for your neighbors and your neighborhood in general, it is Halloween.

When I was a kid, Halloween was a huge deal, or at least I thought it was. Our costumes pretty much consisted of a mask. Or, we went as hobos. Remember when hobos were not politically incorrect? I would love to see a kid dressed as a homeless person today. I think that would be hysterical. Or, maybe not.

I find it funny with my eidetic memory that I cannot remember one Halloween costume I wore as a kid. I guess because I was inside the mask looking out, and we also stopped trick or treating around age nine. Today, they trick or treat up to age twenty-two. My mother was not one to put much effort into costumes the way mothers get into them now, so I think I wore my regular clothes and a mask, and that was it.

Maybe she thought a full-fledged costume would make me Gay or a drag queen. How is that abstinence education working for you, Mrs. Palin?

Around age ten, my friend Jerry from across the street and I would make a haunted house out of his garage for the trick or treaters, and this was a lot of fun, too.

On Halloween, we had the usual hijinks — kids bags being lifted, smashed pumpkins in the street, toilet papered trees and the like. These were to be expected, and a Halloween without such mayhem would be un-American.

As an adult living in apartments, Halloween was not a big deal in Newport News or Florida, but when I moved to Mount Pleasant, the gates of hell opened up, and all the monsters and ghouls were on the hunt. I lived one block from an elementary school, and little did I realize how many children lived in my neighborhood. I went through three bags of candy in twenty minutes then I had to turn off the lights and hide under my bed. They kept knocking on the door until 10:00 pm! I kept hearing in low, growling voices, "Trick or Treat ... trick or treat ... we know you're in there!"

I learned my lesson, and every year after that, I bought ten bags of candy as did all my neighbors. We would dress up for the trick or treaters, and a good time was had by all.

Then came Rockville, and living in a luxury apartment building, I went for two Halloweens with no trick or treaters, not even the man from the third floor whom the nut on the fourth floor claimed was a registered sex offender. The first year, I ate two bags of miniature Mars bars. Someone had to enjoy them.

So, I expected living in a mobile home community to be much like Mount Pleasant. While the average age of our residents is fifty-five, there are about ten teenagers and an equal number of smaller children, plus there are some who babysit their grandchildren while their parents work at night.

I bought eight bags of the crappiest candy I could find — at least crappy to me, so I wouldn't eat any of it. Jolly Ranchers, Smarties, Nerds, Starburst and something called Monster Sticks. Of course, I had to sample one of everything to be sure I didn't like them. I didn't.

Then, I waited, and I waited, and I waited. Around 7:00 pm, the first trick or treaters came. I gave the two of them a handful of candy each. They were very polite and said thank you. Fifteen minutes later, three more came. They were very polite and said thank you. Ten minutes later, Mrs. M's grandchildren came and asked where Esmeralda was. Esmeralda was sitting on the back of the sofa wondering why people were constantly knocking on the door and interrupting her after dinner nap.

Have I told you she doesn't bark when someone knocks on the door? She doesn't even care. Someone could walk in and attack me, and as long as they didn't wake her, she wouldn't care.

I was impressed with the costumes. All were well executed, and my favorite was the five-year-old, complete with perfect bouffant hair piece, dressed like a bride with a veil and train. She looked like a midget bride. Can one say midget anymore? I meant Munchkin. Can one say Muchkin?

Twenty minutes and ten kids later, Halloween in the hood was over.

That's it! No one came from other neighborhoods to trick or treat in our fine community? No teenagers came out trick or treating? Only little kids? All very polite well costumed little kids?

With no more kids, and four unused bags of candy even though I threw a fistful in every bag, I took Esmeralda for her before bed walk. Here is what I noticed. Half the porch lights were out. No one had a real pumpkin, and only one family, a mean father, his stumbling drunk wife, holding a Budweiser tall boy, and their two unhappy children were out. While four or five houses were decorated (including Gay boy's), this was a major disappointment.

What is happening to our country? This is un-American! These people are gun-toting, God fearing Americans! Is there no hope left for our great nation?

I really should not have been surprised. My parents did the same thing once we were grown, and I guess anyone without children figures they did their Halloween time. I am childless — well, human childless — so I am immune to Halloween burnout, and those of my persuasion love Halloween — another excuse to do drag, any kind of drag!

But, come on people. What is Halloween without at least one smashed pumpkin in the street? No one egged a house or toilet papered a tree. Is the economy so bad that people can't even spare one roll of toilet paper? Next year, I'll toilet paper my own trees and smash a pumpkin on my deck.

As Endora would say, "I find this situation utterly boring."

Maybe during Thanksgiving they will drop turkeys from a helicopter. "As God is my witness, I thought turkeys could fly!" — Arthur Carlson, *WKRP in Cincinnati*.

THE BANE OF MY EXISTENCE

In the early 1980s, Lucille Ball was interviewed by a reporter from *Rolling Stone Magazine*. There are two things, among many, about the interview that stuck with me. Lucille Ball would not let them photograph her, and when asked about her hair, she said, "It is the bane of my existence."

I can totally identify. For as long as I can remember, I have had a battle with my hair. I come from a family of good hair on one side and not so good on the other. They say you inherit your hair traits from your mother's side. If her father was bald, you will be bald. If her hair turned gray, yours will turn gray. Whatever.

On my father's side, they have thick, wavy, gorgeous hair, which may turn prematurely gray, but looks great until their last breath. On my mother's side, they either style the few hairs they have into a bouffant or wear a wig.

My hair is thin, semi-curly, dry, and unmanageable. Before I discovered mousse and gel, I always looked like a dirty Q-tip. My hair has never been fashionable. I could never wear it in any style that was longer than an inch and look stylish. I did have a Jewfro for many years but not by choice.

I always threatened that I would shave it all off.

In the early 1990s, when I lived in Florida, my friend Farrah went through chemotherapy. In solidarity with her, I shaved my head. I never felt so free in my life. My hair never looked better ... then it grew back.

For the most part, I decided to keep it short and quit trying to make it look like something it wasn't. I even managed to find a stylist who could cut it every two weeks exactly as I wanted, and here is where my dilemma remains today.

When you have good hair, you can use any shampoo and product and pretty much look presentable at all times. When you have bad hair, you first must find someone who knows how to cut it, and then find products that tame your mane. You must also hope your stylist sticks around for a few years!

Now, I have been to salons, barbers, beauty schools and every hair styling place in between. In high school and college, I went to Jan Mar Beauty School for a $3 haircut. The owner, Evelyn Adams, a lovely woman who died recently, knew me from my job at Baskin Robbins, so she would come over and cut my hair showing one of the students how to do it. For that price, I never complained, although she would cut it very short. But with the dry look, my hair was very manageable at that length.

I decided to let my hair grow a little longer when I taught school to be in style with the big hair of the 1980s. But, I should have known better. No matter who cut my hair, I was back to being a dirty Q-tip.

I did find the first person since the owner of Jan Mar who could cut my hair. She was a beautician at Danny's Hair Loft, and she was fantastic. Then, I discovered mousse and volumizer. I may have looked as if I was wearing a black fuzzy football helmet, but my hair did stay in place. Unfortunately, my new hair dresser moved to Germany, and I was back to trying to find someone who could cut my horrible hair.

I had little to no luck. Just when I would find someone, he or she would move. I was spending a fortune, and no matter who cut it, I looked awful.

In Florida, it took four years to find a stylist who could cut it perfectly after the shaving of my head and the decision to keep it short. He worked in a Cuban-owned shop. The owner had Dairy Queen hair — you know the type, all whipped up and dyed platinum blonde. She would sit at the front desk with her Maltese in her pocket book. Rumor was her bags were packed and ready in the back of the shop, while she waited for Castro to die, so she could return to Havana and reclaim the land her family lost in the revolution. Come to think of it, she was always holding her car keys. I guess she wanted to be the first to return.

Then, I moved to DC, and I was back to square one.

Over the years, I have alternated between barbers and hairdressers, and I have found barbers to be better at cutting my hair. But, that has not stopped me from trying the occasional stylist. I am an optimist, and I am convinced there is a stylist who can cut this wiry mess, allowing me to let my hair grow longer than an inch.

There is an expression in Florida that goes like this: "He's got a big ass charging those prices," which is usually followed by: "This is ridiculous."

You use that expression when someone just starts a business and charges as much as someone with twenty years' experience. For example, a guy graduates from beauty school and on his first job charges $40 for a haircut. "He's got a big ass! This is ridiculous." See how it works.

That is what I ran into. A salon opened next to my gym in what was originally a gallery. I thought I would give them a try. They charged $55 a haircut. I knew I was crazy, since I could get five barber cuts for that price, but I wanted to give them a chance, and perhaps I would let my hair grow out and be somewhat stylish ... or at least contemporary.

I don't know how, but I managed to get the only straight stylist in a Gay-owned shop.

So, there I was being styled by this pierced, tattooed straight guy, fresh out of beauty school, and the first thing he said was, "I have to fix what your last stylist did." That to me is the equivalent of a contractor walking into your house and saying, "Uh oh." Translated: "This is going to cost you."

I said, "Don't tell me that. Just cut me hair the way I asked you." He cut my hair and put in enough product to make it waterproof for a season. However, one washing, and my hair never looked right again. You see, that is the sign of a bad haircut. It may look good when you leave, but if you cannot get it to look right again, don't go back.

I then spent almost ten years trying to find the right barber. No more $55 haircuts for me. And seriously, when did it get so expensive to get a bad haircut?

I finally found a women barber in a gangland barbershop in Mount Pleasant. Sure the MS-13 guys were always in there getting their buzz cuts with their names trimmed into the back of their heads, so you would know who got capped that night. But, she did a good job, and getting my hair cut there gave me street cred. God knows I needed street cred.

Then I moved to Rockville. After one bad barber, I found a Vietnamese barber, named Nick. When I first walked into his shop, there was no one there, so I walked out and asked one of the business owners in the strip mall if he was any good. They assured me he was, and they were right. Curiously, his shop was always empty.

When I moved to Jessup, I tried out a barber near the grocery store. I left the shop looking as if I were headed for the electric chair.

After that, I found myself driving the Beltway back and forth to Rockville for a $10 haircut every three weeks. If you do not live here, I cannot begin to tell you how miserable driving on the Beltway can be at any hour of any day.

It was time for me to "move my life" to Jessup. I could not keep going back to Rockville for haircuts and doctors and veterinary visits and car repairs, etc. I went online and found the barbershop Nick had mentioned when I told him why I kept coming back. They had great reviews.

As luck would have it, they are Vietnamese owned and staffed as well. In my politically incorrect defense, Nick suggested I look for a Vietnamese owned shop, and he did mention this one. Is it racist to be happy when you discover a certain ethnic group owns a business? I mean I wouldn't buy Chinese food from a restaurant owned by Irving Greenberg? Then again ...

A female barber named Sue Anne cut my hair and did a perfect job, and it was only $9! I tipped her $5. As it turned out, she usually does not work Fridays, but the owner was out that day, so she took his place.

Then Sue Anne left. But, Tin took over for her. Tin does a great job, but this middle-aged man always massages my head, neck and shoulders after the haircut in a way that is, how shall I say, sensual? In all my years getting straight hairdressers and barbers, did I finally find the Gay one?

I think he is making passes at me. I could do worse. He does have a steady job in a busy shop.

I can say God was looking out for me. Yes, God has nothing better to do than help me find a good barber, which reminds me of an old joke.

A man goes to his barber before flying to Italy to meet the Pope. The barber gives him the full treatment, including what he, the barber, considers his best haircut ever.

When the man returns, the barber asks what the Pope said to him. The man says, "I kneeled before him, he put his hand on my head and asked, 'Where did you get that lousy haircut?'"

OBEAGLE CARE

I believe it was Al Gore who said his dog gets better health care than his mother-in-law. He was right.

In my further efforts to Jessupize my life, I figured it was time to find a veterinarian close to home rather than fight Beltway traffic for three hours just to get a fifteen-minute exam even though I loved Esmeralda's veterinarian.

Decades of experience had taught me that finding a vet is a bit easier than finding a primary care physician. Ironically, in Florida, I had an easy time finding a doctor, while finding a good vet was quite problematic.

When I first adopted Serena at eight weeks in West Palm Beach, Florida, I went to a vet a co-worker recommended. They were a bit vaccination happy and had me bring her in every two weeks for two months for boosters and the like. She had developed a problem and couldn't keep her food down, and they recommended a tonsillectomy. The price alone scared me, not to mention the prospect of surgery on such a young dog. And do you bring a dog ice cream after that? How do you keep her from barking?

In Florida, a state with very tough animal abuse laws, the Humane Society has retired veterinarians who volunteer their time to conduct exams and minor surgeries, along with spaying and neutering, for around $25 (at least that is what it was in 1995). Having spent a small fortune on vaccines and exams for her stomach, I was running out of money, so I went to a Humane Society vet.

This retired veterinarian in his eighties told me that her diagnosis was the most ridiculous thing he ever heard and in fifty years of practice never once performed a tonsillectomy on a dog. She was diagnosed with irritable bowel and a sensitive stomach and put on prescription dog food, which she remained on for the rest of her life with no more problems until a guest at a party fed her something that almost killed her — but that is another story for another time.

Note: It is not cute to feed someone's dog without asking first. And, if the host has a sign on the buffet that says "Do Not Feed Serena Any Food," pay attention to it.

Yes, I am obsessive and anal retentive. Get over it. As I have told you before, my mother rushed my potty training, and now you are paying the price for it.

I continued to go to the veterinarian at the Humane Society, being that my new puppy was eating all my finances. When I moved to DC, I went to work for a company filled with weirdoes (apparently that is spelled with an "oes").

My boss was a British Royal Family-obsessed hoarder, who was bitter about being single at fifty and passive aggressive as well. Her desk was surrounded by piles of newspapers, and we worked in an open office! She told me she had all the old tires from her car on her balcony. When Princess Diana died, she started spouting off about conspiracy theories and how Diana really wasn't in *that* car.

Her boss was a man they had been trying to fire for two years. His office looked as if a suicide bomber loaded himself up with memos and blew himself up in there. Every time the vice president would come by to fire him, he wasn't in. He always said he was at a funeral, when in fact he was playing tennis. On many occasions, the VP would ask me where he was, and I said he was at a "tennis funeral." One day he came in wearing his tennis outfit and stood at my desk talking to me and farted. He said excuse me and continued with what he was saying. Oh my God! No boss ever — or co-worker of mine for that matter — farted mid-sentence before ... or since.

They ended up firing him by phone. I had the pleasure of cleaning up his office, and I found memos from the Nixon era. How long had they been trying to get rid of him?

They had the worst computer equipment, and mine would crash all the time. I decided to wear my bike helmet at my desk. When asked why, I said, "If my computer crashes, I don't want to hurt my head." A week later, they replaced my computer.

Meanwhile, we had one editor, who as my boss bitterly said, lived a charmed life. She married the perfect man, had perfect skin, gave birth to the perfect baby, lived in the perfect house, etc.

I needed to find a vet in DC, so I decided to take Serena to the Adams Morgan Animal Clinic because it was within walking distance of my apartment. When Ms. Charmed caught wind of this, she got up from her desk (something she never did), walked over to mine and proceeded to tell me how they kidnapped her perfect cat and wouldn't let her have him for two weeks until she paid a ransom.

Did I mention that even some insane people lead charmed lives?

I would make a comment about how they hired nothing but weirdoes, but they hired me, so I better not go there.

Fortunately, I have learned over the years that there are some people who seek drama and aren't happy until they find it. These people also seem to find themselves in situations that are totally unbelievable. Did she seriously think I would believe they had kidnapped her cat for a ransom?

These are also the same people who leave negative comments online on Yelp and Epinion and other sites, while ninety percent of the comments are positive. You know what I mean. "I got a massage from Peter, and he pulled a gun on me during the session because I didn't like the music he was playing. Don't go to him!" Too bad Peter didn't shoot him.

My friend Danny took his dog to Adams Morgan Animal Clinic (a big dog that is still alive at sixteen) and couldn't say enough good things about them, even though he made fun of the one veterinarian who looked like Herman Munster.

They remained Serena's clinic from 1997 until she died in 2009. They always had an opening for an appointment, and they took good care of her. They were especially good when I had to make the decision to put her down.

I wish my experiences with health care in this area were as good as Serena's.

In Florida, as I mentioned, I had a very good doctor. When I had a minor bicycle accident and a few days later started emitting strawberry cream (use your imagination), my doctor immediately diagnosed it as a broken blood vessel caused by the bicycle seat. He said he saw it many times with men in the Czechoslovakian cavalry where he was a military physician. He always had open appointments, never a waiting room filled with dozens of people, and didn't guess at a diagnosis.

When I first moved here, it was a different story entirely.

There was the doctor who had to look everything up in a book — I mean everything. Now, she probably uses Wikipedia to determine what to prescribe.

There was the doctor with ADD who would have you strip down and wait for him then forget you were there. A nurse once told me he had a patient on all fours waiting for a prostate exam, who stayed that way for an hour. I am all for a prostate exam, but who has that kind of time?

Then there was Doctor Colombo. He really wasn't Colombo, but Peter Falk, *alav hashalom*, would have been tapped to play him in a movie. Doctor Colombo would get his prescriptions mixed up. I was on the pill for two months before I realized it. I was so emotional all the time, and my periods had stopped.

There was Doctor Himmler, as I called her. She would yell at me and bark orders. Drop you pants! Up on the table! Quit whining! I always pictured her coming in wearing strap boots and a harness, carrying a whip. Would you believe I went to her for three years? Yes, you would. Moving on …

Finally, there was Doctor Three-Hour. No matter what your ailment or reason for going to him, your visit lasted exactly three hours, and they put you through complete blood work, urinalysis and whatever special they were running that day. I had an echocardiogram when I complained of an earache. I had a pelvic exam when I sprained my hand.

I think they just loved billing the insurance company. The doctor never examined you, himself. He would sit across from you at his desk and write prescriptions based on what you told him you needed. As a result, I have a fifteen-year supply of Viagra. Of course, with the state of my "social life" that could be fifteen pills.

I finally found a good primary physician who unfortunately was in Rockville. But this isn't about me … seriously.

When I adopted Esmeralda, I took her to Adams Morgan Animal Clinic even though I was living in Rockville, but the drive was killing me, so I reluctantly switched to a veterinarian in Rockville, recommended by a co-worker, Nebel Street Animal Clinic. They were fantastic. I actually called Adams Morgan Animal Clinic to apologize for switching. They understood completely.

I was reluctant to switch again, but after much research, we once again found a good veterinarian, Cat and Dog Hospital of Columbia. I found them through a web search. They had phenomenal reviews, with one exception. You guessed it — some drama queen, claiming they killed her cat. Upon further reading, it was revealed that the cat was twenty-two years old. My guess is the cat was past its expiration date, begged for mercy and eventually committed suicide.

Obeagle Care is a success. Please don't repeal it.

FROM ALOOF TO CUDDLER

I have lived with dogs for as long as I can remember. The first dog in my life was actually one I don't quite remember. His name was Lucky, and apparently when my mother brought me home from the hospital, he would stand guard over me. He snarled and sometimes bit whoever came near me, with my mother being the only exception. She must have been the one to feed him. When he bit a meter reader who came within fifty feet of my playpen in the backyard, the decision was made to send him to a farm. I guess he was Lucky. He got out while he could and no longer had to live with my family. He was the only family member I had who protected me. Oh well.

When I was four, my parents gave my brother and me this funny looking dog who was the runt of the litter. Although quite popular today, few people had seen a pug in 1966. Oh My God! Was I four years old in 1966? Where is my Geritol?

Because she was the runt, she was small, and her tail did not curl quite right. We didn't care about that. She was a puppy, and all kids love a puppy.

Anyway, Kelly Gaye Stern, her full name since she came from a long line of champion pugs, was the sweetest dog, and as the name implies, she was a Lesbian. We tried breeding her with a handsome pug named Ralph on several occasions, but she would have none of it. She adored my mother and would whine whenever my mother left the house.

When she got older, she would insist on sitting in a recliner with my mother even though she couldn't jump anymore, so my mother would help her up. My father remarked upon witnessing how my mother would assist her from behind, "That dog thinks you are a Lesbian because you keep sticking your finger up her ass."

As I said, most people had never seen one before, and she would sit in the window all day watching cars go by. Our friends would ask about our funny looking Siamese cat in the window.

And, my mother taught her how to sing "I Love You."

Kelly was also a snuggler. She would alternate between sleeping with my brother and me and always under the covers and snuggled up against our legs. The two of us would watch TV lying on our stomachs on the floor, and Kelly would have to lie down between us.

They say you have not owned a dog until you've been owned by a pug. They are right.

Kelly died at age sixteen. Imagine having a dog from age four to twenty.

Next, came Daisy, the craziest dog ever to grace my world. Daisy was a long-haired Dachsund Yorkshire terrier mix, whom my mother picked out at the Animal Rescue League because she was on top of a dog house barking at all the big dogs. She was tiny when they brought her home, and she had three hairs for a tail.

Daisy was extremely affectionate and loved to sit in my father's lap or sit up next to him in a "beg" position. Whenever anyone yelled, she would run for Dad and seek comfort from their wrath. We would sometimes yell goddamnmit just to watch her crash through his newspaper and sit up next to him.

When we would leave the house, she would take every item from my bedroom closet and bring it into the living room. I wish we had webcams back then because I would love a video of her taking every item one-by-one through the house.

Daisy would usually sleep with my parents because she adored my father. My mother once said, "He comes home from paying golf, pats me on the head and kisses the dog."

She also attacked vacuum cleaners and once punctured the bag while I was vacuuming. Not funny ... well it is now. And, she had a thing for basketballs and could entertain herself rolling one around for hours.

I never saw a dog age the way she did. Her brown and black fur, which by the way, grew to floor length with a long bushy tail, turned completely gray and almost white during her final years. A year before she died, I adopted Serena, a toy parti-poodle.

Serena wanted so much to play with Daisy. Daisy wanted nothing to do with Serena.

Daisy died at sixteen.

Of all the snugglers out there, Serena was the oddest. When I adopted Serena, I swore I would not have another dog sleep in the bed. The first week I had her, I actually was taking care of her and her twin brother Moochy, while they were being weaned from their mother, Venus, who was also a rescue and was pregnant when she was saved from an animal abuser. Before you ask, the Serena-Venus connection was purely accidental since no one had heard of them when I named Serena. She was named for Samantha's cooky cousin.

So, the first night, they whined because they wanted to get into the bed. I made a deal. They could stay in the bed until they fell asleep, then I would put them in their bed. They fell asleep on top of each other. At barely two pounds each, it was hard to tell where one began and the other ended. Serena was black and white (thus a parti-poodle), and moochy all black. I then picked them up with one hand — both fit in one hand — and put them in their bed, and they slept through the night. This went on for two nights until …

My apartment in Florida was the second floor of a cottage, which once served as a butler's quarters. On the way down the stairs on the second morning to put them on the grass to pee and poop, I slipped. I was so worried about the dogs, I did everything to keep them safe, and I broke my foot.

They were fine; I was not. I had a performance with my modern dance troupe that evening. I begged the doctor not to put my foot in a cast. I danced that evening. After returning from the performance, it was bed time.

Same deal as before — fall asleep in my bed then you go into your bed. But, I was tired, and they ended up sleeping with me all night, and after Moochy went back to my friend John's, Serena always slept in the bed.

Now, Serena was also an alpha dog, and I often said our relationship was like that of Joan and Christina. I would say to her, "Why can't you give me the respect I deserve?" and she said, "Because I am not one of your fans!"

She slept where she wanted and had to be touching me at all times, often shoving me right out of the bed. It is amazing how much room a nine-pound dog can take.

Serena also had to sit in my lap at all times during the few times I actually would sit still. However, I was not allowed to pet her unless she wanted to be petted. Did I mention she was alpha?

She went deaf then blind, and I had to train her not to sleep in the bed because she had fallen off a couple of times when she couldn't find the edge. Now, she could never jump that high, so I didn't have to worry about her jumping up on the bed, but …

For three nights, she whined very loudly by the bed near my head all night. All night! Finally, she realized that she wasn't going to get up there anymore, and she slept in her bed for the last three months of her life. She died at age fourteen. Moochy died the week before she did. Venus, their mother at seventeen years old, was still alive. Amazing.

Now, with three snuggling and cuddling dogs, I kind of expected the same from Esmeralda. I was in for a surprise.

Emeralda is a study in what happens when human contact is denied for so long. I read somewhere that because dogs have been domesticated for more than 15,000 years they need human contact and companionship for their psychological well-being.

Since Esmeralda spent almost eight years in a cage, she did not understand what it meant to live with a person, and I expected that. One of two things can happen with a dog with her background; she can become withdrawn, or she can suddenly discover her puppyhood. The bonding, and especially affection, can take as long as a few years to occur.

I have never stuck around long enough for any of the jerks I dated to become affectionate and bond with me, so I had no experience— or patience — in this area.

You already know about her need to escape and the fact that it took almost a year for her to eat in front of me during the daytime rather than wait for me to go to sleep. Now, she looks forward to meal time and eats while I am standing near her, and I don't have to worry about spooking her by walking around. Just doing things in the same room would make her stop eating once she started eating in daylight. Now, she acts like the dogs they used to starve for the Alpo commercials in the 1970s when I feed her. She dances around as I prepare her food.

About the bonding thing. My brother noticed this when I was walking her. She looks up at me the whole time. But that is OK to some extent, but the whole time we lived in Rockville, she would stay in the bedroom, under the bed, while I was in the living room watching TV, unless I closed the bedroom door and forced her to spend her time with me. Then, and only then, she would hop up onto the couch and sleep on top of one of the back cushions and keep her distance.

I was allowed to pet her but only at arm's length. She never, and I mean never, sat next to me. I would constantly kiss her forehead and tell her I loved her, but she was the first dog I've had who does not lick my face. Maybe that is a good thing. A boyfriend did that once, and I still get nauseated thinking about it.

She has never played with a ball. If you throw a ball, she looks at you as if to say, why did you do that? So, bonding through ball tossing was not an option. She does like to run around in circles barking if you do the same thing. If anyone peaks into my windows and sees us barking at each other on all fours, they are surely going to get me a suite at St. Elizabeth's.

But, I had to remember everything I read about it taking as long as a few years for a dog to show affection. Studies are all well and good, but when Mrs. M came over for a visit, and Esmeralda sat next to her on the couch, while Mrs. M scratched her, I got a little jealous. "Wow, she never sits next to me on the couch," I said.

And, I thought I was doing everything right.

Then, everything started to change.

When I would come home from work, she would carry on and run around in circles, howling and barking. She doesn't even do that for Mrs. M. So there!

Esmeralda started following me from room to room, and she had to be in the same room I was in. I didn't have to close a door to a room to get her to spend time with me. I sometimes purposely walk all over the house just see if she will follow me, and she does.

I no longer had to grab her to brush her every night. I could sit on the floor holding the brush, and she would come right up to me. As a matter of fact, if I am fifteen minutes late with her evening grooming, she reminds be by sitting in our spot on the floor and whines. She even comes right up to me for her weekly ear cleaning, and she loves her monthly bath (although she has always liked her monthly bath).

Then, she started coming up to the bed and pounding out "Babalu" with her paws because she wanted to sleep with me. Wow, nobody wants to sleep with *me*.

However, she still kept her distance. In the bed, she would stay on her side or sleep on the other pillow.

Then …

In the middle of one night, she snuggled up close to me and put her head on my shoulder and snored away until it was time to get up. I was so happy that I didn't move because I didn't want to disturb her. This was a breakthrough.

Then …

After dinner, she started hopping up on the couch and sitting close to me, not touching me, but close enough for me to scratch her, especially behind the ears.

And, she started coming up to me and sniffing my face then touching my nose with hers, wagging her tail, then walking away. This is her way of kissing. Esmeralda did this in front of the veterinarian after insisting on sitting on a chair next to mine. The doctor said, "Oh, she really likes you."

Then …

We were watching TV, and I was scratching her and leaning on my left arm with my feet propped up on an ottoman. Esmeralda then lay down on top of my arm and went to sleep. My arm went numb, but I didn't want to disturb her. Her comfort was more important than mine. She even snuggled closer after a while. We stayed like that for an hour.

Now, my world was complete.

BEING A CRAZY MAGNET AIN'T EASY

Just when I thought I had reached my limit in attracting crazies, the gods threw another one my way. And, I must admit this time it was my fault for initiating contact.

One of my neighbors has a gold Chevelle four-door hardtop. I had never seen the owner, and one night while walking Esmeralda (do I ever not mention her?), he was outside, so I asked him what year was his car.

That was my first mistake.

After telling me it was his grandfather's car and it was a 1971 (the square taillights are the clue), I made the mistake of telling him I was president of an antique car club.

When will I learn to keep my mouth shut? I really should carry a clothes pin with me.

He then ran inside and came out with a pile of papers and a pen, and for the first time, I noticed his "outfit." It was forty degrees out that night, and he was wearing a T-shirt, a weight belt, parachute pants, and flip flops. For once, I was the more fashionable one.

"I want to join your car club. Give me your number and the website. Here, write it down," he said handing me the pile of papers and the pen. I wrote down a wrong number and the website with a few letters missing. Forgive me, but we have enough crazy people in the club.

I told myself to say a *Hail Moses* later.

I thought that would be the end of it, but then he said, "I'll walk with you. I want to see your car."

"Oh, I have to go to work now, so I don't have a lot of time." It was 6:30 on a Wednesday night, and I had to lie to get out of this situation.

Now, I would have to say a *Hail Miriam*.

He followed me anyway and then proceeded to tell me his life story.

Sometimes, life writes itself, so here goes:

"My name is Tim. What's yours again?"

"Milton."

"I'm on disability because I was a computer programmer during Y2K and lost my mind after that. That did me in. As a result, I have no short-term memory. I was then an agoraphobic and didn't leave my house for ten years, but once I got over that became a hoarder. I just finished cleaning all the crap out of my house. I have no short-term memory, so I have to write everything down. What is your name again?"

"Milton."

"I want to be your dog walker."

"I have a dog walker, thank you."

"What is your name again?"

"Milton."

"I'm on disability. I have no short-term memory. I was a computer programmer. Y2K did me in. The car belonged to my grandfather. See that house there? I was going to buy it, but it had no driveway. I should have bought it. My mother-in-law lives over there. I don't talk to her. What is your name again?"

"Milton."

"I want to adopt a dog. What is your dog's name? I want to be your dog walker."

"Esmeralda. I have a dog walker."

"Twenty years ago, I gave my wife one of my kidneys. Then they told me she died. Two years ago, I found her. She was alive. I'm on disability. I have no short-term memory. What is your name again?"

"Milton."

"I want to be your dog walker."

"I have a dog walker."

"I was going to buy that house there, but it had no driveway. My mother-in-law lives over there. I'm on disability because I have no short-term memory. What is your name again?"

"Milton."

We then arrived at my house. Maybe I should have walked up to another house and pretended it was mine, but he said he had no short-term memory, so I took my chances.

"Wow. An AMC."

"Well, it was nice meeting you, but I have to go to work now."

"What is your name again?"

"Milton."

"Where is my house?"

"Just keep walking in that direction, and you are the fourth house around the corner."

"OK, that way?"

"Yes."

He may have no short-term memory, but he certainly had long-term memory.

From then on, when I walked by his house, he would say, "Hi, Milton. I want to be your dog walker."

If he weren't so weird, I would ask him more about the dead wife with his one kidney, who turned up eighteen years later. Now there's a story worth publishing.

If I offended anyone with the disability of no short-term memory, I apologize. Oh hell, you won't remember this.

CREAMED CORN AND THE BROWN BAG TURKEY

I am ambivalent about Thanksgiving. It should be my favorite holiday. After all, I was born on Thanksgiving, and I will turn fifty on Thanksgiving, but therein lies the dilemma. When your birthday falls on or near a holiday, especially on a holiday with no specific date, i.e., the fourth Thursday in November, you feel gypped. "We'll celebrate your birthday on Thanksgiving, even though it falls on the Tuesday before."

Maybe this is why I don't make a big deal out of my birthdays since we were always celebrating it *not* on my birthday, and by the time Thanksgiving came around, it was pretty much forgotten.

My brother's birthday was celebrated like the coming of the Messiah. He was the first born, and I was the product of an affair.

I wonder if this happens to people who are born on President's Day. "Oh, we'll celebrate your birthday on Monday, even though it falls on Saturday." I imagine Christmas babies have it worse than anyone. Everybody gets presents, and they probably do not get any extra ones for having their birthday under the tree (but I'll bet they take inventory). January 1 babies must have it bad. After the initial excitement of being born on New Year's Day, for every year after that, your family is hung over at your birthday party. Leap Year babies have it worse — they have quadrennial birthdays, but they are always younger than everyone by multiples of four.

That is the first time I have used quadrennial in a sentence.

Now, I don't dislike Thanksgiving, and as I have gotten older, I have begun to enjoy it even more. However, there is one thing about Thanksgiving that can make it a painful experience: You usually spend it with your extended family. Your own family is fine, but those cousins … don't get me started. Fortunately, our extended family consisted of five people when I was young. They are all dead now.

Growing up, we spent Thanksgiving with my dad's family. Uncle Stanley married a Catholic, so it was Thanksgiving at our house and Christmas at theirs. No matter where we went, we would spend ten minutes at the beginning of the meal discussing food ingredients because of Wendy's allergies, cringe at Jeff's crude jokes, and make sure Carole-Sue was the center of attention, or she would run crying from the table or pretend to be sick and spend the night in her bedroom. My mother would undoubtedly say something offensive to someone to set him or her off, and a good time would be had by all.

Mother once put a ham on the table and told my grandmother it was rare roast beef.

When I moved to Florida, I would come home for Thanksgiving, and by then, it was just the immediate family and my mother's brown bag turkey.

Growing up, we were convinced my mother was a great cook because we rarely ate out. Once I experienced properly prepared foods, I soon realized my mother's cooking was ok at best. Some things were great, but others were … how shall I put this … inedible. Her chopped liver and chicken cacciatore were phenomenal. However, her chuck roast on the grill was disgusting. It was burnt on the outside and raw on the inside. They call this Pittsburgh style. I have never want to visit Pittsburgh.

On one visit home, my mother asked if I would like for her to grill a chuck roast. I said, "I would rather you not make a burnt offering on my behalf." She laughed.

I still do not like steak because she would buy these lousy steaks full of gristle and fat and make me chew them. My napkin would be full of chewed up but unswallowed meat.

Then, there was her *kugel*. I was in my thirties when I finally learned that *kugel* is not supposed to be crunchy. I had made my first one and followed the recipe to the letter. I also learned that *kugel* is delicious when prepared properly.

And, don't get me started on the oily cakes. I am known for my baking, and I have never been able to replicate my mother's oily cakes. I think this had something to do with the fact that she would substitute Sweet-n-Low for sugar. It is a wonder I am still alive.

However, her *pièce de résistance* was her brown bag turkey. A gentile co-worker of my mother's gave her a recipe for roasting a turkey in a brown grocery bag, which is why I never get recipes from gentile co-workers.

Seriously, this is what it involved. You take your turkey and coated it in vegetable oil. Then you stick it in a brown grocery bag, staple the bag shut, and roast it for twenty minutes per pound. There are two good reasons for doing it this way. One, you don't have to baste it.

Two, you can throw away the entire bird because it is already in its own garbage bag.

As a matter of fact, if you adopt this method, skip the middle man and put your turkey out with the trash.

But, here is the best part. After my father would attempt to carve this unappetizing bird, which would have the consistency of drywall, my mother would make the same declaration after chewing her first bite. "I bought a bad bird this year. This is awful. I will never buy that brand again."

Get this. She used this method for twenty-two years and said the same thing every year, including the first year she did this. Are there twenty-two brands of turkeys? The last holiday I spent with my mother was Passover. Her health had been failing, so I came down knowing this would be our last holiday together, and she had actually rallied a bit and was driving again. It turned out to be a nice visit.

The conversation before preparing the turkey, our Passover meat of choice, went like this:

"We have to put the turkey in the bag by ten o'clock ..."

"No."

"What do you mean no?"

"I am making a decision. If you cook one more turkey in a grocery bag, I will never eat in your house again."

Laughter heard from my father between farts while he sat in his easy chair with my dog, Serena, in his lap.

"That is the way I am making it ..."

"No."

"Then you can eat a bologna sandwich."

"I will. In the meantime, we are roasting the turkey my way with no brown bag. Every year, you make it in the brown bag, and every year you declare you bought a bad bird. It is not the bird, it's the bag. I cannot eat another *drivy fertz* turkey. I don't know what goy-friend of yours gave you that recipe, but we are not doing it that way as long as I am here."

"He's right," my father said between farts.

"Who asked you?" my mother said with a smile. "But if yours is dry, you can take the whole thing home with you."

"I will ... and it won't be dry."

We roasted it my way. No bag, perfectly seasoned. The part that drove her nuts was my not letting her open the oven to baste it. It took everything to convince her that opening the oven and basting it only created wet skin and a dry bird.

Needless to say, I inherited my stubbornness and insistence that I am always right from my mother. Lately, I fart as much as my father.

The turkey was perfect, and she even said my chopped liver was as good as hers. That was the ultimate compliment.

That Passover was the nicest holiday our family spent together.

Less than two months later, my mother died, but at least she got to eat one good turkey before she left this earth to help God run things in heaven — or Boca — or wherever Jews go when they die.

I also inherited my need to be in charge from her.

After my mother died, I took over Thanksgiving duties. For the first few years, my father would come up for a visit with my friends for the holiday, giving my brother, who lived near him, a break.

My father was always a pleasure, especially when he would comment on my guests' weight or other physical attributes, and soon, I realized this combination was not working.

Then, we held the first Stern family Thanksgiving since my mother died. My brother, sister-in-law, nephew and father came up. Dad stayed with me, while the others stayed in a hotel. This gave me the pleasure of witnessing my father doing his morning exercises in his briefs with his man boobs flapping about.

I have seen my future, and it is not pretty.

For that Thanksgiving, I decided to go all out. My delicious roast turkey, mushroom bordelaise gravy, cornbread stuffing from homemade cornbread (no bag of croutons crap), cranberry apple relish, pumpkin-sweet potato-carrot mash with molasses and brown sugar, and homemade biscuits.

I asked my brother if my nephew had any favorite food. He said, "Yes, creamed corn."

I hate creamed corn. Creamed corn looks like predigested food. I don't want to know how they cream it. I really don't want to know. But, I wanted him to be happy, so I bought two cans of that dreck.

We sat down to dinner, and I put everything out so beautifully. If I do say so, myself, I set a beautiful table. I have few talents when it comes to entertaining, and working in a five-star restaurant taught me how to set a table. I always take a picture of the table before anyone sits down and messes it up. Everything is color coordinated. I have more table cloths than the Marriot and matching napkins for all of them, enough to make Martha Stewart jealous.

The food looked wonderful, and I thought I had outdone myself. Then someone said it, "Pass the creamed corn." And another, "Yes, pass the creamed corn."

Then, "Oh this creamed corn is delicious." Followed by, "Do you have any more of the creamed corn?"

Seriously? This is your favorite dish on the table? Creamed fucking corn? I should have made Stove Top Stuffing, French's gravy, and opened a can of jellied cranberry sauce!

I thought it; I didn't say it.

If I were suicidal and owned a gun — and knew how to use one — I would have blown my brains out right there at the dining room table, which would have been followed by, "Oh, I hope he didn't get any gray matter in the creamed corn."

"Yes, let me open another can of creamed corn," I said with my best Donna Reed smile. It wasn't even brand name creamed corn!

While I love my family dearly, we are just trash.

I never cooked another Thanksgiving dinner again.

My father died of a heart attack after a battle with Alzheimer's disease a couple of years ago. Now for Thanksgiving, my family comes up to visit, and we go out to eat. Going out was my brother's idea because he doesn't want to bother with dishes. No offense, Alex, but when did you ever wash a dish in my home? Or any home? Wait a minute. Was he commenting on my cooking?

Last year, we had a lovely meal at an upscale restaurant.

But, I now live in a town that allows trailer parks, so our choices are limited. I think I'll make a reservation at Bubba's Liquor, Sports Bar and Grill. I hear they have their own special recipe for creamed corn! We should fit right in.

I ONLY DATE LATIN GUYS

I went on a date with a guy four years ago. We'll call him Randy — not because of his libido but because that is his real name. No protecting the innocent here.

We had what I considered a fantastic time. We talked about a variety of subjects and not ourselves. You know how first dates go being almost like a job interview with the avoidance of subjects like politics, religion and preferred interior design themes. You pretty much spend two hours talking about yourself — a subject I find truly fascinating. The evening ended nicely, and we were going to go out on a second date. However ...

Just before the second date, he informed me that his mother had taken ill and he had to take care of her. I told him that it was very important to take care of her and keep me informed. He even texted with medical updates for a day or two. It is amazing what someone will do to his mother to get out of a date.

It was no surprise that we never did go on a second date. I read the book, *He's Not That Into Me*, so I just wrote it off as one good date with no possibility of a relationship. I am also no idiot. Once the sick mother appeared, I knew I wouldn't see him again.

About a year ago, I had dinner with someone who was friends with him, and I told him about how we never went on a second date or communicated again. And, our mutual friend said, "Oh her. She only dates Latin guys."

Seriously?

This only dating a certain "type" thing has always fascinated me. I could understand his only dating Latin guys if he *was* Latin. But, he's a goddamn blond blue-eyed WASP!

Rita Morena's character in *West Side Story*, Anita, sang in "A Boy Like That" about seeking your own kind. That I can understand. If the guy is Latin and only dates Latins, there is nothing wrong with that. You share beliefs, ethnicity, culture, etc. You never have to explain the ingredients in gefilte fish. Latins don't eat gefilte fish — it was a bad analogy.

There was a time when I only dated Jewish guys, but it is very difficult for two whiny, neurotic men, who are obsessed with pleasing their mothers, while dealing with stomach issues and bad feet to form a lasting relationship. I'm just saying. But, I still date Jewish guys, just not exclusively anymore.

In the Gay world, guys usually date their own kind. Juice heads only date juice heads — that way they can inject each other's asses with steroids. Twinks date twinks, so that one does not crush the other in bed. A-listers date A-listers, so they don't have to show each other how all the buttons work in their BMWs. Hairy bears date hairy bears, so they don't have to feel guilty when they bring home a side of beef from the Safeway. And so on.

What this creates is the "clone culture" where guys are always dating guys who look like themselves. They also only befriend guys who look like themselves. Look at their pics on Facebook. You will notice all the guys look alike, dress alike and act alike. Also, all of A-listers are photographed at parties holding red plastic cups — the ultimate A-list accessory.

The fun part is when one of them starts dating someone else, and you cannot tell the old and new boyfriends apart. You call the new boyfriend by the old boyfriend's name, and things get a little awkward. If you are like me, you diffuse the situation by saying, "I'm sorry, you look just like Brad and Jon and Chris and ... oh who cares? All his old boyfriends look like you, and he goes through them like Kleenex ..." By this time, someone is shoving an *hors d'oeuvre* in my mouth and dragging me away from the situation. Fortunately, I never get embarrassed, nor do I have a filter.

I have never looked like, acted like or dressed like anyone, so I have been spared the curse of clonism. However, this does make being part of a clique impossible, which is fine with me because I have never been one to succumb to the clique culture either. My friends come in all sizes, shapes, colors, ethnicities, etc.

But, this isn't about me ...

A Latin friend of mine was in bed with a guy once, who in the middle of copulation said, "Oh yes! Fuck me with that Puerto Rican dick!" He pulled out immediately, dressed and left.

As he put it, "At that moment I was dehumanized and reduced to my Latin penis." He was right, not to mention the fact that he was Venezuelan.

What is really weird is when you are the subject of someone's obsession. My ex, Philip, is bald, and nothing bothered him more than when someone said, "Oh I find bald guys so hot." I could totally understand this.

My friend Joel once tried to set me up on a date, and the guy said, "I can't go out with him; he's too tall." He had written me off immediately.

That same guy tried to pick me up in the shower at the gym a short time later, and I said, "I can't play with you; you're too short." Of course, I could have kicked myself because he was hung like a ... never mind.

I have had guys come up to me and say, "I just love Jewish men. I only date Jewish guys." These are the ones I avoid completely. They truly creep me out. I expect them to say, "Some of my best friends are Jewish." Oy vay.

Do the guys who only seek a certain kind, who are not what they seek, really think that it is a turn on for the object of their desire? Apparently for some it is.

I recently went to a birthday party with two distinct groups in attendance: middle-aged white men and young Asian men. All were partnered up. Being a writer, I just found the situation fascinating and observed the interactions. In this group, all seemed to have found what they were seeking. I didn't judge, but I thought how limiting life could be if you only seek one thing.

To me, it is like going to a buffet and only eating the beige food.

Now, few people will come right out and say they only date a certain kind to someone who has asked them out, but I have experienced this firsthand. I met a friend of a friend at a party once. We'll call him Rod, not because he had a certain physical attribute, but because that was his real name.

We chatted it up for quite a while that evening, and I finally said, "Would you like to go out on a date sometime?"

He said, "Oh, I'm sorry, I only date Latin guys."

He was Polish!

I ran into him years later, and he was still single. I asked, "How is that only dating Latin guys thing working out for you?"

And back to Randy.

Just the other day, out of the blue, I ran into Randy, and he asked me out on a date, saying it has been a long time, and we should catch up. I agreed to it, thinking maybe he got that only dating Latin guys thing out of his system.

The morning of the date, he texted me that his mother was sick and he had to put her in the hospital.

So let me understand this. If we plan another date in the near future, will he finally kill his mother?

And people wonder why I am still single.

IT'S ABOUT THE EXTERIOR, STUPID

As a Gay man, I always thought home ownership had to do with the interior, being sure your home was color coordinated, fresh smelling and clean and that all one's sex toys were out of sight while still being easily accessible. If you are in a condo, this is all true.

In a house or mobile home, or even a camper, it's about the exterior, stupid!

Had I known before embarking on the trailer park adventure that I would have to do what I had to do today, I might still be an apartment dweller.

In the lot lease, we are instructed to keep our homes clean and free of trash along with hiding our trashcans and recycling bins. We are also told to "wash down" our houses at least once a year. These are easy things to do. I keep my trash cans behind the deck, and I am going to get one of those power wash attachments for my hose to wash my home next spring. I think the Mr. Clean car wash kit should do the job nicely.

But I was starting to have a problem with the trashcan placement. With all the rain we were getting this year, my yard was full of mud, and I was constantly traipsing through a soggy pit to empty my trash and recyclables, not to mention disposal of poop bags. I needed a walkway.

I noticed my cute next-door neighbor (whom I am convinced masturbates to fantasies of me behind those closed curtains — let me have this one tidbit, please) had pavers from his deck to his trash cans, so I decided to buy some pavers to go around my deck to keep my shoes clean. I am legendary for my clean shoes. My friend Dean calls me and always asks if my shoes are clean.

While I was admiring his pavers and measuring them, I heard a voice from above. I was startled and said, "I was only measuring them to see how many I need; I wasn't going to steal them."

No worries; it wasn't God. It was my neighbor.

He was on his roof, cleaning his gutters. And he was pulling out a shitload of leaves.

Earlier that day, I did something I thought I would never do. I raked my leaves — all of them! But, I never considered the ones on the roof or in the gutter.

I asked him, "How often do you have to do that?"

"At least once a year, maybe twice."

I then got on my deck and reached up to see if my gutters were full. Being tall does have its advantages. Oh yes, there were about four inches of leaves in my gutter. I needed to clean them out, and cleaning them meant two things.

I had to climb up a ladder, and I had to get onto my roof — two things I have never done and do not have on my bucket list. I am not afraid of heights. I can stand on a balcony and look over the edge without any worries. However, I am a natural born klutz. If anyone is going to fall off a roof, it is I.

Growing up, I don't think we ever cleaned our gutters, or at least I didn't. I never climbed up on ladders either. I never saw the inside of our attic. Our house had all the worst qualities of the homes of the Munsters and the Addams Family, including cultivated weeds and loose shingles.

I, however, am determined not to care for my home the way my parents did. So, I decided to buy a ladder and clean my gutters.

My neighbor offered to lend me his, but for two reasons I decided not to. His was a little rickety (I'll admit to weighing more than two-hundred pounds), and I don't want to be that guy who borrows stuff all the time. I hate those people.

Does anyone borrow a cup of sugar anymore? In some gay neighborhoods, they borrow a cup of sex.

On the Saturday morning after Black Friday, I showed up at Lowe's when they opened. It was empty (for those who don't know, *that* Saturday morning is the best time to shop). I first found a ladder with a three-hundred-pound weight limit that was on sale, so I put it in my cart and attempted to maneuver it through the store. That wasn't going to work. I knocked six displays over before I asked if I could leave it up front until I was ready to check out. I am so much like Lucy Carmichael in a department store it isn't even funny.

I then went to look at pavers. I found some that were perfect, and I loaded them onto a cart. According to my measurements (and contrary to belief, this Gay man does measure, and I measure exactly), I needed forty-eight of them. They weighed twenty pounds each. The cart weighed nine-hundred-sixty pounds, and I pulled that bastard from the garden center all the way to the front of the store where I had my ladder and green bungee cords. Did you expect me to buy any other color?

Just so you know. I was the only one in the store, and no one offered to help me. Of course, I didn't ask for help either. I never do. I am the perfect martyr. I should be in the Bible somewhere. — maybe hauling stones in ancient Egypt then falling off a pyramid to my death because I wouldn't ask for help.

I checked out then I pulled my car up and proceeded to load it up and strap the ladder to the roof with my new bungee cords. There were some Girl Scouts setting up to sell cookies who watched me the whole time. They giggled when I tripped and almost landed face first into my pavers. I made a note to buy some thin mints.

If you don't know me, you are not aware of the fact that I drive a thirty-year-old station wagon. I loaded the car with no help, and with each paver, the back went down a little more, and once all were in, it was almost bottomed out. I then strapped the ladder to the roof rack, again with no help. I even wore a plaid jacket that morning. I am a Lesbian in a Gay man's body.

After buying a box each of thin mints and lemon cookies, I made it home, and it was like driving uphill the whole way. I took a picture of my car because I figured no one would believe I did this, especially my mechanic.

Once I arrived home and after I took the picture, I walked Esmeralda very quickly. I was sure my rear leaf springs were going to collapse if I waited any longer. Then, I emptied out the pavers and laid out my walkway. It turns out I had measured exactly. And, I do get to keep my Gay card because my measurement ended in "eight." Think about it.

That went well. However, now came ladder time.

Again, I am not afraid of ladders, just falling off them. I am, however, afraid of spiral staircases. I don't know why, but I conquered that fear when visiting the Baltimore Washington Monument with my friend Louis, which is also an obelisk (not Louis, the monument), and climbing the spiral staircase to the top. Going down was another story, and I almost had to change pants at the bottom. So ...

I used the bathroom then I mustered up the courage. At first, I thought I could put the ladder beside the house, climb up a couple of steps then reach up and clean the gutters that way, but even I couldn't reach that far.

With my cell phone in my pocket in case of an emergency, my wallet in my pants, so they could identify the body, and the ladder on the deck, I decided it was either now or never. I climbed up and looked at the roof. I climbed up one more step then another. With the grace of a goony bird, I clamored onto the roof. I am sure that was a sight to behold.

I was on the fucking roof! I looked around. I was on top of the world. OK, it was only nineteen feet up, but I did hyperventilate slightly then I sat down and scooted to the edge to clean out the gutters. Fortunately, I was wearing gloves even though no one told me about the gunk under the leaves.

Scooting on my fat ass, I managed to complete one side and only had two near misses. I then looked to the other side thinking those gutters couldn't be full because the leaves tend to fall on one side of the house. Oh was I an optimistic idiot. There were more leaves on the far side than the side I just cleaned.

I then walked over to that side, looking like Lucy Carmichael and Vivian Bagley putting up an antenna, and again on my fat ass, cleaned that side.

The whole time I was thinking, "I am going to fall off this roof and die, or I'm going to have to call the Fire Department to get me down." The second option didn't seem so bad.

I'm really surprised I didn't throw up for the first time since 1997.

Then, I was done, but I was now stuck on the roof. A neighbor walked by with his dog, and I asked him if he would hold the ladder for me. Thank God, I live in a trailer park. Everyone is so friendly and willing to help. In Rockville, they would have acted as if they didn't hear me.

He held the ladder, and I somehow got down in one piece.

Also, no one told me how wet shingles get. My pants were soaked through my ass, so I took a shower immediately to avoid getting a yeast infection on my bum.

When all was said and done, I was informed there is an attachment for the garden hose for cleaning gutters that you can use without leaving the ground.

Why do I always find out about these things after the fact?

Cross one item off my bucket list — after I put it on there of course.

The thin mints were delicious, all of them. The lemon cookies were crap, all of them.

CHRISTMAS IS THE JEWISH CHRISTMAS — THE EIGHT MYTHS OF HANUKAH

I love Christmas with all the songs, decorations and lights, especially the lights, and the tackier and more overdone the house, the better.

When we were kids, our parents would love to take us around in the car and look at all the lights. This is where I first learned the word *umbeshrian* — which according to my mother, meant overdone.

We even had a Christmas tree in our house when I was little, and when my mother accidentally barbecued the den one December, she was most upset about the loss of her Styrofoam snow man with two elves standing next to him.

Now, that I own my first home, I have also strung up some lights — blue and white of course, to celebrate the season. Before you start in on me about decorating for a Christian holiday, keep reading ...

(About ten years ago, I gave a *drash* during Shabbat services on Hanukah, where I presented for the first time my "Eight Myths of Hanukah." A few years after that, I was asked to present them again. For your reading pleasure, I present them for the third time.)

Introduction

Many people do not realize that Jesus was not born on December 25. He was born September 11, 3 BCE, which on the Hebrew calendar for that year was Elul 1.

To make a long story short, in the year 380, Pope Damasus I made it his goal to have all Christians in the Roman Empire yield to his authority, and he convinced the Emperor to issue an edict requiring them to practice the religion of Rome, Catholicism. Damasus I was also seeking to lure the people away from the pagan rituals honoring the birth of the sun god on December 25 at midnight by demanding attendance at a memorial in honor of Christ's death — in other words, the Mass. The people confused this Mass with the pagan solar birth rituals conducted at that same time, and gradually, the Christ-Mass became associated with the Nativity, hence, Christmas. Somehow,

131

many of the symbols and customs remained, most notably, the Christmas tree and fruitcake.

Did you know all fruit cakes were actually baked before the year 380? That is why they are so dense and hard to slice.

In the United States, Christmas wasn't even celebrated during our country's first ninety-four years because in England, it was celebrated with excessive drinking and lewd and lascivious behavior. Not unlike a Tuesday night in my home.

As a matter of fact, Washington crossed the Delaware on December 25, 1776, to attack the British in Trenton because he knew the Red Coats would be hung … over.

Americans wanted to reject all things British, so Christmas and afternoon tea were the first to go. I wish we kept the tea.

Congress met on Christmas day every year until after the Civil War. Americans complained there were no federal holidays, so on June 26, 1870, Christmas was officially made a federal holiday. However, you can thank the Jews for something else. We invented the weekend. You know: God worked all week then rested in Boca.

So, to all my Jewish friends out there, hang up those Hanukah lights this weekend because Christmas is not a religious holiday; it is a federal holiday, and we want to be patriotic!

Now, I present:

The Eight Myths of Hanukah

1. *Hanukah is the Jewish Christmas.* False. How many times have I been asked, "Is Hanukah the Jewish Christmas?" Let me set the record straight. Christmas is the Jewish Christmas. Mary and Joseph were Jewish, Jesus was Jewish, and at least one of the Wise Men was Jewish — the one that brought the fur.

2. *Hanukah is the holiest of Jewish holidays.* False. Hanukah isn't even a religious holiday. The holiest of Jewish holidays is April 24, Barbra Streisand's birthday. The second holiest Jewish holiday is December 29, the wedding anniversary of Steve Lawrence and Eydie Gorme.

3. *Hanukah is another Jewish holiday where they tried to kill us, they didn't, so we eat.* True. Also known as the Festival of Lights, Hanukah is an eight-day Jewish holiday commemorating the re-dedication of the Holy Temple (the Second Temple) in Jerusalem at the time of the Maccabean Revolt of the second century BCE, which brings us to …

4. Hanukah commemorates the miracle that one day's worth of oil lasted eight days in the Holy Temple. True. But, this is hardly a miracle because I witnessed my grandmother doing the same thing with one tea bag.

5. During Hanukah, children get a gift every night for eight days. False. If you grew up in my house, you got a gift the first night, then for seven nights, you heard about how awful it was to grow up during The Great Depression. The ritual of gift giving is actually very American, since Jewish children in this country are totally exposed to Christmas customs.

6. Hanukah is a holiday when Jewish people eat bland, colorless foods that are fried in oil and difficult to digest. True for ALL Jewish holidays. On Hanukah, we eat latkes (potato pancakes) or *sufganiot*, if you are Sephardic. *Sufganiot* are similar to jelly donuts. I am part Sephardic, so I like donuts, just not jelly ones.

7. There are many popular songs about Hanukah, and Jewish people know the words to all of them. False. Other than "Dreidel, Dreidel, Dreidel," there are no other Hanukah songs we can sing, except for "The Hanukah Song," by Adam Sandler, which brings us to Number 8 ...

8. Steve & Eydie and Barbra Streisand have recorded Hanukah albums. SO NOT TRUE! Would you believe Steve and Eydie have recorded a Christmas album, and Barbra has recorded not one but two Christmas albums?! And all those Christmas songs we hear on the radio are mostly written, and oftentimes performed, by Jews! Oy vay! This brings us back to myth Number 1, proving once again that Christmas is the Jewish Christmas!

So, from my Trailer Park to Yours, here is wishing you a very Happy Jewish Christmas and a Merry Hanukah!

HOW ALARMING

Remember when people first started installing car alarms in the 1980s, and they would go off all the time in the middle of the night every time someone walked by one of their cars and farted? Were you one of those people who wanted to go outside with a baseball bat and beat the car to a mangled bloody pulp? Julia Sugarbaker did that on an episode of *Designing Women*.

You knew who had a car alarm because they had a fob. Now, everyone has a fob. Mrs. M lost her fob one day and asked me if I knew anything about getting one replaced. I said, "Do you see what I drive? My car uses a skeleton key."

I never had a need for a car alarm. My car is insured for three times what it is worth, which is equal to the price of dinner for two. If someone wanted to steal it, I would hand him the keys, turn around and say, "Gee, officer, one minute it was there and next thing I knew … oh, when … three days ago" (I want to give them time to get away, so I could collect).

House alarms are also very popular now. My upstairs neighbor in Mount Pleasant, the one who would hire twinks to walk his dog, had one. When the dog would whine because the dog walker didn't show up, I would go upstairs with my key and set off the alarm. I just realized something. He gave me a key but not the alarm code. What was that about? Anyway, the police knew me by name. I would open the door, and three minutes later, they would show up, and we would have a good laugh.

My parents had a house alarm. Once, while visiting, I came back late — in our family that means after nine o'clock — and I set off the alarm. Their code was the year they met and the year they got married — 5354. I kept doing it backwards. Oh, they're dead, so you can't rob their house now. And you wouldn't have wanted to. A burglar broke into their home once and redecorated. I think his parting words were, "Enough with the Chinese tchotchkes!"

Which brings me to my home …

The problem with living in a trailer was I didn't know if I needed an alarm, and if so, should I get a car alarm or a house alarm. Think about it. A thief could break into my house or just drive off with it. "We've spotted him on Route 1. Yes, an F-150 with a singlewide hitched to the back. He's doing around twenty mph. We're in hot pursuit." Then you sing "Bad Boys, Bad Boys" very very slowly.

I have been the victim of three crimes in my life, which means I should be done for now. In 1988, my car was stolen. Later that same year, my apartment was robbed. In Atlanta in 1993, I was mugged at gun point after which I threw up in the back of a police car while being driven around trying to find the culprits — like that made any sense.

"Oh yeah, officer, there he is walking down the street with a gun in his hand and my wallet in his back pocket." UrrUrrrUrrrrraaalphh. "Oh, sorry about that. Someone's going to have to clean that up."

The thief stepped out of the passenger side of a car at a crosswalk and pointed his gun at my head. Seriously, it took a gun to steal $27 and my license. They were driving a white Chevrolet Cavalier; no wonder they were mugging people.

I manage to survive four months without an alarm. Then Daylight Savings Time ended, and I was leaving for and coming home from work in the dark. And for the first time in my life, I have four exposed walls. And more importantly, Esmeralda is alone until Mrs. M comes to get her around ten o'clock for her first walk and around three o'clock for her second walk.

My things, I don't care about. All my dreck can be replaced. My dog — that is another story. Do what you want to me. Touch my dog, and you'll regret the day you left your mother. Don't fuck with my dog! I'm from Hampton Roads, Bitch!

I got that out of my system.

So, I decided to call that alarm company with a short attention span — ADT.

The representative showed up fifteen minutes late, and the first question I asked was whether the police would do the same. You know I have no filter.

I offered him a seat, and he said, "Nice house. Did you have it professionally decorated?"

He could have sold me a motion detector for the toilet after that compliment! No one has ever accused me of hiring a decorator.

He then went over all the packages and asked what in my house was important to me. I said, "Nothing. This is to protect my dog because thieves take little dogs like her and use them for pit bull training, and I don't know what I would do if someone stole my dog. I don't care about my stuff. That can be replaced."

"You are getting an alarm for your dog?"

"Yes."

He knew then to keep his opinion to himself or he wasn't going to sell an alarm system. I picked a basic system, while Esmeralda just watched. He asked, "Does your dog ever bark? Are you sure she's a beagle?"

"Yes. She just prefers to observe rather than comment. We're polar opposites."

Not even a chuckle. How do people get through life without a sense of humor?

I chose a basic system for the doors and one motion detector for the dining room. The way my cooking is received, if someone is still moving after one of my meals, it will be truly alarming — unless I serve creamed corn, a family favorite.

Then he needed a $75 check for Howard County. What? I have to pay the county in order to get an alarm installed? Apparently, in Howard County, yes.

The following week, the alarm was installed by my first cute installer. Be it a contractor, plumber, handyman, you name it, I always get the trolls! After a few hours, he showed me how it worked, and that is when I became alarmed.

I didn't know that when leaving the house, the damn thing would let out a high-pitched beep for one minute. The first time he tested it, Esmeralda was under the bed in less than three seconds.

"This isn't going to work. You need to remove this thing. I bought this for my dog, and now it is scaring the shit out of her."

"Mr. Stern, that is how it sounds."

"You mean I can't lower the volume?"

"No."

"Then rip it out of the wall."

"Seriously?"

For every problem, there is a solution. He didn't have one, but I did — the owner's manual. I read it — in front of him. You can lower the volume of the beep by pressing two buttons, and I showed him how.

Some things in this world never change. Cute still equals dumb; too bad it doesn't always equal hung.

I wonder how many people out there have dogs under the bed because their alarm's beep is too loud.

The other thing Esmeralda didn't like was the lady's voice. "Alarm, stay, exit now." For the first week, every time the lady would speak, Esmeralda's ears would go down, and she would sulk away from the thing. It was like in *Sybil*, when Joanne Woodward played the tape of alters to Sybil, and she heard her alter with a voice like her mother's and went under the piano, reverting to a fetal stage.

Something tells me Esmeralda was abused by a woman — a morbidly obese woman with a cigarette. Once while walking her in Rockville, a morbidly obese, chain-smoking woman exited her car, and I said hello. The minute Esmeralda saw her, she took off on her leash and dragged me three blocks. Or maybe Esmeralda worried I was straight and into morbidly obese, chain-smoking women? No, I think it was the former.

Esmeralda finally became accustomed to the voice. Now she just stares at it waiting for it to say more.

But here is the best part.

The $75 check was for the inspection fee. And this is how that works. The county sets up an appointment from 9:30 am — 4:30 pm. On the day of the appointment, the inspector shows up at 9:35 am, walks into your home, looks at the control panel, and says, "OK, that's it." Hands you a card saying approved and leaves.

For $75, I expect a happy ending.

Apparently, this is some old rule from the days before wireless to be sure the control box is not a fire hazard or something like that. The inspector said it was ridiculous, and he did about ten of these a day and was usually finished by 10:30 am.

I want his job.

NO ONE TOLD ME
ABOUT THIS PLACE

Take away my Gay card now. I hate shopping. There, I said it. Walking down aisles, browsing around, trying on clothes, looking at this item, looking at that, not knowing what you're looking for ... uucchhhh.

When I go into a store, I know exactly what I want, I find it, I buy it, and I leave. This has driven many of my friends crazy. They like to browse and look around. If I don't see what I came to buy immediately, I ask for help. If they don't have it, I leave. And, I have been known to leave my friends in stores. Once I had to send a search party into an antique store for my friend Frank.

Wait a minute! I get to keep my Gay card. Straight men never ask where anything is or for directions. I always ask for help in stores and directions when I'm driving. I don't have time to get lost.

A few weeks ago, I needed to get a purple sweater for Spirit Day in Solidarity with LGBT Youth Who Have Been Bullied. I walked up the street to Filene's Basement, back to the men's department, found a purple and a green sweater, paid for them, and returned to my office. Six blocks round-trip with a purchase in between took me twenty minutes. One of my co-workers could not get over it. She didn't even realize I had left.

I don't mind going to discount or grocery stores to buy what I need. I just do it as quickly as possible. I can grocery shop for a month's worth of food in thirty minutes and redeem my coupons in the process. I go to Target and Walmart at least once a week. I go in, get what I need and leave.

But, don't ever take me to a mall. Oh my God! I am convinced that if you are evil in this life, you spend the afterlife in a mall. I don't know what is worse, the parking, the crowds, or the stores that sell nothing I want. Take Spencer Gifts. How many black light posters of Kiss do I need? Can you tell it has been thirty years since I went to a mall?

With the exception of those two sweaters, I usually buy my clothes online, especially shoes since I wear a size fourteen, and no one carries that.

I refuse to walk into a shoe store. I don't know how many times I heard, "We have up to size thirteen, and they fit large?"

My answer, "If they fit large, they would be size fourteen."

My favorite was at Virginia Beach in the early 1980s, at one of those shops that sells flip flops (now they call them thongs and wear them with formals). The clerk looked at me as if I were Lurch and said, "We keep the larger sizes upstairs."

My question, "Aren't you afraid the first floor ceiling won't support the weight of all those heavy shoes?"

Speaking of Lurch. When I was fourteen, I took a four-week tennis course in the summer, and the instructor, who couldn't stand me, kept calling me Lurch. I told him if he didn't stop, I would sign up for four more weeks. He didn't. I did. And, he never taught tennis again.

Back to shopping. I do admit I love discount stores. K-Mart, Target, Walmart, you name it. I may shop quickly, but I do it with a smile. Bargains always get my juices going.

Want to seduce me? Show me a price tag that says "50% OFF"!

My mother worked in a high-end women's clothing store called La Vogue, but she loved cheap stores. In Newport News when I was growing up, there was store called King's. I don't know if they had King's where you live, but let me try to describe it for you.

Have you ever been to GC Murphy, Co.? Or a K-Mart in a really bad neighborhood? Imagine a store that makes those look like a boutique. Even the parking lot was full of potholes. My father used to say that they should open an alignment shop next to King's.

I still remember piling into Mother's red Corvair and going to King's. I loved King's. They also had a grocery store attached to King's that was separated by those plastic strips you see in walk-in freezers. The grocery department was so trashy, the meat department only sold road kill.

I'm not kidding. She bought a chicken there that to this day I swear was a fat pigeon.

Mother once bought me shirts from King's. One was yellow with white bands on the collar and sleeves. After one washing, the bands fell off; after two, we couldn't find the shirt in the washing machine.

Too bad. I really liked that shirt. The yellow went so well with my skin tone.

Anyway, back to shopping. I had yet to do any real landscaping. However, even I was getting tired of my home looking as if someone parked a camper in an empty lot, so I took a trip to Walmart to look around their garden department — in December!

Their garden department wasn't even open. I then drove over to Lowe's, but all they had were Christmas trees. You can't plant those.

On my way to the Metro every morning, I pass by a place called Behnke Nursery. They always have a sign out front that says what kind of greenery they have on sale. I know absolutely nothing about plants, except that one should trim his bush regularly but never remove it completely because a little grass on the playing field is a good thing.

I decided to drive down to Beltsville (yes, we do have a city called Beltsville — it's near the Beltway of course). As usual with any of my shopping adventures, I knew what I wanted, and I was determined to get it in as little time as possible. I wanted six planters, and six bushes to go in them to surround my deck.

I grabbed a cart, walked in, and I immediately asked where the hard plastic pots for planting outside were. A friend told me not to get clay pots because they crack, and crack is whack. The clerk showed me where to look.

Then, I saw it: "All pots, 50% OFF." I thought I was going to have to change my underwear. I looked at all the pots. I browsed. I pondered. I laid them out as I envisioned they would be around my deck. I walked around them at different angles. I turned my head and back again to see what kind of first impression they would have. And being Jewish, I turned them over to see where they came from (which is why flying saucers never land on Jewish lawns — I stole that from Joan Rivers).

What the fuck was I doing? Was I shopping? Was I enjoying myself? Was I taking my time?

I was!

Why didn't anyone tell me about this place? If I had known what fun this would be, I would have landscaped something twenty-five years ago!

After picking out my pots, I asked for help from a young fellow who looked like Louie Anderson. He showed me the bushes. And there it was again, "All bushes 50% OFF." I needed a cigarette!

He helped me pick out six bushes. Then he showed me the right kind of potting soil, and he even helped me pick out the right kind of crushed marble to line the area between my walkway and my house.

I was spent.

I paid for everything, loaded up my car and drove home with a smile on my face and the inability to see out the passenger side or rear of the station wagon.

But, don't get too excited. I managed to complete the entire shopping trip and unload the car in ninety minutes. Hey, it's a start.

The following weekend, I returned to Behnke Nursery and bought six more bushes to plant around the house, and I was home in an hour. I just cannot resist a 50% OFF sale, and I now know I do like to shop — in nurseries and lawn and garden departments or whatever they call them!

My neighbors love my landscape design — or they just love the fact that I finally did something. Who cares? I'm happy.

I cannot wait until spring, when I can buy flowers or bulbs or annuals or — I have no clue, but I'll learn. I hope Louie Anderson is still working at Behnke Nursery then.

TABLE FOR ONE?

All of us have dined alone, but not everyone in a restaurant. I have been single a long time ... a long, long time. By my latest calculation, I have eaten more than 19,709 meals alone (the actual number was 19,710). When I added up those numbers, I was reminded of the penultimate *Mary Tyler Moore Show* when she adds up all the dates she's had — more than 2,000 dates. It is then she decides to go out with Mr. Grant.

If you are single, you have also eaten quite a few inappropriate dinners — and don't go denying it. For example, a quart of ice cream, an entire extra-large, meat lovers pizza or even a family-sized bucket of fried chicken with all the sides. You can do this in the comfort of your own home without anyone knowing what you did. That is until you waddle into the office one Monday morning, and you bang into all the cubicles with both hips.

More things single people have done are: eat all three courses out of one very large bowl while sitting on the couch watching that TLC series about the morbidly obese; eat an entire meal over the sink while waving at your neighbors from the kitchen window; or worse, stand in front of an open refrigerator with a spoon, opening all the leftover containers one by one, consuming their contents, and flinging the empty containers into the sink before moving onto the next one, until none are left.

I, for one, have done none of the above, and I dare you to prove otherwise. Uuurrrppp.

However, and I say however a lot, not many single people have eaten dinner in a restaurant alone. I single out dinner because stopping for breakfast or lunch and eating alone does not seem to be a big deal to most people. How self-conscious can one be about eating a corned beef sandwich, two cream sodas, and six dill pickles in seventeen minutes? I can tell you — not very.

Dining alone is not a problem for me, but as a twenty-year veteran of the restaurant industry and being a resident citizen of the United States, I can understand why some do have a problem with dining single on this side of the pond.

Going to a restaurant alone in the New World is a different from experience from dining on the Continent. Americans are uptight people, and some of the people who are paid to serve us are the most uptight of all.

It usually starts with the host or hostess who greets you with "just one?" I never met a single childless restaurant hostess or one who was in a happy relationship. They don't understand someone who isn't tethered to another living being via reproduction or a one-night stand turned twelve-year live-in relationship after a bender at the local western bar. Yes, I generalize about hostesses, so sue me.

Then, the bitter hostess does this. She looks at the reservation book nervously, even if the restaurant is empty. Then she looks at the dining room as if she never saw it before. Several minutes later, you get, "Follow me." You then follow her all over the restaurant. She is confused. What do you do with one person? This is unnatural. Everyone comes in pairs or four-tops, or groups of eight or more. Never "just one." You end up seeing sections of the restaurant the owner doesn't even know about, and finally she seats you. She doesn't look at you directly. She puts the menu down and looks for a waiter. And you hear, "He is alone over there." Then, she points.

It is at this point when I want to scratch my armpits and fling my feces at the next person who walks by since the staff stare at me for a minute as if the hostess just seated a monkey in the dining room.

As a former waiter, I know how some of the staff react. Some of the single straight waiters sigh and wait on the single guy as quickly as possible to free up the table. Do you need to get through dinner quickly because you have theater plans? Split your group into singles. They will rush you out of there, you will have time to look for a good parking space, and you won't miss the overture.

Some of the waitresses will flirt with you and linger until they find out you're Gay. Married doesn't matter whether it is the guest or the waitress. Gay assures you a quiet meal. So, any straight guys out there. If you just don't want to be bothered while you eat dinner, start the conversation with, "My husband, Trent, recommended this restaurant."

But if you got me for a waiter in my day, you were treated like any other patron and not rushed. Have I mentioned I am perfect? I also had eaten my share of meals alone in restaurants. I was also the only waiter who would wait on the biker groups. Wild and loud, but the best tippers in the world! It pays not to have hang-ups.

We are a country that views single people with suspicion while at the same time being obsessed with marriage and relationships. Not our own marriages and relationships — everyone else's. No matter where on the political spectrum you sit, as an American, it is your duty to be obsessed with everyone else's marriage. When they say your marriage will ruin marriage as an institution, you point out their multiple marriages, eleven-hour marriages and seventy-two-day marriages. When they say your marriage is forbidden in the Bible, you point out that on that same page it says you can't eat pork, yet they served ham biscuits at their wedding, which brings us back to restaurants.

Europeans don't have the hang-ups we do. The women go to topless at the beach with more body hair than Robin Williams. The pear shaped men with bird arms and legs wear bikinis. Their politicians have affairs, and their only concern is what the mistress is wearing.

They also don't care if you eat single in a restaurant.

I have been to Europe three times, twice alone and once with a cheap partner, who didn't want to spend money on food, so he ate Powerbars for every meal, while I stopped at street vendors. We were in Paris! We never walked into a restaurant! Don't travel with a Southern Baptist.

My first trip was to Austria to visit my friend Caroline in Salzburg. I loved it. I ate about half of my evening meals alone, and I never ran into the bitter hostess syndrome. I wasn't seated in a dark corner or a table by the water closet. I sat in the dining room with the other human beings. No one rushed me. My favorite restaurant was this adorable Greek bistro. The staff and I would hold a conversation with my limited Greek and German and their fluent English. I was given samples of specials and invited to taste different wines. For once, I ate alone in a restaurant and didn't finish my meal in twelve minutes, while they cleared and set my table for the next party before I could get one arm into the sleeve of my coat.

If single restaurant patrons in the United States were always treated this way, we would have fewer bad marriages because dining alone would not be an unpleasant experience and one wouldn't seek out bad relationships just so he could try a new restaurant. I have interesting theories.

I have had some interesting experiences in restaurants, especially while traveling this great land of ours.

In Tallahassee while on a business trip, a waitress was so nervous about having a single diner in her section that she spent fifteen minutes explaining how a salad bar works. She must have thought it was my first day out of the crate. The restaurant's salad bar had six items, two of which were dressing. I decided to dine somewhere else.

In Suffolk, Virginia, after an all-day business meeting, a hostess kept trying to seat me with other people. "Are you sure you wouldn't want to sit here? They seem like a nice couple." "How about here? Their kids, other than that one, seem well behaved."

In my best Greta Garbo, I said, "I want to dine alone."

While in Horsham, Pennsylvania, on another business trip (do you see why I now put "no travel" on job applications?), a hostess kept looking behind me for more people, no matter how many times I said, "One." Then she asked if I wanted to place a to-go order. I guess no one ever sat alone in her restaurant. I stayed, and I dined for two hours. That drove her crazy! The portions were small, and the food was lousy.

So, this year for Christmas, I had no plans. I couldn't decide if I wanted to pop a Lean Cuisine into the microwave or go out to eat. By mid-afternoon, after editing a terrible manuscript for almost seven hours, I decided to go out for Chinese food. Not only would I be a single Gay Jew in a Chinese restaurant on Christmas, I would be in a restaurant full of Jews, being that it was in Columbia, where more than a few Jewish families live.

I cleaned up, got dressed, very nicely, I might add. After all, it was a federal holiday.

I walked in, and the hostess said, "Just one." She then looked at the reservation book, then at the half empty dining room, and said, "Follow me." I then followed her from table to table as she stopped or hesitated or changed her mind. She then conferred with a fellow staffer in their native tongue, I am guessing Mandarin, and then she gave me the reverse tour of the restaurant, until she finally seated me against the wall in a two-top. She found my waiter, whispered in his ear, and pointed at me.

Some things never change.

EVERY DIET STARTS ON MONDAY AND ENDS ON TUESDAY

At the beginning of every year, those of us who belong to a gym have the privilege of sharing our space with the Resolutionaries. Fortunately, I go when the gym opens at 5:00 am, and even the most dedicated Resolutionaries rarely make it that early. Another advantage to working out that early is that we only have to deal with a few Resolutionaries until the first really cold or rainy morning. Once that occurs, we never see them again. It is the only time of year, I pray for bad weather.

But this is not about the Resolutionaries at my gym; this is about resolutions.

Through the years, I have made my share of resolutions, and I have broken almost all them.

Last year, I decided to take a different approach. Rather than declare resolutions I knew I wouldn't keep — whisper my opinions, be more patient with stupid people, quit rolling my eyes during meetings — I made goals. I thought goals would be easier to achieve than changes in a middle-aged personality.

Apparently, I was right.

I only established three goals: lose fifty pounds, buy a mobile home, and write a blog about my experiences once I bought a mobile home.

That actually turned out well. In four months, I lost fifty pounds, and afterward, I looked like Larry King in every picture someone took of me. I have since regained fifteen of those pounds, which are now a part of this year's goals.

You know I achieved the other two goals, or you would be reading pornography right now.

They say if you want to make God laugh, make plans. I don't know if that is entirely true, but let's take a look back at one of the major plans I made in my past life.

During job interviews, the one question I do not like is "Where do you see yourself in five years." I always give the same answer. "Five years ago, I didn't see myself sitting here interviewing for a job I need but really don't want."

I don't say that. What I do say is "Sitting where you are and asking someone else that ridiculous question."

Here is why I hate that question? If my life had turned out as I had planned, right now I would be sitting in a writer's room working on a hit sitcom. I was supposed to be a comedy writer — the Carl Reiner or Rob Petrie of my generation.

I spent the first ten years after college jumping from job to job because becoming a comedy writer was my goal, and jobs were just for paying the bills. By age thirty, I realized the time had come for me to get serious about a career because my writing was not going to support me — it still doesn't.

Everyone I knew had moved ahead in their lives with homes, families, luxury cars, and I was living in a studio apartment, working three part-time jobs, fresh out of a really bad relationship, and driving a beat-up Plymouth Colt.

That was when I entered publishing, and nineteen years later, I am still doing the same job. I often make the joke that a trained monkey could do what I do because I have been doing it for so long that there is no longer a learning curve. In that time, I have worked for six different companies on four similar government contracts (only a Beltway Bandit would understand six companies and four contracts). With each new company or contract, the players sometimes change, but the job never does.

But, I am happy I made the decision to shuffle my priorities, or I wouldn't be writing this from my first home. I would probably be watching TV in an efficiency apartment with weekly rates, waiting for my shift to start — and still driving that Plymouth Colt. I would be that waiter the college kids on the staff point to and say, "God, don't let that happen to me."

I waited on tables for so long (even part-time until my late thirties) that I had more tuxedo shirts than Dean Martin.

For those of you who haven't pursued a career in the arts, this is foreign to you. I have a friend who has pursued an acting career for thirty years. He, in fact, lives in an efficiency apartment and watches TV while he waits for his shift to start. Do I pity him? No. I admire him. He still goes to auditions; he gets the occasional walk-on or commercial work; and he has never given up. He's happy.

But, what happens when someone like us flip flops his priorities? Three things from what I've observed.

One: You become so career focused, applying all your energies on your job that you end up a huge success.

Two: You last five minutes in a nine-to-five job and go back to your initial priorities.

Three: You don't lose sight of your dreams; you just make them part-time, weekend dreams.

At the age of forty-one (eleven years after my career flip flop), my first book was published, and now, at the age of forty-nine, you are reading my sixth book. I may not have become a television comedy writer, but I did become a writer.

In 2011, I made an important decision. Now when people ask me what I do for a living, I no longer say I am a communications manager on a government contract. I say, "I am a writer."

They don't need to know that I work two jobs to pay the bills and support a ridiculous antique car habit, so I can live in the lap of trailer park luxury in city called Jessup.

Back to the goals. What are mine this year? I told you about the fifteen pounds.

My other two, I won't say out loud, but let's just say they have a lot to do with this manufactured home I own and love and where to go from here.

I aim to achieve them.

My favorite poem:

Dreams by Langston Hughes

Hold fast to dreams
For if dreams die
Life is a broken-winged bird
That cannot fly.
Hold fast to dreams
For when dreams go
Life is a barren field
Frozen with snow.

Happy New Year!

THE LOUD TALKERS

There are loud mouths, big mouths and loud talkers.

Yes, there is a difference, and they are not to be confused with those who have loud voices. I have a voice that carries — a loud voice if you will. When I whisper, they can hear me in Paraguay. Growing up, this caused me a lot of problems. If a group of kids was carrying on, I was the one who got yelled at because my voice was the loudest and the only one they could heard.

In musical theater, it was a godsend. I never needed to be miked. I was once called a male Ethel Merman. I am still trying to figure out if that was a compliment. In situations where someone leaves his lights on, they always come to me and ask that I get everyone's attention and make an announcement. For this reason, I never talk on my cell phone on public transit. No matter how hard I try, the whole world is going to hear my conversation.

Loud mouths blabber everything to everyone. Tell a loud mouth a secret, and the world will know it in less than twenty-four hours. From across a crowded room you hear, "My wife tells me you were fired. I bet you never saw that one coming."

Big mouths also blabber, but they tell your secrets to whomever you are nearest. You are standing in a bar, next to a really hot guy, and the big mouth walks up to you and your future ex-husband, points to you and says to Mr. Right, "You should have seen this guy last week. Scratching like there was no tomorrow. Crabs are a bitch I always say. Don't you?"

Loud talkers are different. They are just loud, and what they have to say has nothing to do with you. They won't tell your secrets because your life is of no interest to them. The more boring their lives, the louder they get.

The loud talkers always pop up when you really don't want to hear anyone else's chatter. They love busses and restaurants. For some reason, they don't ride trains. People read or sleep on trains.

Back in the day, the loud talker was the big guy in the big suit in the middle table of the restaurant going on and on about his latest business deal. If you listened carefully, you learned that he sold ball bearings. Not that there is anything wrong with that, but how fascinating can ball bearings be? I guess to another ball bearing salesman — very. I have a friend who sells ball bearings.

Today, the loud talkers use their cell phones to let the world know all their business. One day, I was sitting next to a man on the bus, and behind us, a relatively attractive young woman was carrying on a very loud conversation on her cell phone that went like this:

"I don't know why I cannot meet the right guy ... I never get a second date ... These guys have issues with commitment ... I call them the next day, and they don't answer their phones ... You should have seen how the last one dressed ... I usually screw them on the first date because I never seem to get a second date ... He couldn't get it up."

I said to the guy next to me, "It is a wonder she gets a first date."

Then there was the woman who spent twenty minutes explaining the difference between corn and tortilla chips or something like that. When she got to her stop, she was still talking and held the door, so she could finish her explanation before stepping out into the rain. Without realizing it, I said out loud, "Get the hell off the bus," and of course, everyone heard me — and smiled.

When I was a teenager, I would get my hair cut at a beauty school, I told you about earlier. One day, a woman I knew was in there getting her hair set. Mind you, a hair cut cost $3 and a wash and set cost $7. Her style was similar to Jackie Onassis in the 1970s. Picture shoulder length hair that is teased and combed straight back with a thin ribbon wrapped from underneath the back then behind her ears and tied in a small, tight bow at the top of her head. While they were finishing her "do," she kept saying in the loudest voice as she retied the thin bow, "It is a classic style. I have been wearing it like this for years. It will never go out of style. I get compliments all the time."

Well, everyone looked at her, and I need not tell you what they were thinking.

The sad thing is I knew her, and I also knew her husband was going through some difficult financial times, so I figured she was overcompensating. I also did not tell anyone I saw her there. In spite of what my mother would say about my being a big mouth, I wasn't.

And speaking of hair, the other day I was at my new favorite barbershop getting my $9 "do," when this young guy walked in and started his loud talking. He was sitting two chairs down from me, and I heard — well, everyone heard:

"I bet you never expected me to let my hair get this long. I don't use shampoo anymore. I figured my hair would get nasty, but you can see it isn't at all." The barber cringed. "I don't wear deodorant anymore. I want my body to sweat."

Obviously, he didn't know the difference between deodorant and antiperspirant or how they work. I'm glad I was two chairs away.

"Yeah, I moved back home. It's great. I take care of my little brother. My mother cooks for me and does my laundry. It's great."

That isn't what your mother said.

"I quit college. Who needs an education? I work in my uncle's take-out across the street. It's great."

How lovely.

While he was getting his hair cut, his parents were dumping all his belongings onto the curb, fumigating his room, and changing the locks.

As I always say. Life often writes itself.

I DON'T EVEN PLAY
A DOCTOR ON TV

I like to volunteer, but there is a problem with how I go about doing it. I think it has something to do with my being a know-it-all who constantly wants to correct things because I am always right. There are other factors involved. I like being in charge, and my ultimate goal is to be a benevolent dictator with unilateral authority over a tropical island country with nothing but pretty people as my loyal subjects. I read *The Secret*, so this is attainable.

My volunteer history works something like this. I join an organization. I do a couple of things for them, then I offer my unsolicited opinion on how something should be done, then I do it myself because if you want something done right, do it yourself, then they ask me to serve on their board, and then I become president of the board for longer than anyone else in the history of their organization. The amazing thing is that all the above steps leading to my unanimous election as president usually take less than six months. I am not kidding.

If your organization needs a newsletter editor or booth designer, that is my favorite pathway to your leadership. Be warned.

Lucy in the *Peanuts* comic strip once said while sitting in her psychiatry booth, every eleventh person is a natural born leader. That means the birth order is ten followers, one leader. I mentioned this earlier and quite often because I believe it to be true.

For example, I can sit quietly during a group exercise with strangers at our home office, and they will all ask that I be leader before I open my mouth. And, I accept.

Once I become president, everyone complains about how I act like a dictator, try to do everything myself, and offer my unsolicited and unfiltered opinions, but for some reason, they keep asking me to run again. I offer to let any one of them have the job then they tell me how much they appreciate what I do. Whatever. I totally understand how all the Kim Ills and Ungs have stayed in power in North Korea for so long. No one else wants to run things. And they say democracy is the preferred form of government. Hah!

I wonder what Lucy says about the ratio of dictators.

Even a dictator gets tired. After five years as a synagogue president, I was burned out. Less than a year into my volunteer retirement, I was the newsletter editor for the Straight Eights, the oldest Gay car club in the United States (for those who don't know, straight eight is a type of engine and sort of a play on words). Within a year of that, I was elected president of the car club, and I am still in that position today.

In case you are wondering, this sort of thing happens at work, too. When I first entered publishing, I was working as an $8.50 per hour part-time proofreader. In six weeks, I was running the department, and this pattern continues to this day as well, except in the corporate world there is a glass ceiling for dictators, but I aim to break that.

This year, I made a pledge to continue volunteering without becoming part of the leadership. Let's see if I am successful.

The way I intend to achieve my goal is to volunteer for small tasks, go in, do my thing, keep my mouth shut, and leave. There are people who know me well who just did a spit-take.

I belong to the Scleroderma Foundation. My mother died from complications of Scleroderma, an autoimmune disease in the same family as Lupus and Rheumatoid Arthritis. The name means "stone skin" in Greek. With Scleroderma, your body attacks itself by overproducing collagen, and your skin and internal organs turn to stone. The actor, Jason Alexander, whose sister has the disease, is a national spokesman. Bob Saget's sister died from the disease, and he produced a movie of the week about it several years ago. For some unknown reason, the majority of Scleroderma sufferers are Jewish women and Black men.

As a member of the foundation, I get emails with opportunities to volunteer. Recently, they had a booth at the NBC4 Health Expo at the Washington Convention Center, and they needed to staff it for two-hour intervals. I decided to volunteer, and I made up my mind just to show up, do what they ask, and leave.

The NBC4 Health Expo is free to the public and huge. They have a kid's soccer field, aerobics demonstrations, vision and hearing screenings, blood pressure testing, HIV testing, etc. Since it is free, it attracts a diversity of attendees, so you know with me there staffing a booth ...

I arrived ten minutes early, and the couple staffing before me, gave me the run-down of which pamphlets to give out first, and what to tell people. Surprisingly, I was the only one volunteering alone. Well, not surprisingly. This happens to natural born leaders as well. We get assigned solo tasks by people who don't even know us. I have never met the man who was in charge of the booth, yet he made me the only one in two days of slots to work alone. See, the number eleven thing even happens in cyberspace. For me, that is not a problem. I do my best work alone.

Once left on my own, I studied the booth design. The Gods were testing me. The pamphlets were neatly stacked, but the display, a four-by-two tri-fold, was a disaster. It was set off center, had no central focus, and it was visually unappealing. Now, old Milton would immediately have contacted the organizer and offered to redesign their display and stage all their future booths, and we all know how that would have ended.

New Milton took two aspirins and did not say a word.

People came up to the booth and asked about Scleroderma, and I explained what it was and forced them to take brochures. Interestingly, the only ones who knew what it was either had a friend or relative with it or were health professionals who had witnessed its effects.

Then the other aspect of my wonderful life took effect. My crazy magnet went into high force field. They all found me.

Crazies love three things: free stuff and an audience ... and, of course, me.

You should have seen all the people with their free canvas tote bags carting around more pamphlets than a Jehovah's Witness. Being stuck behind a booth, I had nowhere to hide. And being at a disease booth, I suddenly became a diagnostician. Who knew there were so many hypochondriacs in the world?

Once I described Scleroderma, seventy-five percent of the crazies thought they had it. At one point, I had an audience, including one well-dressed woman whose wig was pushed back too far. It took everything in me not to adjust that thing.

The *coup de grâce* was the morbidly obese woman who lifted up her pants leg to show me a spot on her inner thigh and asked if I thought she had it.

I looked right into her eyes and said, "Honey, I don't even play a doctor on TV."

Thanks to some small mercy, my shift was finally up, and my replacement came to relieve me. She took one look at the booth and said, "That display needs work."

I said to myself as I walked away, "She must be a number eleven, too."

YOU CALL THAT A SNOW STORM?

The change of seasons, some love it, some hate it. For the past two winters in the DC Metropolitan area, I'll bet a good portion of the residents hated it. I love it.

As you know, I lived in South Florida for five years, where people ask, "The weather?" and you reply, "Yes." I never pulled out my winter coat the entire time I was there. The drawback to living in Florida is that it is the Jewish Gateway to Heaven. Basically, you move there to die. Running errands is synonymous with being in a funeral procession.

Ironically, they ship your body back via Federal Express, so you can be buried within twenty-four hours in the land of the living. You die there, but God forbid you should be buried there. I think Florida has two cemeteries, one of which has six plots, four of which are for sale.

It is all about visitation. What is a better way to guilt your children than to be buried where they have no excuse to skip putting a rock on your stone at least four times a year?

When I first moved back to the Eastern Seaboard, I arrived on Martin Luther King Day 1997 with temperatures in the teens. Two days prior, I was wearing shorts in eighty-degree weather. My poor Serena looked at me as we exited the car and said in French, "*C'est quoi ce bordel?*"* She was a toy parti-poodle, and my friend Sarah told me I got that right. Poodles are French if I lost you there for a minute.

I admit that I thought the same thing. But within a day or so, I was glad to be back in the land of the living rather than the balmy hospice by the sea.

The next day, I pulled my red winter coat out of the steamer trunk and put it on for the first time in five years. No one told me that everyone in DC wears charcoal gray. Not black, not navy, but charcoal gray. I was the six-four freak in the red winter coat on the bus. You know me. I didn't care.

After my first year back, I realized I really did like the change of seasons. Serena got somewhat used to it, too. We had our share of snow storms. In March of 1999, we got a doozy — three feet of snow in twenty-four hours.

I actually went to work via train then bus to our office in the armpit of Maryland — Rockville, in the middle of it (I actually worked in Rockville for three years, while still living in DC, which should have been a warning not to move there). There were maybe twenty of us at work, so the company bought pizzas for everyone. One of my co-workers, who lived behind our offices, called in saying it was too dangerous to walk, but when I told her we had free pizza, she was standing behind me before I could hang up the phone. I asked what took her so long, and she said she had to tie her boots.

By 2:00 pm, I decided it might be best to go home. I stepped out of the office and prepared to walk the half mile up to the White Flint Metro. When I stepped off the curb, the snow was up to my waist, and I immediately thought of Serena home alone with me freezing to death on Rockville Pike.

God heard my call and sent a bus with a lady bus driver who looked like Morgan Freeman in drag. The bus driver opened the door, and I asked where her bus was going, and she said, "Silver Spring Metro." If you don't know the area, the Silver Spring Metro is clear across the county from White Flint, but it was either that or die in Rockville. I also knew I could catch a bus from Silver Spring to my street.

This is going to sound sexist, but women bus drivers are the best. She navigated that bus through one residential street after another and didn't slip once. I almost kissed her before I thanked her and alighted.

My next bus was also driven by a woman, and by 4:00 pm, I was home. Funny how two-hour commutes don't freak us out around here.

I was greeted by a happy little dog. I put her sweater and leash on, and I opened the door. She took a flying leap and disappeared. It was funny, and even she got a kick out of it. One of the best pictures ever taken of us was the next day after that snow storm.

We had our share of snow in the years that followed, including 2002 when it snowed every Friday, but nothing compared to my first winter in Rockville. A little less than a month after Serena died in December 2009, we had one storm followed by two storms and close to five feet of snow. I was stuck on the fifth floor of Rockville Town Square for a week. The Metro was not running above ground, the streets weren't plowed, and everything came to a complete stop.

I was so desperate for food that I almost bought a chicken at CVS.

To keep myself entertained, I taught myself the lyrics to every song written by Harold Arlen. I think one of my neighbors committed suicide by jamming an ice pick into her ear.

The following winter, Esmeralda's first outside of Mississippi, we had an ice storm followed by a snow storm, and I had a beagle who didn't want to go to the bathroom outside. Upon first seeing snow, Esmeralda said, "Bloody hell!" Beagles are British.

So, now we live in a trailer park in Jessup, and I want to experience all the seasons during my first year as a home owner, but Bloody Hell, we are having the mildest winter in years. *C'est quoi ce bordel?*

Don't get me wrong, I don't want a paralyzing blizzard, but seriously, no snow at all?

We did get a small dusting of about an inch or two this past weekend. It did require a bit of shoveling and cleaning of the cars, but it was hardly worth writing home to Mom about. However, there was enough to make things icy dicey for yours truly.

I drove to a friend's house the night after our "big" storm, and he said to watch out for a patch of ice near his porch. Being the study of poise and grace that I am, I slipped on that very patch and went asshole over teacups. I was up on my feet in seconds.

When I was a dancer in Florida, my choreographer knew what a klutz I was, so he taught me how to fall properly; therefore, I wasn't hurt. My friend said it was both the funniest and most amazing thing he had ever seen.

I just wish someone would catch me on film when I do that, so I can win $10,000 on *America's Funnies Home Videos*.

There is still hope. God once sent me a bus with a lady driver; maybe if I pray enough, put ice cubes in the toilet and sleep with my pajamas inside out, God will send me at least eight inches ... of snow.

/Apparently "what the fuck?" in French. It was on the internet, so it must be right.

SOMETIMES YOU DON'T WANT TO GO HOME

My brother recently sent me something that got me thinking. It was a picture of the house where we grew up. I've told you about that house. My father used to joke that we had to do $10,000 in repairs before they would condemn it. That is the house where we were not allowed to answer the phone because it was probably a bill collector.

The picture brought back memories of course, which I immediately considered when studying the photograph. I saw the tree in front of the living room window that my mother and I planted. I noticed they never replaced the boxwoods that were under the bedroom windows, which I removed in 1984, much to the chagrin of my family after they asked me to remove them then forgot they asked me to remove them and raised hell when I did. Twenty-eight years later and there are still no bushes in their place. I saw they painted the shutters back to their original color — brown. They were painted green in 1967. I remember the painter drove a Ford Econoline — the Falcon-based van. The crap that is stuck in my head. Vaysmir.

In the 1980s, my mother had them painted gray by a painter who would take his shirt off the minute he arrived and worked with his sister and brother-in-law. They got paint everywhere, and some of it actually landed on the shutters. My brother and I painted the brick because Mother said she would pay us. We still have not been paid. And she's been dead for more than a decade.

Let me tell you a little about this house in the Ivy Farms Neighborhood of Newport News. First, the neighborhood was one of many to pop up in the late 1950s and early 1960s to accommodate the families with their cute little baby boomers. I am one of the last of the cute baby boomers, but I have never been little.

What few people knew at the time was that the neighborhood was built on the old city dump. What made it even more special was that the builder used scrap to build each house. My father once worked for him and told us how the man would stop his car to pick up nails and wood then use them in a new house. Whenever you wanted to replace a window or door, you would find out nothing was a standard size and no two in your house were the same.

Like most of the developments of the day, there was a mixture of about four or five different models. There were two single-story layouts or in some cases a split ranch with the same layout as the one story; in the split ranch, the bedrooms were located "upstairs" — a total of three steps up. We had one of those. The others were two story houses.

The homes had modestly large rooms, usually a separate family room, and one and a half baths. My nephew upon seeing the house as they drove by said, "It looks small." I never thought of it as small. My brother explained my nephew never had to share a bathroom. We were four people using one shower. Not at the same time. This was Newport News, not West Virginia.

Today, I live alone with two full baths.

Of course in the era of McMansions, these homes look like mother-in-law cottages, but I still prefer a modest ranch to an overpriced McMansion.

We spent the better part of two decades fighting mold inside and out especially since the brick was painted white. That white brick is an interesting story ... or not.

When my mother became pregnant in 1962, a surprise to *all* parties involved for reasons that could fill an entire book (read my novel, *Michael's Secrets* — shameless plug), my parents decided that an apartment would not cut it anymore. They didn't want to live near the other Jews, who always knew each other's business (for reasons that would fill a *Torah* scroll), so my mother picked out this lovely neighborhood when they chose to leave Stewart Gardens. Aunt Anita and her family had already moved there, and three other Jewish families moved there after we did. The bulk of the members of the tribe, however, moved to Hidenwood. Same kind of house, better neighborhood.

Apparently, my mother spent a great deal of time picking out a burnt orange brick for the house. The two houses on either side of ours were being built at the same time, and the one on the left had red brick, and the one on the right had pink brick, or the other way around, or one had orange, who can remember as I was *in utero* at the time. Anyway, pregnant Harryette and her two-year-old son, Alex, drove over to the house in their brown 1958 Ford Country Squire to check on the progress, and all the construction workers were standing in front of the house shaking their heads.

As it turned out, they had bricked up one side of the house with the brick from the house on the right, and the other side of the house with the brick from the one on the left, but never even used the brick my mother picked out, which was still sitting in the front yard. The foreman, upon seeing my expectant mother and her little son, suggested they just paint the brick white and for all their trouble they would fence in the back yard for free. Mother took the deal, and she always said she was an idiot for doing so because they could have easily knocked down all the brick and started over. I always wanted to sandblast the white paint to see what a house with two different colors of brick looked like.

The present occupants don't even know this story, so imagine if on a whim they decided to remove the white paint. I would love to be there when that happens.

This story always fascinated me because if I were having a house built and something like this happened, I would get out of the deal as soon as possible.

My parents were never accused of being shrewd.

We had the only house on the street with white painted brick for many years, and white brick shows mold. My brother said it still does.

The house was not insulated either. You could actually see someone's hair blowing when they sat by one of the windows. Nana's wig would even shift while she would struggle to light a Kent cigarette in the breeze of one of those windows. In the summer, it was an oven with only two window air conditioning units. When we had central AC installed, it would never cut off from May to September.

As crappy as that house was, it did have a very nice layout, and the galley style kitchen was its best feature. Four people could prepare a meal in that kitchen without even bumping into each other. There was no exhaust fan, garbage disposal or even a dishwasher, but many a holiday meal was prepared in that kitchen, and hours were spent cleaning up afterward.

The main draw for the neighborhood was the elementary school, South Morrison Elementary, where I was the fifth grade valedictorian in 1974. Thank you. Oh, you didn't congratulate me. My bad.

And that is where this story becomes depressing.

South Morrison, an award-winning elementary school, is now an abandoned building, which once was a haven for crack whores, or so I have been told. The city is trying to decide what to do with it. Surrounding it are abandoned, boarded up and in some cases, burned down apartment buildings. I used to deliver papers to the tenants of those apartments, many of whom would not pay their bills.

The bank at the top of my street, where I opened my fist checking account, is now a police substation. The community pool has been filled in, and the rest of the neighborhood looks like a set from an Eminem video.

Jack Carter used to joke that he grew up in such a bad neighborhood that you had to go six blocks to leave the scene of a crime. Well, that is my old neighborhood now. One childhood friend relayed how crime has completely taken over with people being shot on a regular basis.

I don't have many great memories of growing up there, but it was my childhood home, and I find it sad that what was once a decent neighborhood with a great school is now a place you wouldn't want to visit at any time of day.

Ironically, that was the only stick-built home I ever lived in, and now officially in the worst neighborhood from my past. That is saying a lot considering all the apartments I rented in many a dicey area.

And the best neighborhood? The one I live in now as a Gay Jew in a Trailer Park.

Life is full of ironies.

MOONSHINE AND BEEF JERKY

Sometimes, I think my life is one big giant sitcom. Maybe because I watched nothing but sitcoms growing up, and I continue to love them. One of my many exes actually arranged his house like the set of a sitcom, and when we would have conversations, he would wink and smile at the imaginary audience. And, people wonder why I have remained single for so long.

Lucy Ricardo once said, "Some people are cut out for champagne and caviar. I'm more of the beer and pretzel type." If that is the case, then I am "moonshine and beef jerky."

Recently, a friend of mine invited me to a birthday dinner for his sister, which was being held at a restaurant I did not know. I had never met his sister or anyone else who would be there, but I was up for the challenge of hobnobbing with strangers in a fancy restaurant. Little did I know how fancy it would be!

I told Frank (you know my friend Frank who kept me from taking the shuttle to St. Elizabeth's on moving day) where I was going, and he said, "You will need to wear a jacket and tie, or a tie, or a jacket." I panicked. Although I don't wear jeans, I also don't wear jackets and ties. My wardrobe is sort of dress casual even when I go to the supermarket. I decided to call the restaurant, and they told me it was business casual, but I couldn't leave it at that.

"Do I need to wear a jacket?"

"No."

"Do I need to wear a tie?"

"No."

"Do I need to wear dress shoes?"

"They would be preferred."

"Are kakis acceptable?"

"Yes."

"Can I wear them with this smart looking off-white mock turtleneck sweater I just bought on sale at Sears?"

"Yes … sir I am busy, and I need to go."

She hung up so fast that I couldn't ask if the brown and beige argyle sweater with the V-neck would be a better choice. I felt like Sally Rogers getting ready for a blind date when she asked, "Should I wear the dress with the low V neck or the one with the high slit in the skirt?" Buddy Sorrell said, "Wear the top of one and the bottom of the other."

When she arrived for the date at Rob and Laura's, with a mink stole on, she came in yelling, "Where is this tall, handsome, PRIEST you wanted me to meet?" Laura forgot to tell her that the man, a former beau, turned out to be a priest.

Rob, went to take her mink stole, and she screamed, "No." So, we knew which dress she wore.

After getting some wardrobe clarification, I looked at the menu online. Oh my God! The lowest priced entrée was $48, and everything was *ala carte*. I wasn't sure of protocol when being asked to a stranger's birthday party, so the afternoon before the big event, I cashed in my 401K just in case I, the stranger who came to dinner, would have to pay his own check. Who needs a retirement, when you can eat prime rib and spinach soufflé for close to $100?

Let me back up a bit. I like diners and dives — not the show, actual diners and dives. Over the years, I have found that some of the worst meals I ever ate were the most expensive, with a few exceptions, and some of the best at the greasy spoons and truck stops, with no exceptions.

My family was not known for fine dining, probably because in Newport News, Virginia, there was little of it when I lived there. The fanciest restaurant around was Nick's Seafood Pavilion on the York River, which I believe closed in 2005. The waitresses would wear Greek influenced uniforms made entirely of bed linen. Bed linen makes for heavy costuming, so the waitresses were all built like East German basketball players.

Going to Nick's was considered a major treat. No reservations were allowed, you waited in line for some time to get in, and the lines were arranged by the number in your party. The food was expensive by Virginia Lower Peninsula standards, but it was good. And where else could you get an iceberg lettuce wedge salad with thousand island dressing for $20? The view of the river from the main dining room was magnificent. The place was filled with all kinds of authentic Greek art, and the dining room had heavy linens and fancy silverware and plates.

On one of our last visits there, I ordered a scallop dish. The portion was not that large, and my mother went on and one about how I didn't know how to order in a fine restaurant. I couldn't take it anymore, so I said, "How could I know how to eat in a fancy restaurant? The fanciest place we've ever eaten is Uncle Jimmy's Pizza?" My father thought that was funny. Even funnier was that half of Uncle Jimmy's was a Laundromat. Once when we ate at Uncle Jimmy's, Nana got so excited because they were one of the last places to serve instant Sanka. Nana's favorite restaurant was the Hot Shoppe at Van Ness in Washington, DC. That should tell you how fancy our family was.

I spent almost twenty years working in the restaurant business, and the fanciest place that ever employed me was the Rod & Gun in Delray Beach, Florida, where I got my first exposure to New York Jews, the stories of which would fill a blog and book of their own.

We had fancy linens and uniforms, a stellar wine list and French cuisine, but we also had an early bird menu with soup, salad, coffee or tea and dessert for $15.95. It was hardly five-star.

I bought a present for the birthday girl based on her love of cooking and inability to settle on a favorite color and drove my 1983 AMC Eagle Wagon to eat, excuse me, dine the way the other half does.

Upon finding the restaurant, I saw they had valet parking, and I could just picture waiting at the end of the evening for the valet to try to start a car with a carburetor, so I decided to park in the garage next to the restaurant, which was also part of the Ritz Carlton. I parked next to the most expensive BMW I could find. I love scaring people.

In spite of the hostess's reluctance to help with me with my wardrobe, I wore the off-white sweater, kakis, dress shoes, and I topped it off with this olive blazer-coat combination I picked up when a big and tall shop went out of business years ago. It sort of looks like a blazer but doubles as a coat and it has shoulder pads like Joan Crawford's. And when in doubt, I ask, "What would Joan Crawford do?"

"In three months, I was one of the best waitresses there. I took tips and was glad to get them. And at home, I baked pies for the restaurant." OK, not a sitcom, but *Mildred Pierce* is a great movie.

I arrived before my friend, so I waited near the hostess stand, and I am glad I did not take wardrobe advice from her. She was no older than twenty-five, but she was wearing a flower in her head as if she was the long lost White Pointer Sister. If I weren't meeting a bunch of strangers, I would have called her over, yanked that flora from her head and fixed her hair. It took everything in me not to pull out my styling pick and Aquanet (I'm old school).

My friend arrived, and we were seated with the rest of the party. Introductions were made, and for the first time in a long time, I did not sit at the head of the table. I am a number eleven, and even strangers tend to put me at the head of the table. But I was a stranger in a strange land (subliminal Jewish reference), so I sucked it up and made a note to claim my rightful place at the table next time I ate with this group … if there would be a next time.

Now, you know I love my own family, but they are just trash.

In this group was a former high official in law enforcement, a high ranking congressional employee, an attorney, two real estate developers, and a man at the other head of the table who looked at me with suspicion. He was only six years older than I but looked to be twenty years older, so I knew he was straight. Poor straight men; they don't age very well — probably because they live with straight women.

I looked in front of me, and there were two napkins — one black and one white. I asked my friend why, and he said the napkins are based on what you are wearing.

I asked if they had gingham.

There were three glasses in front of me, one for water, two for wine. I guessed red or white. I was correct. Thank God this wasn't one of those places with seventeen forks. There is nothing worse than eating macaroni salad with a shrimp fork. I am the one who always gives up the incorrect fork to the waiter and then has to eat his steak with a soup spoon.

The birthday girl loved the gift I bought for her kitchen, and one of her friends asked where I got it because she wanted one. I said a boutique store near where I live. I didn't have the heart to tell her it was from Walmart. I made a note to get her friend a set next time I was there.

Then, we ordered cocktails. Someone ordered a Belvedere, which I thought was a drink butlers enjoy. Apparently, it is type of martini. I sipped it, and it was yummy! Other fancy drinks were ordered, and the waiter looked at me. I felt like Paula (played by Penny Marshall on the *Mary Tyler Moore Show*) out on a date with Lou and another couple, and after everyone ordered, she said in her best Penny Marshall voice, "A beer."

I asked what they had on draft and ordered a Belgian beer, which was served room temperature. I commented that it was like the beer I drank in Belgium (might as well let the better half know I have traveled abroad), but the waiter informed me that something must be wrong with the tap as it was supposed to be cold. I decided I liked it like that, and he comped it anyway. I'll bet it cost $30 a glass.

Dinner was lovely. I had the lamb chops, but you will be happy to know I did not pick up the bones and suck the meat off them, but it took everything in me not to!

I did learn one thing about the other half. No matter how fancy the environment, get a few drinks in them, and they get just as trashed and trashy as the rest of us. The nouveau riche, what can you do? People are people.

The birthday girl's husband picked up the check, so I was able to restore the funds to my 401K.

Afterward, my friend asked how I enjoyed the evening with his crazy family. Crazy? Oh honey, if that had been a meal with my family, someone would have cried, someone would have thrown a plate, and someone would have left in anger without paying. And that would have been dinner for two!

I always said dinner with my family was like a meal in a mental institution. My father used to laugh at that as well.

After eating a meal that cost twice as much as my mortgage, I returned to the trailer park with personality!

I did forget to bring the lamb bones home for Esmeralda!

Next time.

EXCUSE ME, LADY —
IS THAT MY DRESS?

The hardest thing to do is get a straight man in drag. The second hardest thing to do is get him to take off the goddamn dress!

For Gay men, the easiest thing to do is get him into the dress, and when the night is over and the tips are counted, getting him out of the dress is the second easiest thing to do. Watch *RuPaul's Drag Race*, and you will see how quickly the queens take off their wigs and makeup.

I admit it. I have done my share of drag over the years and as recently as six months ago. We had a party to celebrate Lucille Ball's 100th birthday, and I went as the *Here's Lucy* Marionette. It should not be a surprise that I skipped over Lucy Ricardo and Mrs. Carmichael; after all, I have never been like everyone else. There I was in a tuxedo jacket, ruffle shirt, white bow tie, top hat, red wig, full make-up, black stockings, six-inch stilettos, and NO PANTS. I walked down the street like that!

Upon seeing the photo, Lucie Arnaz told me I made her day — probably because she had seen her share of Lucys in the chocolate factory, doing the Vitameatavegamin commercial or fresh out of the grape vat. Did I just drop a name? Yes, I did. Even a Gay Jew in a Trailer Park knows a few celebrities personally. *Puff, puff.*

At the end of that evening, I made a decision. Well, to be honest, the mirror made a decision. Drag has three phases: Fierce, Amusing and Tragic. Up through age thirty, it can be fierce. Up to age forty-five, it can be amusing. The secret is recognizing when it becomes tragic, and honey, that night, I saw it clear as day.

In drag, I look like my maternal grandmother, Nana. All I need is a wig, a Kent cigarette, and a couple of Oh-my-Gods, and my brother will swear he is seeing a ghost. The sad part is that as I age, I continue to look like Nana — as she aged. All I needed that night was a fresh cup of instant Sanka and coke-bottle glasses, and the picture would have been complete.

For anyone who has ever worn drag, there is that first moment in his life when he put on a dress. OK, you are about to be told something no one, not even my closest friends know. My first moment was age nine, and it was my homophobic mother's fault!

If she were alive today and knew what I did, it would kill her. If she is listening or reading this from wherever she is, this is going to be priceless!

In the house where I was raised, I only had the use of half my bedroom closet, as did my brother. My father kept half his clothes in Alex's closet, and my mother, who never threw anything away, kept half her clothes in mine. Do you see where this is going?

When you are an oddball kid and spend a lot of time alone in your room living a fantasy life that is much better than reality, you have to find ways to entertain yourself, and that is what I did.

Not only did my mother keep half her clothes in my closet, but also she kept half her shoes, and even better, a complete wardrobe of hats, gloves and wigs. It was a future drag queen's dream.

I didn't have to shop for anything, which at age nine was a good thing, since I did not have a driver's license, nor did I have a job.

When I was sent to my room, I was more than happy to oblige.

My mother was a fashionista in her day, so not only were the clothes plentiful, but also they were fabulous, and most were left over from the late fifties and early sixties, my favorite fashions of all time. She was tall, and I was tall for my age, so we were the perfect match, both size twelves. Today, a twelve is an eighteen. Every mother wants a daughter, so they can share clothes. I wonder if every Gay boy wants a mother who's into fashion?

There was a flower-print sundress with a sweetheart collar that I must say I looked fetching in, especially with the brown wig, multi-colored pumps and big straw hat. There was the blue knit dress with the big buttons down the center that went really well with the blue shoes with four-inch heels and open toes. My mother was a size ten shoe, and at age nine, I was a men's nine, so I could squeeze into her shoes … for a while.

My favorite was the full green skirt, with shiny gold leaves etched into the fabric that went with an off the shoulder light green top and green shoes. I could not get over how good I looked in that one, and little did I know what I had done when I danced around in my room in that outfit.

But, the drag show was not to last very long. I continued to grow, and by age eleven, my feet were too big for the shoes (a sad day when that happened), and my waist too big for the skirts and capris (which with my yo-yoing weight was no surprise). My career was over.

When I was sixteen, my mother decided to clean out some of the clothes, and when she came upon the full green skirt with the shiny gold leaves etched into the fabric that went with the off-the-shoulder light green top and green shoes, she looked at them and said, "This is what I wore when your father and I were married."

OH MY GOD! I had on my mother's wedding dress, and I didn't even know it! It took everything in me not to laugh! How many boys can say they had on their mother's wedding dress? OK, it wasn't a white wedding dress, but my father was her third husband, so it still counts. All the pictures of their wedding were in black and white, so I never made the connection. Then, she pulled out the flowered sun dress, which I found out she wore on their honeymoon. Could this get any better?

By that point, I had not worn a dress nor heels in at least five years, and it would be almost a decade before I did again. I thought it was out of my system by that point.

When I first came out, most of my friends were drag queens and bar flies. Sadly, only two of my friends from that time are still alive. I loved them all and still miss them.

One night back in the day, there was an AIDS charity event where I was volunteering, and I was asked if I would do drag to act as MC. At that point, I was twenty-five, six-four, and two-hundred-twenty pounds. I protested, saying I couldn't do glam drag, but funny maybe.

This was before six-four RuPaul became a household name. I saw RuPaul in Atlanta before the polish we now know, and giirrrll, she was a hot mess!

They put me in a black suit dress that looked as if it came out of Maude's closet, a black teased up wig with a flip, very heavy make-up, and at that moment Sylvia Rose was born. The year was 1988. Sylvia talked with a heavy New York accent, smoked Benson & Hedges and said the most awful things to people. I loved her. I found it amusing that after all those nights prancing around in every article of clothing my mother saved from the early years of her third marriage that this was the first time I did this in public.

Needless to say, I was a hit. Who is going to argue with me, and the way everyone was drinking, who would remember?

For the next four years, Sylvia would come out to host an event on occasion, and then she retired. I never had to shop because the girls always had something for me to wear, most of which I suspect was stolen from their grandmothers' closets. The shoes I bought myself from a drag queen shop in downtown Norfolk, Virginia, where they didn't even blink while a six-four, former football player, walked around in heels to be sure the size seventeens fit. I need to re-visit that store someday.

Speaking of grandmothers. When Nana died, my mother donated all her wigs to Goodwill. I would kill to have those wigs today. They were *real* hair, professionally coiffured by Don's Wigs of Newport News, teased to the heavens to be closer to God, and just magnificent. Uccchhh, when I think of the money I could have gotten for those on Drag eBay ...

But, I digress ...

When I moved to Florida, I decided to go as Bea Arthur one Halloween, and for the first time, I had to shop for my own dress. So, I did what any respectable drag queen would do, I went to the Hadassah Thrift Store. I figured it would be the closest to my childhood closet I could get. I pawed through the racks like Ethel Mertz in Gimble's Basement, and in five minutes, I found the most perfect frock. It was pink satin with layers and layers of chiffon overlaying the dress and sleeves to hide my less than perfect figure — exactly what Bea would wear.

They sold it to me for $15. As I was leaving, one of the *yentas* in the shop said to the clerk who rang me up, "How could you sell that dress to a man for $15?"

My friend, Stan, loved that dress, and when Halloween was just a memory, he asked to borrow it, and being the generous sort I am, I lent it to him.

Bitch cut off the sleeves! I could have killed him!

I told him he could keep the dress. I look like a member of the East German women's swim team when I go sleeveless.

Over the years, I picked up a few other frocks. One from Sears — in the 1990s, they had a great big girls' department. That black dress lasted a few years, then I wanted to go as Endora one Halloween, so my friend Sandy made me my first custom made dress — a multicolored shift that mimicked the one Endora called a Lilly Arlegge original in the "Jack and the Beanstalk" episode. Complete with wild red wig, purple shoes (I died a pair of my black ones) and perfect Endora make-up, I was really pleased with myself. So pleased, that I decided to go to the restaurant where I worked, in Delray Beach, to show off my costume.

The owner asked me to go up to a table of old Jewish women and ask them how their meal was. So, there I was, a six-ten Endora (the heels added six inches), standing next to the table, and I asked in my best Endora voice, "How is your dinner?"

And one of the ladies answered, "The salmon is a little dry."

No one even blinked. Seriously? This make-up took me three fucking hours, and all you can say is the salmon is dry?!?

The owner asked me what they said, and I answered, "The salmon is dry." Then, I left for my party, where a few people thought I was Madge the Palmolive Lady.

Upon my arrival in DC, I finally had a chance to break Sylvia Rose out one more time, and Endora joined her for a Purim Party at Bet Mishpachah. I had to explain to one old queen who Endora was and the premise of *Bewitched*. I then asked for his Gay card.

I think my best drag costume was Joan Crawford in the *Mommie Dearest* wire hanger scene. Everyone got that one. There I was hair in curlers, white band around my skull, bathrobe, night cream, a dress on a wire hanger in one hand, and a can of Bon Ami in the other. We had an acquaintance who fancied himself a movie buff, and he was the only one at the party who could not guess my costume. He said, "Are you Endora?"

I should have dressed as Madge the Palmolive Lady.

By then, I was approaching forty, and frankly, my feet couldn't take the heels anymore. So, I retired my drag costumes until the Lucy party this past year, but I didn't discard them until …

With limited closet space in the trailer, I decided it was time to let someone else enjoy my haute couture, so a couple of weekends ago, I donated all of my girlie stuff — all of it. However, I did keep the shoes. Hey, I can't just quit cold turkey!

One day in 1985, Mother and I were out to lunch, when she said, "Don't look, but that woman over there is wearing one of Nana's dresses we donated to Goodwill." Of course, I looked. My first thought was *why is this woman shopping at Goodwill?*

This past Sunday, I was out shopping at Home Goods, the one my friend Lydia suggested in Gambrill, Maryland, and while I was wheeling my cart down the aisle, I just about screamed, "Girrrrl, she didn't!"

This woman, obviously fresh from church, was wearing my black fedora complete with zebra print hat band that I actually fashioned myself. It originally had no hat band, but I found a zebra-print scarf that I wrapped around the hat and let dangle off the back. At first I thought it was a coincidence, until I saw her dress. It was a black knit dress with a black and gray striped bodice, and a black and white striped knit jacket. She was even wearing two strings of pearls.

Bitch was wearing my dress and hat! The hat was meant for a different outfit, but those were definitely my old clothes.

I couldn't stop staring at her. I wanted to criticize her, but she was really pulling it off, and I was a little surprised I didn't think of wearing that hat with that dress, myself.

I wanted to say, "Excuse me, Lady, is that my dress?"

Instead, when she looked over, I said, "I really love your outfit."

She smiled and said, "Thank you."

And people make fun of my taste in clothes. If they are good enough for church … wait a minute.

I wonder if she is on the committee to support a ban on Gay marriage? And there she is, sitting in a meeting in the church basement wearing the clothes of a former drag queen!

Life can be sweet!

WHAT'S IN YOUR BASKET?

Remember the episode of *Designing Women* when Suzanne said to Mary Jo in the supermarket, "Two guys, one cart, fresh pasta ... figure it out"? Do you look in other people's carts at the supermarket? Of course you do.

Have you ever had to go shopping for a strange combination of just a few items and hoped no one would look in your basket? Of course you have, and you wouldn't be reading this is if it didn't happen to me.

I love looking in other people's carts, especially those of weight challenged mothers with weight challenged children. Was that politically correct enough? Roseanne, when she did stand-up, said fat mothers were the best because they had the good snacks. No one hangs out at the house with the skinny mother.

No one would hang around our house. One, because we were the crazy family every neighborhood has and points out when friends and relatives come to visit, and two, our mother was constantly on a diet. Everything in our house was sugar free. The woman used Sweet n Low instead of sugar in *every* recipe. To this day, I never eat in a restaurant that advertises "home cooking." I stole that line from Alan King, *alev ha sholem.*

When the fat-free craze started, we adopted that as well. There is no food worse than fat-free cream cheese. Cream cheese is fat! Remove the fat, and you have caulk.

My mother's grocery cart was filled with Fresca, Tab, Sweet n Low, bananas, chicken, chuck roast (which I have told you she would burn on the grill), cottage cheese, and tomatoes. Oy vay.

Mother was on Atkins when it first came out, and I remember going with her to the G.C. Murphy Co. lunch counter at Newmarket Shopping Center in our 1965 Corvair, where they had those cool orange punch machines, and her ordering a hamburger omelet with a side of cottage cheese. I don't care how fat and desperate I get (and I have been pretty fat and desperate in my day), I will never order a hamburger omelet with a side of cottage cheese. Occasionally, she would convince my father to go on one of those diets.

No wonder my parents always had gas. For years, I thought we had an invisible pet duck. Think about it.

179

Back to the market. I am a very efficient grocery shopper as I have told you before, but this does not preclude me from observing other people's food choices, especially in the checkout line.

Before I criticize others, I do have one problem when I shop. I can buy $200 worth of groceries and still have nothing to eat. Seriously, I will come home and empty my bags, which will contain cleaning products, Kleenex, toothpaste and other personal hygiene items, and only find a bunch of bananas and three fresh donuts that I will eat very quickly over the sink before disposing of the evidence. Esmeralda gives me the look that says, "I know what you're doing."

As a kid, I had to sneak fattening snacks, and although my parents are not watching anymore, I still eat junk food when no one is around and pretend I never do. Then I say, "The dryer keeps shrinking my underwear."

I usually get stuck behind the fat mother (yes, I said fat this time, which is ok because my shrinking underwear is cutting off my circulation). I love their carts, which usually have frozen pizzas, frozen chicken nuggets, six or seven boss bottles of soda (do they call them boss bottles anymore?), ice cream, four of five bags of Doritos, a hunk of unidentifiable red meat, pork chops, and a jumbo pack of toilet paper. They are going to need that toilet paper. Amazingly, there are no — and I mean no — fruits and vegetables in the cart. However, next to the cart is a little fat kid that is so hyped up on sugar that the mother is constantly shushing her and saying no when she grabs candy bars. Seriously, no candy bars? Well, I guess she has to draw the line somewhere.

Behind me is the former supermodel, a seventy-something woman in a velour track suit, whose face is pulled so tight that when she turns her head she has an orgasm. In her cart are fruits and vegetables of every variety and color, various nuts in bags, enough Crystal Light to drown a giraffe, and a bottle of Geritol. I wonder if she has an invisible pet duck, too.

Between major shopping excursions, all of us have to run in for a few items, and these fun people can be found in the express or self-checkout aisle. There you find the husband buying tampons.

Now, I never had a period, although many of my friends would argue otherwise, but I have never understood running out of tampons. Maybe this is because I have a dozen toothbrushes, at least seven back-up tubes of toothpaste, bottle after bottle of mouthwash, shampoo, and body wash, bottles of dog shampoo and canine ear cleaner, enough detergent to wash the Baltimore Ravens' jock straps for a year (who wouldn't want that job?), and dozens of other bottles of cleaning products for windows, floors, countertops, bathtubs, toilet bowls, etc.

If there is ever a nuclear war, look for the really skinny but immaculately clean Gay Jew and his dog next to the very clean park space where his trailer was vaporized. I may die of starvation, but I'll be damned if I die dirty!

So, women of America, how in the hell do you run out of tampons? Or, do you do this to torture your menfolk by sending them out for tampons? Amazingly, they never run out of maxi pads. If my Aunt Flo visited me every month, bitch, I would be prepared.

Well, I can usually find something I need at the grocery store, since I rarely buy food, but one morning this week, I needed only two items. I drove over to the store right after the gym at 6:00 am and walked into Weis on a mission. I was pronouncing it "weece" until my neighbor corrected me and said it was pronounced "wice." I asked the manager, and he said he pronounces it "we is." I'll go with "wice."

Where was I? Oh yes, my two items.

There I was with my hand basket. I love the little hand baskets because they discourage me from buying even more bottles of detergent. I had my two items, and I looked over to the bakery department, and what did I smell, fresh donuts! They come out fresh at 6:00 am! There *is* a God.

Hey, I just came from the gym ... shut up.

I went to self-checkout, and I scanned my bag of donuts then my next two items. At that hour, the cashiers are not available, but one is around to help, and she likes to bag items for the few people who come in to shop. She is also the weird one they put on that shift to keep her away from most of the regular customers and the other staff. When she bagged my items, using my canvas shopping bag, she gave me a strange look.

What, you never saw someone buy donuts, Fleet enemas and double-A batteries before?

CLOSE COMBAT

I have never been in a fight. OK, I was beaten up a few times as a kid, once by a neighbor whose mother told him I threw a mud pie at their 1965 Oldsmobile, when I was five. He was eight. Yes, I threw the mud pie, but in my defense, I was aiming for my friend Jerry. I missed. This woman held onto that for the entire day, and that afternoon, when the school bus dropped her son off, she came out, said something to him, pointed at me, and next thing I knew I was on the ground getting my ass kicked. I didn't throw any punches because I was too busy guarding my face. Every drag queen knows "Never the face, never the face!"

My father, the original Mister Macho, who tried to make Robert Conrad look like a flaming sissy, once gave my brother and me boxing lessons using the cushions on my mother's mid-century modern teak couch. All I learned from that experience was that my father knew nothing about boxing.

Funny thing about my father, he always talked about all the fights he got into as a kid in Brooklyn. Once saying, "I've been beaten up by guys smaller than I, and I've beaten up guys bigger than I." Actually, he did not say, "I." He said, "me." I just felt like cleaning up the grammar.

What is it about Brooklyn? Everyone who grew up there said they fought every day, yet none of them have cauliflower ears or crooked noses or missing teeth. Is everyone from Brooklyn full of shit?

He also told one story about how three Marines beat him up when he was in the Navy. Apparently, they called him off a bus full of recruits, took him into a room, told him to straighten up his hat, turned off the lights, then punched him in the stomach. All mayhem broke loose in the dark, and when they were tired out, they cleaned up in the bathroom and had a good laugh.

My father also told the story about the guy in the Navy who never bathed, so he and two other sailors were ordered to take the guy into the shower and scrub him down with brushes. This was thirty years before the Village People made their first appearance.

OK, a fight in the dark, and four naked sailors in the shower. Interesting.

Of course, he always followed these stories with the one about how he fell asleep in a Jeep, and the guy driving it reached over and fondled him. He immediately had him stop the Jeep, beat the guy up, and left him wherever they were in the desert. I have two problems with this story. Anyone who has ridden in a World War II era Jeep will tell you the only way to fall asleep in one is to be dead or passed out drunk. And what were two sailors doing driving a Jeep in the desert?

Needless to say, I did not inherit my father's mortal combat history. I have also never been fondled in a Jeep. My loss.

I did manage to talk myself out of more fights than you can count on two hands, two feet and an open zipper. I have never punched anyone in my life. This is not to say I have not wanted to. I have also never put my fist through a wall, but then again, that is a very straight thing to do. Straight guys love to punch walls and doors.

My friend Chris always said that one day I would get into a fight, and when I threw my first punch, all the rage I have held onto for years would come out, and I would end up killing the guy.

When I was ten years old, my mother thought it would be a good idea to enroll my brother and me in Judo classes at the Jewish Community Center. OK, Judo at the JCC — I am not even going to go there, but you can imagine all the Jewish mothers sitting on the sidelines watching to be sure Irving didn't get injured or sweaty and that he had a nosh when class was over. OK, I went there.

Our mother just dropped us off.

At the time, I thought it might be fun to horse around and learn to fight at the same time. However, Judo is not a martial art for those needing to learn how to defend themselves. The translation for Judo is "gentle way." How often do you get into a fight in your pajamas? In addition, to engage in Judo combat, your opponent must also be barefoot in pajamas, and you must grab the collar of his pajamas in a certain way in order to throw him. But if he throws you, you must land on your back, throw out one arm and yell, "Hiyah!" with an accent on the "yah." Seriously?

I am amazed I can remember that since it was forty years ago.

"Excuse me, sir, who just broke into my house, will you put on this snazzy white robe, take off your shoes, tie this lovely pastel belt around your waist, stand with your feet parallel and shoulder width apart, and let me grab you by the collar and throw you over my shoulder? Oh, and don't forget to flex your knees a bit and bounce on the balls of your feet. Thank you."

No offense to Judo enthusiasts, but even at that young age, I found this martial art to be useless for self-defense. I wanted to take Karate, but that would never be taught at a Jewish Community Center because you might poke or kick someone's eye out. Or worse, you might injure your hands and not be able to take piano or violin lessons or hold a pastrami sandwich again.

By age eleven, my career in white pajamas was over. I did get up to yellow belt, but to go beyond that, I would have had to fight someone, and again, I am not a fighter.

Several years ago, while living in Mount Pleasant (which was neither a mount nor pleasant, discuss), they started offering Krav Maga classes at Bancroft Elementary School, next door to where I lived. A friend of mine's partner, a Lesbian of course, took the course and loved it. I would chat with the instructor as she would head to her car, and she tried to get me to join the class, but at the time, I really had no desire for mortal combat.

For those who don't know, basically, Krav Maga is an Israeli self-defense technique that roughly translated means "close combat." It is a combination of boxing, martial arts, and other fighting techniques intended to take down your opponent as quickly as possible, so you don't miss the early bird special with soup or salad, coffee or tea, and dessert. Jews are nothing if not efficient.

My idea of fitness has always been weight lifting and running. I used to run five to ten miles a day in all kinds of weather until a fateful morning in 2007. My bad hip slipped (there is no other way to put this), and I ended up having the sidewalk for breakfast. Now, being the Neanderthal that I am, I immediately got up and started running again.

Archeologists say Neanderthals had a very high pain threshold evidenced by the fact that their bones are full of self-set fractures. A Neanderthal could fall hundreds of feet chasing a Woolly Mammoth, break a foot, reset it in seconds, and keep running. I am the same way. I have reset at least two broken toes. I told a doctor neighbor how I did this once, showed him the black and blue toe, and he got squeamish and almost barfed in front of me.

I knew immediately something was wrong. My shirt was covered in blood, and when I reached up, I realized a part of my face was bleeding as I had a four-inch wide, two-inch deep hole in my chin. I took off my shirt, held it up to my chin and walked home. This was 5:00 am on 16th Street in Washington, DC. No one stopped or noticed me. Upon arriving home, Serena, who was by then completely deaf, had no idea I was home. I showered then drove myself to the emergency room at Washington Hospital Center. Fortunately, it was empty that morning, and they took me right in.

The doctor could not get over the fact that I showered and drove myself over. He asked if I was in pain. I wasn't. He also asked about my swollen fingers, which apparently I had sprained in the fall. I didn't even realize I did. I then relayed my Neanderthal factoid, but I think a part of him thought I was on some kind of controlled substance. He checked my pupils and seeing they weren't dilated came to the conclusion that I was just a freak of nature. Big surprise.

Thus ended almost thirty years of running. I tried cardio machines, but moving in place and getting nowhere to me is the most boring thing one can do. Cardio machines gave me heel spurs, and you probably guessed, they make me whine, too.

Going back a dozen or so years, at age thirty-two, I decided to take dance classes, beginning with tap, then ballet and modern. I wasn't all that good, but I did manage to dance for a season with the Palm Beach Opera, only because they needed someone over six-feet tall to dance with one of the women members of the ballet, as we were called. I wasn't a women member; I was just a member. The choreographer retired at age forty after trying to choreograph me. Some people make shoe salesmen cry; I do the same thing to choreographers.

I took dance for many years, but when I moved to DC, transportation and getting to a class after work proved impossible; thus ended my dream of becoming the next Ken Berry. Besides, Kinney Shoe Stores were out of business by then.

I did try a class at a studio a year before I left DC, but I was the only guy in a class of thirty twenty-five-year-old women, and frankly, I did not feel like continuing.

In the armpit of Maryland known as Rockville, there was no way to have any extracurricular activities because it took two hours to drive three miles.

But now, I live in Jessup, where I can go grocery shopping during rush hour and still be home in time for Diane Sawyer.

Some guys deal with a mid-life crisis by buying a car or changing their wardrobe, so they have more street cred. I guess my sudden need to try something totally outside my comfort zone is my way of dealing with the approaching date of my fiftieth birthday. I started thinking about taking a boxing class. It looks like a great workout. I still go to the gym every morning and have not missed a workout since 1977, but frankly, weight lifting is starting to bore me, and I only workout for thirty minutes now just to maintain, and I cannot wait to be done.

I have no desire to bungee jump, parachute, race a car, ski, grow a beard, wear bikini underwear, or date a younger woman, but I thought hitting someone would be a fantastic stress reliever. Working as a government contractor, I tend to think about hitting people all the time.

One Sunday afternoon a few weeks ago, I was watching a *Jersey Shore* marathon on MTV, and there was an advertisement for Krav Maga Maryland, and they mentioned a studio in Columbia, which I could spit at from Jessup. I also knew where it was because there is a great Asian-fusion restaurant in the same strip mall. I could drive there in seven minutes any time of day, and I could stop at Walmart on the way home. Win-win. The next day I called about classes.

I met with one of the trainers that week, and he explained the classes and the schedule and asked me what I did for a living and why I wanted to do this. I gave him the quick version of what you just read, and I signed up. After signing up, he took me over to where they sell the equipment and told me I would need padded gloves and a cup. I understood about the gloves, but I didn't understand the need for a cup. Apparently, there is a lot of crotch kicking in Krav Maga. "Excuse me, could we amend that contract I just signed?" He didn't grab the cup and show me which one to get, he pointed from a distance.

I said, "I haven't put it on yet, so there is no reason to worry about touching it."

I informed him that I would shop for those items elsewhere to get a better deal. I stopped at Walmart, and they had the same brand cup and gloves for one quarter the price, so I bought four of each. That way I could clean them after every use and not miss a class.

On Saturday, I arrived for my first class, wearing my new cup and gloves. Being a Saturday morning class, there were about forty of us in there, and thankfully, a range of ages from thirty years younger than I to around ten years younger than I. Yes, I was the *alta cocker* in the room.

Everyone, including me, was wearing black sweat pants and black or gray T-shirts and tennis shoes or those weird socks with the toes in them that I find creepy. I was the only one in Chuck Taylors, except for the instructor. Yes, the tall drink of twenty-something water teaching the class shared my taste in shoes. We had a connection; he just didn't know it yet.

There was one exception — there always is. One guy was barefoot, wearing red short shorts, a pink shirt, and aviator glasses. He also had the Tom Selleck mustache. I pictured him living in the house at the end of the cul-de-sac with a train set in his basement. I made a mental note not to partner with him. No need to be the crazy magnet during my first class.

The class started with running around the room for five minutes, then push-ups, then running backwards for another five, and guess who ran backwards right into me, knocking me on my fat ass? Yep, my magnet brought the weirdo right into me. He couldn't knock someone else over. It had to be I? I bounced up immediately, as I always do, and kept moving.

We then ran sideways then did these jumps with push-ups between, and I thought I was going to die. The class was only thirteen minutes in, and I was going to have a heart attack in a studio in a strip mall in Columbia, Maryland. I could see the obit. "Obscure writer and Gay Jew from a trailer park collapses in Hebrew self-defense class during the warm up. No film at eleven."

I somehow caught my breath, and the punching began. My partner was a guy who was shorter than I but could punch me through a wall if he wanted to. You hold a pad in front of you, while your partner punches you in combinations you call out, but my favorite part was when you say down, he drops and does five push-ups while you run to another part of the room, and he has to find you and begin punching you again. Then you switch. The theory behind this is that most fights happen because you see a loved one being attacked, and you might get knocked down and have to chase the guy.

To be clear, I am not chasing anyone. The only running I do now is to the 7-Eleven for a pint of ice cream.

At one point, the instructor came over to give me pointers, and I told him it was my first class. When I took dance, I told them it was my first class for almost six months before they finally caught on. He asked how tall I was and then showed me how to adjust for my height. I never knew punching someone could be so much fun — no wonder straight people get into bar fights all the time.

At the end of that exercise, he told us about fighting people at different heights then said, pointing to me, "Your opponent could be … how tall are you?"

No matter where I go, I get pointed out as the freak. I can never just disappear into the crowd. Whatever.

The workout is so intense that you are drenched in sweat, and the entire class stinks of BO, but that is half the fun!

The class ended with a very intimate moment. He asked us to pick someone who was nearest to our size. I got as far away from Jeffrey Dahmer as I could and picked out this six-foot-two, twenty-three-year-old, hunkalicious slab of masculinity. Then we were instructed to lie on our backs, while our partner got into a push-up position above us, wrap our wrists around his neck then allow him to crawl across the floor dragging us all the way. Once at the other end of the room, you switched positions. I was the second fastest one in the room. And honey, I hadn't had that much fun with a man's arms around my neck since Bush choked on a pretzel.

Thank God, I was wearing a cup.

I could not wait until the next class.

WAS THE SALESMAN PRETTY?

One of my favorite episodes of *Everybody Loves Raymond* was when Raymond bought a vacuum cleaner from a door-to-door saleslady, and Debra asks if she was pretty. He says, "Yes, but you should see this machine."

I once read that good looking people make the best sales people, but in the same article, it said that good looking people also make the worst telemarketers because they are not used to rejection.

As the saying goes, "You have a face made for radio."

To be clear, I have nothing against unattractive people. I firmly believe that anyone with the right grooming and wardrobe can be attractive. If you take a good look at unattractive people, you will notice they have done everything possible to make themselves unattractive. This is especially true with many teenagers who adopt hairstyles and make-up applications that do nothing to make them good looking, oftentimes achieving a repulsive effect.

If it were not true that anyone can make his or herself attractive then how come on *Good Morning America* they can make over some shluub in an hour? The results are usually phenomenal with one exception. The dresses. They get the hair and make-up right, and if they put the woman in slacks, she comes out looking damn good, but who picks out the dresses? It's as if they raided the dumpster behind the Goodwill Thrift Store for rejects.

Another point is that attractiveness has nothing to do with weight. I have seen the most beautiful fat people and the ugliest skinny people, and every one of them either worked to make themselves attractive or just crawled out of bed wearing an "I don't give a shit" T-shirt.

I have been told I am attractive since I was a little boy by only one particular demographic — middle-aged Jewish women. The yentas love me. I have worked to maintain my looks for my demographic by doing a nightly ritual that involves the mixing of Oil of Olay with formaldehyde and sleeping in a hyperbolic chamber. Oh honey, this doesn't just happen. And although I don't wear the most fashionable clothes, I also never go out looking sloppy. I don't wear jeans, and I never even go to the grocery store without hair and wardrobe in proper order and a healthy layer of moisturizer on my face. And, the middle-aged Jewish women still wink at me in the produce section while squeezing their melons.

I also have the cleanest shoes in town. As I have said, my friend Dean always asks me, "Do you still wear spotless tennis shoes?" When your feet don't touch the ground, it is easy to keep your shoes clean.

I even look spotless when I go to Krav Maga class. I always win best hair.

In high school, I sat in eleventh grade homeroom and watched as every boy was nominated for the Homecoming Court except me. I wasn't the guy whose name was scrawled in some girl's notebook, although through Facebook, I did find out a former male classmate had a crush on me. To think I could have had a better time at the prom.

Since my look is an acquired taste, I have never been called sexy, but then again, sexy has nothing to do with looks as much as it has to do with essence. Have you ever noticed there are some plain people whose bones you want to jump in public and some very good looking people whom you wouldn't consider boning even if there was a monetary reward in the end?

I have a friend who is attractive, but not what one would call a knock-out, yet everyone who says hello to him wants to screw him. It is funny to watch how guys react to being introduced to him. He doesn't have a killer body or model hair or even the snazziest wardrobe, but he must put out a scent that is a mixture of a porterhouse steak and musk (I stole that from the *Golden Girls*). I think I am the only person in the world who is immune to his lure.

I am glad I am not sexy or put out a natural fragrance. I don't know how I would handle the responsibility of having sex with so many people. Oh the burden my friend must bear.

Although I state anyone can be attractive with just a little effort, there are those who have a natural beauty that is just breathtaking. You know the type, male or female, they walk by, and you just cannot help but stare at them. If they say hello to you, you exhibit the symptoms of a mild stroke. You know you do.

However, I don't.

What I do is flirt.

I know there isn't a chance in hell one of God's perfect creatures will rock my world, so I figure I have nothing to lose, so I flirt. And I can flirt with the best of them.

But sometimes, my flirting gets me in trouble.

Take Valentine's Day. Seriously, take Valentine's Day and never let me have to live through it again.

On the way home from work Valentine's Day night, I performed my Milton is alone on a special day ritual. I stopped and bought a bucket of fried chicken with the intent of eating every damn piece of that succulent meat then having a large piece of cake for dessert. And, of course watching some TLC show about the morbidly obese during my meal. Sometimes, I don't even use a plate; I just stand over the sink and throw the bones into the disposal.

If I spend any more special days alone, I will be on one of those TLC shows as they slice away a wall of my trailer and carry me away on a flatbed.

I arrived home with my chicken and cake and immediately took Esmeralda out for a walk. As we turned the corner, I spotted a guy in a winter coat similar to mine who was wearing a badge and holding a clipboard, and he was one of the beautiful people. He was no older than twenty-five, no taller than five-six, with short brown hair and a smile that would make angels sing.

All of you would have had a stroke.

I flirted.

With my brightest smile, I asked, "What are you selling?"

He said, "Look, our coats match."

See, even some beautiful people have questionable taste.

As it turns out, he was selling some kind of alternative provider for my electricity that was going to save me 1.7 cents a kilowatt per something or other. It sounded good. OK, it sounded wonderful coming from his beautiful mouth. I gave him my address.

Fifteen minutes later, he was knocking on my door.

I said, "Your wife must be mad about you working on Valentine's Day."

He didn't respond, instead getting into his shpiel.

We sat at my dinette while he explained what I was getting and how for a year I would be getting my electric bill as usual but my power from a competitive supplier, and five minutes later, I was signing a contract while looking into his beautiful brown eyes. Yet, I still didn't know what the hell he was selling.

I also noticed something else since I rarely get a chance to look so closely at the face of someone half my age. There wasn't a blemish, a line, a wrinkle, a crease, not one flaw at all.

God, was I ever that young?

He also told me he sells health supplements that are organic through his side business. I told him to come by the following week and tell me about those as well.

Interestingly, I didn't want to bone him, just look at him.

Then, he was gone, and I still didn't know what the hell I just bought.

Later that evening as I stood above the sink eating my fried chicken, Esmeralda looked at me and asked in Beagleeze, "Was the salesman pretty?"

STRAIGHT MEN
PLAYING WITH KNIVES

For as long as I live, I will never completely understand straight men — not the kind who feed a comedian lines, but the ones who knock their women over the head with a club and drag them back to the cave. To me, most straight men are just cave men with a better wardrobe.

For example, I like to watch a football game on occasion, but I don't throw food at the TV screen or wear a jersey or even care who wins or loses. I just like the science of the game. But, straight men can talk about a particular football game until the key players have retired and had their knees replaced. There is a guy who comes into the gym every morning, and for forty-five minutes argues with the guy at the front desk about a football game. Not even the past weekend's game, but one game that has him irked beyond belief. The Super Bowl was two or three weeks ago — who remembers — and this guy still comes in and argues about every play that occurred. I have never seen him workout. He stands there holding his gym bag and yelling about this pass or that tackle or this kick. He reminds me of what a restaurant owner I know always says, "The customer has gone home and already shit out his dinner, and you are still complaining about him."

As long as we are talking about football, I have to complain — big surprise. For a sport that is full of man on man contact with lots of bone crushing, blood spurting and grunting, what is up with Astroturf and stadiums with roofs? I watched a game a month ago (I don't know who was playing, I switched channels and the game was on, so I stuck with it for an hour), and one team was wearing pristine white uniforms. It was the third quarter, and no one had a mark on him. Not a blood stain, not a mud stain, not even a wrinkle. You call this football? Where's the mud? Where's the rain? Where's the snow? And they call us sissies.

I had an electric football set as a kid (the NFL Electric Football Tudor Board Game), and my toy players got dirtier than these guys.

Remember those electric football games. Basically, you set up the teams, put the felt football in the quarterback's bent arm, flicked a switch, and the damn thing vibrated until you couldn't make heads or tails of who was doing what to whom, but you kept setting it up and flicking the switch because at seven years old, it took you so little to entertain yourself and you liked things that vibrated.

Now, I like staying clean as much as the next guy, but football today is hardly a sport. Every time one of these spotless players catches a pass or makes a tackle, he has to do some kind of dance followed by a fist pump. This is when I scream at the screen, "Stop your showboating and get on with the next play!" And with the curse of instant replay, we have to watch this spectacle over and over again. With the money they are making, they need to play in all kinds of weather and get dirty and bloody and break a few bones. What is amazing is golf is more manly than football these days. These overweight fashionably challenged country club members will take their shoes and socks off to stand in a bacteria filled pond to get the right shot from a bad lie.

Where are our modern day gladiators? They are playing baseball. Thank God for baseball. At least they still have dirt on their uniforms and skinned knees, but I am sure it won't be long before they come up with Astrosand, too.

Bet you didn't know a flaming queen would know something about sports? I just don't talk about them. When the game is over, it's over, much like my relationships.

Back to straight men. As you know, I am taking Krav Maga, and as usual with my obsessive compulsive personality, I have rearranged my schedule, so I can take a class every other day because God forbid I should miss one, or I would end up doing my Wonder Woman circles and have a mini-nervous breakdown. I could give Rain Man a run for his money.

What this class has done is really expose me to straight men in a group setting, and it is fun to observe wildlife in its natural habitat. The last time I was around so many straight men in a group setting was when I played football, but that was a long time ago in a universe far, far away. I always played center with the quarterback's hands always up my crotch. No wonder I miss the game so much.

There may be some Gay men in the Krav Maga class, but I'll be damned if I can figure them out. I have the worst Gaydar of anyone on the planet with the exception of my friend Charles. He compensates for his bad Gaydar by assuming all men are Gay and then figuring out who is straight.

How bad is my Gaydar? When I lived in Mount Pleasant (which was neither a mount nor pleasant, discuss), I had a neighbor, cute guy, who was always working in his yard shirtless and had the complete Gay look. We would talk every time Serena and I would walk by, and he would chat with me when he walked by my place. I asked him to dinner, and he said, "What is this about? You know I am straight."

I answered, "I know you're straight, I was just asking if you wanted to grab a bite sometime." As I walked away, I cursed myself for once again having bad Gaydar. And honey, this is the least embarrassing situation in which I have found myself.

So here I am in this class, and I have taken classes at all different times, so I have been exposed to many straight men or so I assume. There are also quite a few women in these classes, but with one exception, I am sure they are all straight. My Lesbigar is much better than my Gaydar. After all, I drive a Lesbian magnet.

Granted this is a self-defense class, but I cannot be the only person in this class who is taking it for its fitness benefits, or do all these people find themselves in situations every weekend where they need to defend themselves in a fight? The instructors always talk about bar fights.

"OK, you find yourself in a bar, and a guy throws a punch at you. This is how you deflect the punch." They speak as if everyone goes out on Saturday night and finds himself in the middle of a brawl. My favorite was the instructor who said, "Last Saturday, I was at the Green Turtle, and this guy wanted to fight me. He went into a wrestling stance, so I kicked him in the face."

Who are these people? You kicked a guy in the face? Do all straight men have to learn these skills? Is this why in straight bars they use plastic cups and in Gay bars they use fine crystal?

I find all this fascinating. Do straight men go out looking for trouble? Do they grunt like Tim Allen? Maybe it's because they don't shave their balls. Having all that hair down there must make them angry.

Gay men don't get into fistfights. In all the years I went to Gay bars, I only saw one act of violence. A guy threw a beer bottle at his boyfriend during an argument. He missed because he threw like a girl. Everyone scooted out of the way, and he was escorted out. No punches were thrown, and we went about our business and continued dancing to C&C Music Factory's latest hit. I think they only had one hit.

But, here is my theory. Straight men are very possessive of their girlfriends. If a guy even sees another guy looking at his girlfriend, he immediately feels threatened and goes into attack mode, and what culminates is a fistfight. For Gay men, if another guy looks at your boyfriend, you feel flattered because he is obviously jealous of what you have, and what culminates is a threeway. So you see, straight men use their fists, and Gay men use their penises.

When straight men do a threeway, their biggest concern is crossing swords. For Gaymen, it is the lighting.

Another thing I have never understood is why straight men like *me* so much. Seriously, following middle-aged Jewish women, this has been my second best demographic. I have not been in the closet since Mary Tyler Moore tried three times to launch a variety show, so they know I am of the pink persuasion. The instructors know I am a flamer. One of them, a creative writing major in college, just bought my latest novel. They never have a problem touching me when showing me the proper way to throw a punch or kick a guy in the face. I have noticed they are hesitant to touch any of the other guys in the class. I am also the guy who took ballet and modern dance from the only two straight instructors in South Florida. They loved me.

See why is my Gaydar so screwed up? I don't know if they are being friendly or coming on to me. Even at my jobs, the straight guys always love me. Maybe it has something to do with the fact that I am comfortable in my own skin and can talk auto mechanics and sports with the best of them. I confuse them. Who knows?

But, as much as they love me, I will never fully understand them, and yesterday, I really was confused.

The subject at the end of the class was what to do if your opponent has a knife? Seriously? Are these guys going out every Saturday night and reenacting scenes from *West Side Story*? Oh my God! I get it now!

Oh … wait a minute; it can't be that easy.

Anyway …

The instructor told us how many people are stabbed and don't realize the attacker had a knife until it is all over because it happens so fast. Then he talked about these knives you can pull out of your pocket that open immediately. He asked, "How many of you carry a knife to work?"

There was a show of about eight hands. Some of the people in the class are in law enforcement, but don't they use guns? He then said he has co-workers (notice the plural) at his day job who play with their knives all day.

I had to ask, "Where in the hell do you work that people are playing with knives?" He just smiled.

Can you imagine walking by a co-worker's desk and seeing him playing with his switchblade? Maybe, if you are a receptionist in a meth lab.

One cannot enter the government building where I work with a peanut butter sandwich without being questioned because apparently the biggest threat to national security is a peanut butter bomb.

A few weeks ago, CVS had a sale on batteries — buy one get one free. I ran over there at lunch time, and I bought six packages of batteries. Upon entering the building, I was questioned as to why I bought so many batteries and why I was bringing them into the building as if it is any of their damn business.

"They were on sale."

"But sir, I don't understand why you need so many?"

"I'm single, and I don't get out much."

They let me go through. Yes, I buy a lot of batteries.

So, bringing a knife to work would be completely out of the question. Or would it? I think I'll put a cleaver in my backpack and see what happens.

A THREE-HOUR TOUR

Gilligan's Island has been in syndication forty-five years, yet whenever someone over-packs for a trip, the first thing he is called is Lovey Howell. Her name was actually Eunice Wentworth Howell.

I used to be a light packer. I spent a week in Austria in 1992, and I traveled with one carry-on bag. I don't know how I did it. I also traveled from Germany to Austria and back again with no GPS, cell phone, computer or fluency in German.

Try that today.

When we had our goodbye luncheon at my last government project, the event coordinator declared I was the best packer she ever met. Only one person raised an eyebrow. Apparently, I can pack a lot of stuff into a small space. I have a talent; I don't question it; I just accept it. As a matter of fact, friends ask me to pack their trunks for trips. Yet, I am still single.

I still can pack for a trip in about fifteen minutes. Yes, I am also a fast packer. You never knew what hit you.

Oh, he didn't just go there.

However, somewhere along the way, while my packing skills have remained, I have become Mrs. Howell. When did I suddenly start needing so much stuff? Recently, I had to go on an overnight business trip, and I brought enough underwear for a month-long safari, even though I don't have a bladder control problem. Also, my size fourteen shoes can take up an entire suitcase on their own, but when did I start needing four wardrobe changes for every day of a trip? It's a good thing I don't travel very often even though I can still pack all that stuff into two suitcases. If one of my bags ever explodes, there will be a brief disaster.

After my last over-packed trip, I decided to a look back at those glorious family vacations we took in the 1970s. My brother is gonna love this.

Arnold and Harryette Stern loved to spend money the few times they had it, and there was a time when vacations were the recipients of their retirement, our college and everyone's grocery funds. Since they didn't have money very often, there weren't that many family vacations. Thank God for small mercies.

Forgive me all you loyal family vacationers, but I cannot think of anything more horrible than a family vacation. My friend Chris used to claim that all divorces were the result of a family vacation. Think about it. You spend twenty-four hours a day for seven days with people you normally see for fifteen or twenty minutes a week. I worked in restaurants in Williamsburg, Virginia, for close to a dozen years, and I never saw a happy family on vacation. Never. I still remember the one mother who came up to the bar, ordered Scotch straight up and proceeded to tell me that she was glad she didn't carry a gun on this trip. Not only did they have three kids in tow, but also both grandmothers, who apparently did not like each other. I asked her one question, "What the hell were you thinking?" Her answer was to order another drink.

If Jews learned anything from Moses and Zipporrah, it is never to take your extended family on a trip. Imagine traipsing through the desert for forty years with more than half a million of your closest friends and relatives following you. Moses didn't go up the mountain to talk to God; he went up there to get the hell away from all those whiny Jews.

What we also learned from Mr. and Mrs. Moses was that Jews always vacation where it is hot. One of our family vacations was to Miami in August. Seriously, and we stayed at the Aztec hotel for one night. It was such a dump that my mother left an unflushed present in the commode before we moved to the Thunderbird Hotel.

As you can see, I come from really classy stock.

Now, let me tell you about a typical Stern family vacation. My mother would bake by the pool covered in Coppertone, smoking cigarettes and reading a book, while my father played golf, and my brother and I swam in the ocean. We knew better than to bother either of them. At night, they would go to an expensive dinner, and my brother and I would be on our own. I don't remember our doing much of anything as a family, but my parents were married for more than forty-six years, so while this sounds like a strange vacation routine, perhaps they knew something other families didn't? We spent as much time together on vacation as we did when we weren't. Stick with me; I am trying to find the positive in all this.

The funny thing about our vacations was how much they packed. Of course, the portable bar was the most essential item, and the first thing that was opened upon arrival. After that were my mother's things, which would only fit into a complete set of Sampsonite, three wig boxes, a Hollywood-sized make-up case, and four garment bags. All of this would fill the car's trunk, and the rest of us were on our own. Maybe this is when I learned to fit a lot into a small space.

The most bizarre vacation was the trip they took to Cape Cod after dropping us off at Nana's in the Van Ness North Apartments, in Washington, DC, in the summer of 1972. At that time, my father drove the prettiest car I think he ever owned — a 1967 Mercury Monterey four-door sedan, which was seafoam green with a black vinyl interior. We called it our *Hawaii Five-O* car. The trunk of this huge car was filled with Mother's things, and for this trip, they put one of those poles across the back seat and hung up what had to be half of both of their complete summer wardrobes. My brother sat up front, while I squeezed into the back, against the passenger-side door, with all those clothes taking up ninety-percent of the space as we drove to Nana's from Newport News. I couldn't see beside me, and I started to cry. When they asked why I was crying, I told them I felt like a piece of luggage because the three of them were up front, and I was squeezed among all these clothes and wig boxes as if I wasn't part of the family.

Their trip was for only five days. Who the hell needed all those clothes?

And for the five days we stayed with Nana, she carried on about two things: Aunt Flossie's divorce and why our parents were spending all their money on these ridiculous vacations. We did get to see the Panda's when they first arrived at the National Zoo. About that, Nana complained that they needed a bath. The next day, on the front page of *The Washington Post*, there was a picture of the pandas getting a bath.

When they returned to pick us up, somehow they had managed to fill the car up with more stuff, and we were also hauling Nana's black and white RCA television home since she bought a Sony color set to replace it. There I was in the back seat again — this time with a television banging into my head.

I made two vows on that trip. I would never go on a trip where I ended up in the back seat competing for room with someone else's luggage and used appliances, and I would never travel with a middle-aged Jewish woman.

While I do pack quite a bit for the few trips I take these days, I leave the wig boxes at home, and I leave enough room for me to see out the rearview mirror. And yes, on the rare occasion when I do sit in the back seat, I still cry.

IT ONLY HAPPENS ON SITCOMS

Picture it. New York, 1951. Ethel pokes her head into Lucy's open window, and Lucy tells her to come right in. Ethel then sits down and finishes Ricky's breakfast.

Picture it. New Rochelle, 1962. Millie just walks into Laura's house without even knocking and starts yammering right away.

Picture it. Binley Woods, Warwickshire, a village east of Coventry, 1991. Hyacinth steps outside and insists Elizabeth pop in for a coffee at 10:15. As soon as the coffee is poured, Elizabeth drops a cup from the Royal Dalton with the hand-painted periwinkles on the floor.

Picture it. Chicago, 1975. There is a knock on Bob and Emily's door and Howard just walks in and starts complaining.

Picture it. Jessup, 2012. There is a knock on my door, and Mrs. M comes in for a chat in the middle of the afternoon with Buddy, her beagle-basset hound mix, who proceeds to hide all of Esmeralda's chew-bones, while she watches without a care in the world. They stay for more than an hour.

And you thought neighbors only dropped by unannounced on sitcoms.

I remember sitting at a party in West Palm Beach in 1992 (yes, I remember the year), and we were having a heated debate about whether *Hazel* was a sitcom or documentary. The thesis of one of the debater's arguments was that the show was never funny. I had to agree. It was annoying, but never funny, but for some inexplicable reason, when I see a rerun of *Hazel* on TV, I have to stop flicking channels and watch it. I don't laugh; I just observe and wait for a scene with one of their cool 1960s Fords. Mrs. B drove a Falcon at one time!

Anyway, in the middle of the argument, someone mentioned how Rosie (played by Maudie Prickett), Hazel's best friend, would drop by unannounced. Then we got into a discussion about how on sitcoms friends drop by all the time without so much as a phone call or an invite. All of us agreed that this was a violation of protocol, with one exception — the host, my partner, whose house was arranged like a sitcom set and who in the middle of conversations would turn to the nonexistent audience and wait for a reaction. I swear he got one once, then Marc Daniels yelled, "Cut."

Seriously, how many of you just knock on your neighbor's door to sit down and have a chat? I'll bet none of you. The only time I knocked on a neighbor's door was if he left his headlights on.

Once in DC, I saw a guy in a van ram into one of my neighbor's cars. I called the police with the license plate number then knocked on the victim's door to tell her what happened. It turns out the van was stolen. A week later, she knocked on my door and yelled at me for giving the police the license plate number because if the driver had not been identified, she wouldn't have had to pay a deductible, but because of me, she had to pay $500. I vowed never to knock on someone's door again.

Ceiling or wall yes, door, no.

In an apartment building, you never show up unannounced unless you are delivering a package that arrived in your mailbox by accident, but you never expected or accepted an invite for coffee. In a way, this is strange. Or is it? Maybe we never did this in apartments because we can hear everything through the walls and showing up at someone's door unannounced would get you sucked into their drama.

And who wants to be sucked into their drama? Oh right, every guy I ever dated.

Now, I haven't lived in a stick house in decades, but I don't remember just knocking on someone's door to come over and have a chat. Once in all the years we lived on Dresden Drive, my mother went over to Mrs. Ruble's and sat down to have a smoke with her and Mimi Smith. We were playing outside her house, and somehow, everyone ended up at Mrs. Ruble's. But that was a very rare occurrence indeed.

Then, I saw *The Long, Long Trailer*, and in that movie, it turns out that in a trailer park showing up unannounced is a common occurrence, but wasn't that a 1950s version of an RV park? Or did Marjorie Maine really live in a trailer park? Oh, wouldn't that be cool?

But that was a movie, and my life is more like a sitcom. So here I am, the Gay Jew in the Trailer Park. Just as I have in any neighborhood where I lived, I know everyone by name and most of their back stories, which helps when walking Esmeralda and saying hello, and we do stop to have a conversation on the sidewalk all the time, but that is not like showing up at someone's house.

Soon after I moved in, I came back from a winery tour, and I wanted to give a bottle of wine to Mrs. M for walking Esmeralda while I was out for the afternoon. I called first. When I went over with Esmeralda, she asked me why I called, considering it too formal. She said just come over next time. And, Esmeralda and I sat and chatted with Mrs. and Mr. M for an hour about nothing in particular.

I should have realized the protocol since Mrs. M stopped by a couple of times to watch me put together furniture soon after I moved in.

Two days after the wine delivery, Mrs. M knocked on my door and came in. I offered her a cup of coffee, and in the middle of the conversation, I mentioned how Mrs. E's next door neighbor was having some financial difficulty. Within seconds, she and I were knocking on Mrs. E's door to get the 4-1-1. I asked if we should have called first, and Mrs. M looked at me as if I were insane. I know that look; I get it all the time. Mrs. E invited us in, and we had another cup of coffee and discussed how we could help her next-door neighbor.

Apparently, I was not well versed in Mobile Home Community Manners. In my new world, one does not call first. One just knocks on the door. I've tried to analyze this. Could it be that our homes are closer together than in gated or stick-built neighborhoods but not on top of each other as in apartment buildings? Our streets are wide enough to drive a house down one; they have to be. Maybe our lack of fenced-in yards has something to do with it? Could it be that the average age in my community is fifty-five, so we are of the same generation?

But that was my problem. I was analyzing too much. Face it, trailer park people are just friendlier and more like family. And there is a big reason why. No social ladders to climb. No one is A-list or D-list. We are all T-list. Even if you live in a singlewide as I do, you are just another trailer park queen enjoying life.

Hyacinth with her slim-line phone with automatic redial would never survive in my community.

So, if you want to live where your neighbors look out for you, and at times, watch your every move, then come on down and buy yourself a manufactured home in a mobile home community.

And honey, once you move in, you better be sure to have a pot of coffee going at all times. After 5:00 pm, make it decaf.

THE WHORE OF BABYLON

Elaine Boosler is one of my favorite comedians, and she used to have a routine about coming home after a one-night stand, wearing the same black dress, and mother's shielding their children's eyes while they watched her do the walk of shame like the Whore of Babylon.

All of us have done the walk of shame, but depending on where you live, the level of shame varies quite a bit. In the city, the only onlookers who warrant your concern are the homeless people, and chances are some of them have showered more recently than you have. Most of them also have a hat to cover the headboard bump in their hair. How many times have you said, "Why didn't I put a hat in my purse?"

If there is room for last night's underwear, there is room for a hat.

My mother dated Seymour at around the same time my father dated Devera. Then by some strange crossing of stars, my parents were married and Devera and Seymour were married within two weeks of each other. Through the years, we always heard the story of my mother's hose ending up in Seymour's glove compartment after a wild night of drinking. Due to the ickiness of anyone's parents' sex life, I never asked any of the parties involved to elaborate.

There was also the story of Mother and Devera driving one car while Dad and Seymour drove behind them. Mother looked in the rearview mirror and Dad was driving, then she looked again, and Seymour was driving. Those were the days of bench seats; but still, the visual was disturbing for any number of apparent reasons.

But again, I digress ....

Back in the day, I did any number of walks of shame, but that was back in my twenties. Remember your twenties? You could be out all night, come home, get one hour's sleep, shower, dress for work, and put in a double shift then do the whole thing all over again the next night.

Then you turn thirty, and your body betrays you immediately. All of a sudden you need to get to sleep. You are still working the same job, but for the first time in your life, you say, "I have to work in the morning."

Your potential repeat casual sex partner, whose name you still have not requested and wouldn't have remembered anyway says, "Didn't you have to work in the morning last week?"

"Yes, but last week, I was twenty-nine years old."

"Oh, happy birthday ... how about a quickie in the parking lot?"

Unless you own a Nash Ambassador (the car that turns into a bedroom), I have no possibility of doing it with you in a parking lot. I have always been too tall for the back seat, and don't even try the front.

When I did the walk of shame, it was in an apartment complex. Nobody cared or noticed what time I came in or left. This has advantages. You never have to explain where you were or whom you were with, and depending on your closeted status, you don't have to change Bob's name to Betty.

The disadvantage is that on the off-chance your one night stand was the best sex you ever had, no one is there to ask you where you were last night, so you can tell him about the wild fabulous sex you had while being tied to a bed and tickled with a feather duster.

Do you know what S&M would be for someone like me with Joan Crawfordish OCD? Tying me to the bed and rearranging my furniture while spilling coffee on the kitchen counter.

I once had a trick who moved two items on my coffee table while I was in the kitchen getting us drinks, and when I sat down, I put them back where they were without saying a word. I'll bet he was scared at that point — probably thought I was a serial killer. I get that a lot.

When I think of the tricks whom I invited to my home or vice versa back in the days before the Internet and cell phones, it is a wonder I was never robbed. Actually, it isn't. Whenever I got lucky, I made sure to tell a friend, have the friend make a mental picture of my latest conquest before we left the bar, and reminded that friend to call me first thing in the morning to be sure I was alive.

For those of you who do the Internet pick-ups, be sure to have the person you are hooking up with call you, so his number is on your cell phone. Then write the number down and put it in a place where the coroner or detectives will find it.

And you thought you wouldn't learn anything today.

My tricking days are long gone. Sometimes I feel like Shelly Winters, who said after a life of debauchery and sleeping with every well-hung leading man in Hollywood, "I am done with sex," and from age forty-eight to the end of her life, she no longer had relations.

However, after reading both her autobiographies, I think her vagina was just tired … or fell off.

When we put my father in an assisted living facility after the onset of Alzheimer's, he became the Casanova of the senile set. While his mind was gone, his body was that of a man twenty years younger, and he was the only man in the place who wasn't in a wheelchair. He did more women than a sex addict at a sorority reunion. He also had the advantage of not having to remember their names, and if he did one twice, it was a whole new experience. My brother nicknamed him "*Yencing* Matilda."

When he died, every woman in there sat *Shiva*, and it wasn't even a Jewish facility.

There is no walk of shame in a nursing home either. His mother, Grandma, also had Alzheimer's, and she had a boyfriend who used to wait for her in her bed. They were introduced every night.

In a mobile home community, things are a bit different. All of us know each other's business just by seeing whose car is parked out front … and for how long.

For example, Ms. K has a boyfriend who owns his own plumbing company. His truck is out front all the time, but one morning, there was a Chrysler 300, and Mrs. M said to me, "Well, looks like she picked up a new one."

I immediately thought about how I would handle explaining a strange car in front of my house all night.

I briefly dated someone we'll call Mr. Wrong, and he stayed overnight after the second date. When he left, he texted me that two of my neighbors across the street were watching him from their windows.

I knew who, Mrs. M and Ms. K.

I also knew someone would ask me something.

Before she did, I had to wonder how this would affect our relationship. Mrs. M is Esmeralda's dog walker, who is also a devout Catholic and a good friend now, but I know nothing of her politics. Her husband is crazy about me because of my old cars and my love of gadgets that sell for only two easy payments of $19.99, and as you know, straight men are one of my demographics, but Mrs. M is not a middle-age Jewish woman, my other demographic. However, she has been to a party at my house when it was full of queens and dykes, and she fit in just fine. But this would be the first time she would encounter Gay sex on her block. Or would it?

Mrs. M came over within fifteen minutes with the excuse of having a smoke behind my house, so her husband wouldn't catch her. I still cannot believe he doesn't smell her Marlboro Lights on her person.

"Did you and your friend have a good time last night?"

"Yes, we ate dinner at this really nice Asian restaurant then saw a movie."

"We were wondering if those are ski racks on his truck?"

"Yes."

Imagine if I answered, "Yes, we fucked all night. It's a wonder I can walk the dog this morning!" Don't you wish you could do that just once?

Apparently, she wasn't freaked out at all. And when his truck no longer appeared in the hood, she didn't ask any questions either, but there is something curious going on because ...

This past weekend, a friend of mine drove quite a distance to see a play with me, and I told him to stay overnight since he wouldn't get home until after 2:00 am if he drove back.

The next morning, we went out to breakfast early then came back to my house before he left.

Fifteen minutes later, I was taking Esmeralda out for her second walk, and Mrs. M drove around the corner and pulled up next to us and asked, "Did you have a good time last night?"

While there were no details worth sharing besides seeing a play and having dinner, do you think she was just hoping to get something juicy? Or is a Gay Jew in a Trailer Park something she never before encountered?

Next time, I'll give her all the details. Unfortunately, I am so boring in bed that she might wish she never asked.

NEVER LEAVE THE HOUSE WITHOUT LIPSTICK

Aunt Minnie once told me that she and her sisters, Aunt Honey and Grandma, never left the house without wearing lipstick. Nana told me she never walked down the street without a hat and gloves. My mother said that when her father found out she took up smoking he told her never to walk down the street smoking a cigarette — only hookers do that.

Judging from how people dress these days and their other habits, you would think they were all just a bunch of trashy hookers. And that includes the men as well.

I love the TV shows of the 1950s and early 1960s when everyone dressed up to do anything including yard work. Remember the opening sequence of *Leave It to Beaver* when he is mowing the grass? He is wearing kakis! High water kakis, but kakis nonetheless and a button down shirt. Remember when Lucy got her head stuck in a loving cup? Ethel wouldn't go on the subway with her until she changed out of her jeans. I love that episode.

Have you seen what people wear on the Metro? Now we are lucky if their jeans are pulled up past the bottom of their asses. I absolutely hate that look. I don't get it. It is unattractive. It looks stupid. Will it ever end? Have you seen one of those teenagers (and since it has been around for more than twenty years — adults) try to walk or run? If they only knew that their solidarity with prison folk has to do with taking it up the ass, they might go back to wearing high-waisted pants.

I heard that there is a whole generation with hip problems from trying to walk in pants that are cinched at the knees. Good. Dumb asses.

Anyway ...

Since my parents never gave me any advice, except to not get married nor have children. Well, they never said that, but after living with them while growing up, I surmised that was the wisdom they wished to impart. Most if not all of my sage advice came from my grandmothers and other elderly aunts. My grandfathers died before I was born, so my biggest influences were gray-haired or wig wearing old Jewish women with too much lipstick and always appearing

213

surrounded by a thick cloud of smoke. I was almost eleven years old before I realized neither grandmother, nor their sisters, were related to Endora.

And you wonder how I turned out the way I did. It is no mystery to me.

Of the many things I learned was that one never went out without wearing a girdle, had her face on, and her hair done. I cannot imagine what they would think if they were alive today. I can proudly say I try never to leave the house without all three.

You want to see slobs; go to a supermarket in the middle of the day, during the week. You would think these were the people who work from home. Oh no. These are housewives ... excuse me ... stay at home moms. It is a sea of faded ripped jeans, flip flops and fried red hair. What is it with dying your hair a cross between magenta and burnt sienna and then never bothering to wash or comb it? Seriously?

The strangest thing is all of them, and I mean all of them, have manicured nails. The nails are green, blue, black, and purple, but I'll be damned if they are not professionally manicured. So, they don't have a comb at the beauty parlor where they get their nails painted?

Even when I am running a quick errand at 6:00 am after the gym, I am put together, and I have a hat on to cover my bed head. As a matter of fact, I am the only guy in the gym at 5:00 am who wears a hat to cover my undone hair, but you can be assured that the hat coordinates with my choice of shorts and shirt on any particular day. Since Krav Maga classes take place mid-morning, by then, I have showered and primped. I usually win best hair, and no matter how much I sweat, my hair remains in place. I wouldn't have it any other way. Yes, my Krav Maga outfit is also color coordinated although one day I made an odd choice of a yellow T-shirt with charcoal sweat pants. I was experimenting. Fortunately, no one commented, but I still won best hair.

With the exception of the 6:00 am grocery run that takes place maybe once a month, I have never run even the simplest errand without having the three elements mentioned above ... until recently.

Yesterday, I decided to be creative and put pebbles under my deck inside my walkway to spruce up my front yard (I have somehow become a landscape designer), so I showered, put on an outfit Beaver Cleaver would have worn to mow the grass, kakis and a button-down shirt, and drove over to Lowe's to pick up nine bags of pebbles.

Amazingly, well not that amazing if you know me, I managed to load the bags on a cart then wheel them to my car and load that four-hundred-fifty pounds of pebbles into my car without getting a speck of dirt on me or breaking a sweat.

Honey, they don't call me a queen for nothing. Being Jewish doesn't hurt either.

Once, I arrived home, I changed into an old pair of sweats and a stained sweatshirt I save for these lawn care tasks in fifty-degree weather and proceeded with my project. Depending on temperature and humidity level, I have just the right outfit, including coordinated older pairs of Chuck Taylors, which are clean of course. You never know who is going to drive by!

After an hour, it became quite obvious that I did not have enough pebbles, and by them I was covered in a layer of pebble dust, my hair was no longer perfect, and I didn't even want to know how my face looked, but I needed to return to Lowe's for more rocks. Esmeralda, who was lying in the grass observing me, managed to stay perfectly coiffed and looking pretty as ever the entire time.

Time was limited since I had dinner plans with my friend Frank, so I did something unthinkable. After taking Esmeralda inside and grabbing my wallet and keys, I hopped into the car, looking as if I just crawled out from under my deck, which I actually did, and drove over to Lowe's for nine more bags of pebbles.

Quick shopper that I am, I rushed into the garden center, grabbed a cart and went straight back to the pebble area. The store was empty, so I was able to load up another four-hundred-fifty pounds of pebbles, wheel the cart up front and pay in less than fifteen minutes. Then, I quickly wheeled the cart to my car, and no sooner had I opened the lift-gate and started loading the bags, when I heard, "Milton!"

Damn me for driving a thirty-year-old station wagon! You just can't hide something like that.

I turned around, and standing there was a guy I dated briefly a few years ago, and next to him was his life partner or lover or latest boyfriend or trick from the previous night.

"How have you been? This is Rod." Or did he say Robert or Rocky or Richard?

"I've been good."

We chatted for just a few seconds, and as they walked away, I heard Ricky, or was it Ralph or Renaldo, say to him, "Looks like you dodged a bullet."

At that moment, I felt Grandma, Nana, Aunt Minnie, Aunt Rose, Aunt Anita, Aunt Flossie, and Aunt Renee roll over in their graves in unison, and I swear I saw a large cloud of tobacco-smoke materialize overhead.

Even Endora was disappointed.

I KNOW WHY
THE STRAIGHT MAN SINGS

I like boobs.

There, I said it. The fact is I know a lot of Gay men who like boobs. It isn't a sexual thing; it's an appreciation for thing of beauty ... and power. Surprisingly, I know a lot of Lesbians who also like boobs. Who knew?

Why do guys like me like boobs? One reason — jealousy. I am jealous because women can accentuate the one thing that makes straight men crazy anywhere, any place, any time and not get in trouble.

Mary Jo on *Designing Women* discovered the power of big boobs when she tried on a pair of falsies. Men did anything she asked. As a co-worker of mine said, "You got the goods; you get the service."

Do you have a big presentation in front of room full of potential male clients? Ask Sally Rogers for her low cut V-neck dress. Chances are you'll not only get the contract, but also referrals.

Harriet Lane, niece of President James Buchanan, the first woman to be called First Lady, and subject of the book, *Harriet Lane, America's First Lady* by Milton Stern (I've heard of him), learned early on the power of her bosom. She had the neckline on her inaugural gown lowered two and a half inches. By doing so, she became the most influential fashion icon of her time, and the most powerful woman to live in the Executive Mansion during the nineteenth century. She convinced many a Congressman to push legislation through the chamber. If you don't believe me, buy my book.

Men can't do this. We can't walk into a room full of potential female clients wearing a pair of pants with a low cut V-neck ... uh waist. That would be sexual harassment. And if a man has nice hairy pecs, he can't wear an open shirt to get attention unless he takes a time machine back to 1975 and wears a leisure suit to work.

Want to distract a straight man and turn him into a babbling idiot? Have a big breasted woman stand in front of him. Works every time.

Which brings me to my second reason we like boobs. People look at them. You think they can help themselves, but they can't. Even straight women look at boobs. Of course, when they look at them they are asking themselves, "I wonder if those are real?"

When I did drag, I made sure I had the biggest, firmest rack you ever saw. And even though I was a six-foot-nine-inch man in a dress, my boobs still got the most attention. Straight guys would grab them, Lesbians would drool over them, and Gay men would compliment them. And these weren't those horrible breast plate titties the drag queens pay hundreds of dollars for today, these were plush dog toys stuffed into a size fifty-two, double-E bra! I didn't even have nipples!

Even though Serena was wondering what happened to two of her soccer balls while I was out, I still enjoyed the power of big boobs. My jugs had everyone's attention.

The third reason I like boobs is they are beautiful. When I see a sex scene in a movie, I cannot stop studying the breasts, and I have learned to appreciate nice breasts. I went with my friends Mindy and Ellen to see *Frida*, starring Salma Hayek. When she first took off her top, I said to Ellen, "Now that is a nice pair of breasts." And she said, "They certainly are." Ellen also has a nice rack.

Once on the Metro, this young woman was standing with her boobs at my eye level and wearing a tight sweater. She had the most perfectly shaped and sized breasts, and I wanted so badly to touch them. I don't know why. It isn't as if I had never touched boobs, although it has been more than twenty-five years. The last girl whose boobs I touched is a fan of mine, and I can honestly say they were very nice breasts, and I am sure they still are!

My boob obsession almost got me in trouble the other day in the office. One of our clients, as we call the government employees for whom we as contractors provide a service, is a young, attractive, recent college graduate who is a real go getter and really gets things done — a rarity in the federal workforce. She also wears fashionable clothes and rather low cut tops. I am not sure whose attention she is trying to get because in her agency, the majority of the workforce is middle-aged women and a sprinkling of some of the most unattractive men on planet earth. She does wear minimal to no make-up and a fashionably short hairstyle. Maybe she's into middle-aged women. Or, she dresses like that to get things done.

I had some materials for her that were too large to email, so she came down to get a CD from me. I didn't know she was standing behind me until she said my name. I grabbed the CD and swung my chair around, and the next thing I knew my nose was within inches of her beautiful cleavage. Her top was cut to almost the bottom of her sternum. In those few seconds, I realized a few things.

God has blessed her with a bounty of mammary goodness. Not only are her breasts large, but also they are perfectly formed and firm, and I'll bet anything they are real. Of course, she is at that age when all the body parts are still where they are supposed to be as opposed to my age when everything is a few miles south of its original location.

If I walk around the house naked, I get rug burns on my testicles.

I also realized that I couldn't lift my eyes from the sight before me. While I was holding and waving the CD above my head in the hopes she could grab it, I continued to stare at those lovely tits. They were just magnificent.

It is a good thing she was in a hurry because the last thing I realized surprised me. I wanted to bury my face in that fertile valley and play motor boat.

Now, I know why the straight man sings.

One last thing: I was a bottle baby.

LOOK WHO GOT OLD AND FAT!

The good thing about Facebook is you get to become a self-centered narcissistic ass who thinks every aspect of your dull existence is worth sharing with the world in the hopes of getting a reality show based on your life. Of course, that thought never occurred to me.

Ahem.

The other good thing about Facebook is that you can look through the photo albums of past flames and remark on their non-graceful aging and expanding waistlines. Of course, I would never do that.

Ahem.

A recent study showed that people who have more friends on Facebook have higher self-esteem, and many people base their self-worth on how many Facebook friends they have. Of course, I would never base my self-worth on the number of Facebook friends I have.

Reality check.

I use Facebook to promote my books and blog and to write bizarre posts about the crazy things — and people — I encounter as I lead my bizarre, everyday life. And, I base my self-esteem on how many people comment on my posts. I also like to post pictures of my landscaping attempts around my trailer. After all, I am the Gay Jew in the Trailer Park, so you must — absolutely must — see what I am doing to flame up my singlewide, whether you like it or not. Hint: click on the "Like" button.

Facebook uses me to see how long it takes an optimist can become a bitter old queen. According to the results of this experiment, it takes about three minutes for the conversion to be complete. Some would argue there is *no* conversion to complete.

A lot of us use social networking to catch up with — or more specifically — find old friends from our past, and this is where our parents had it a lot easier. There is something about losing touch with people that makes life so much better. But in our world of constant contact and updates on our everyday comings and goings, too much information is definitely contributing to our shorter lifespans. See, it has nothing to do with the economy or the national debt or lack of universal health care.

There is a reason God made the Earth so big: so we could move away and not look back. Did we learn nothing from Mrs. Lot? Salt causes hypertension, and so does looking up your old friends and lovers.

Take it from someone who is approaching fifty and still single — stop looking back!

Here is how our parents received an update on an old flame:

"Remember that redhead with big tits you dated in high school?"

"Yes. How is she?"

"Dead."

See. No drama, no curiosity. Just the facts.

As an historical researcher, I cannot help but look up old friends to find out where they are, what they are doing, whom they have married and divorced, how many kids they have, and lately, who is now a grandparent. I still refuse to believe I am old enough to have contemporaries with grandchildren. They must be foster grandchildren or there is a typo in the photo captions.

In my research, this is what I have discovered.

The guy who told me he couldn't see me anymore because he found Jesus and had become straight and was going to marry a woman married a woman, had a kid, moved to the northwest, divorced the woman, married a man, put on at least fifty pounds, and has not aged well.

The guy who told me he couldn't see me anymore because he met someone else, moved to the Midwest with his new boyfriend, broke up with him, moved to the West Coast, is on his third boyfriend, put on at least fifty pounds, and has not aged well.

The guy who told me he couldn't see me anymore because he was actually dating someone else at the same time, just celebrated a milestone anniversary, traveled the world, and bought a house with his Mister Man. And yes, he put on at least fifty pounds and has not aged well. Actually, he is more buff than ever, but his unattractive face does look much older.

To me, none of them look happy. Oh sure, they are smiling in all their photographs, but I can see the pain and misery they are experiencing. I know unhappiness when I see it.

As Queen Elizabeth I said, "We have no need of the looking glass! The look on your face says enough."

If you look me up, you will notice I have not put on a pound and have not aged a minute. Using a high school picture of me on the beach as my profile photo doesn't hurt matters. However, it might be difficult to believe my dog, Daisy, is thirty-one now.

Surprisingly, with the exception of the ex-Gay who became Gay, finding the old nasty ass bastards didn't bother me. The problem with Mr. Ex-Gay was over the years he would send letters to my family looking for me, and they would forward these strange letters where he professed his love of Jesus and how happy being straight was for him. Included in each letter was a picture of him running a marathon or doing some other physical activity shirtless. Talk about confusing. Now, he is a big old Gay man living on a ranch with his flamer of a husband. I have never met his husband, but from the pictures, I can tell he is a flamer. The smile and head angle always give it away. However, he is still a homophobe and has a real problem with any outward appearance of Gayness as one can observe from his Facebook rants.

A piece of advice. If you use a current profile picture, delete any photos of you on Facebook that are more than three years old. There is no reason for anyone to see how much you've aged. If you can see them; they can see you.

They say people are getting more plastic surgery now because they can see how they aged on Facebook. Chin implants are the most popular procedure.

You could do what I do. In the car collector world, I am known as a "twenty-footer." I do not allow close-ups. I have a contract like Lucille Ball's in *Here's Lucy* — no close ups and always use a filter.

Past lovers and friends aside, there is another aspect of Facebook that drives me crazy. I call it "The Invitation Was Lost in the Mail" album, and it appears every Monday morning.

There you are sitting at your desk, eating a muffin (that is as big as your ass) as quickly as possible before any of your officemates arrive. You are perfectly rested because other than running a few errands, you had no weekend plans and stayed home Saturday night eating an order of sesame chicken and a pint of Chunky Monkey while watching *Keeping Up Appearances* on PBS. You log onto Facebook, and what do you see? A friend of yours, and not just a Facebook friend but an in-person friend, has posted pictures from a party he attended. Not only do you know the host, but also every other goddamn nasty ass guest who was there.

How nice for him. How nice for everyone.

If it weren't for Facebook, you would probably have a good Monday, but now, all you can think is "Why wasn't I invited?" "Did I offend someone? Oh, that couldn't be it. I offend everyone." "What is wrong with me?" "Why am I not loved?"

Then, you sniff your armpits. No, everything smells all right there.

Now, if you had fewer Facebook friends, you would find fewer pictures of your friends attending parties, and you would have higher self-esteem. So you see that whole theory about the number of Facebook friends is bullshit.

I am convinced all those people holding red plastic cups and smiling while attending their fabulous parties aren't really happy and are full of shit as well.

Bitter, party of one!

POOP WAR OF 2012

I believe more people are concerned about dog poop than any other issue facing our nation today. Not only is the owner concerned when his dog does not poop or poops too often, but also not a day goes by for a yardless dog owner without someone making a comment about where or when his dog poops.

David Letterman once made a joke that if an alien landed on Earth and saw a man walking his dog and witnessed the man bending over and cleaning up the dog's poop, he would consider the dog the more intelligent being.

I would never in a million years want to change a diaper, but I have no problem putting a plastic bag over my hand and picking up dog poop, which is also when the Jewish mother in me comes out, for I am concerned with firmness, consistency and color. After all, the colon is the window to your health. This is why whenever you come back from the bathroom in a Jewish home, everyone asks, "Are you ok?"

As an apartment dweller and now a trailer park queen, I have never had the luxury of opening a door and letting my dog go out into the yard. That means, by my crude calculation, in twenty-six years I have bagged 23,725 pounds of poop. That is a lot of shit.

I am so glad I always had small dogs. I do have a rule: I will never have a dog whose poop is bigger than mine.

My friend Charles has a very large and beautiful chocolate lab named Eleanor Roosevelt, Ella for short. Ella is now sixteen and still going strong. She also tap dances when she is excited. Once when I was staying at his house for a book signing, I remarked that having a dog that large was like having a pet horse. Ella's head is as big as mine. I offered to walk Ella and my Serena together, and he said to take a large bag because her poop is enormous. I prayed she would not have to go. Unfortunately, she did. For the first time in my life, I gagged while cleaning up poop. I should have brought a shovel and a cart.

My friend Ed once had a Great Dane, named Gable, in a New Jersey apartment! He told me he mastered the art of holding a Hefty bag below his dogs poop chute and catching all he had to offer. That story made me gag.

The worst thing, however, is when you take your dog for a walk and three blocks from your house you realize you forgot to grab a bag.

This is also the time your dog decides to take a dump in the mean old man with a shotgun's yard. And just as your dog finishes evacuating, he steps out his front door, and you say as quickly as possible, "I forgot my bag; I'll get one right now and be right back."

The beauty of having a small dog is that you can pick her up, run home, grab a bag, come back, and clean it up before he has a chance to reload.

Having female dogs presents its own problem. Amazingly, people who don't own dogs do not understand biology. They think all dogs lift a leg when they pee. If they see a female dog squatting to pee, they assume a present is being left for them. Once in Mount Pleasant, a lady screamed at me, "Are you going to clean that up?"

I screamed back, "Not without a sponge." She then ran out to her yard to find the offending shit pile but was shocked when nothing was there. She thought I was a magician.

Esmeralda doesn't just pee. She has to find the perfect spot and then perform figure eights for a minute before finally squatting and taking a long luxurious piss. More than once in my new neighborhood, I have had to explain that she is a female dog and they squat rather than lift a leg.

One night after dinner with a friend, we were walking Esmeralda, and she started her Dorothy Hamill compulsory figures. I had just remarked about how friendly my neighbors were when this old man with an oxygen tank yelled at me, "That dog isn't going to shit in my yard; is it?"

We immediately walked to another spot, and my friend remarked that not everyone was friendly. I informed him that every neighborhood has the mean old man with a shotgun, or in our case, an oxygen tank. Did I mention he was smoking at the time? Another reason we chose to scurry out of there.

Before she poops, Esmeralda trots laps back and forth then walks in circles. When I first adopted her, I didn't know this, and I thought she was trying to walk in the other direction rather than where we were heading. I don't know how many times I nudged her back in the direction we were going and wondering if she would ever poop outside rather then immediately upon returning to our horrible apartment in Rockville.

The first time I realized what she was doing and she finally did poop outside, I said jokingly, "Praise Jesus." That was a mistake. "Praise Jesus" became our command for taking a poop, and even though I am Jewish, I prayed to Jesus that no one would ever hear me say that to make her poop outside. Fortunately, she quickly got the hang of things; I figured out her bowel movement schedule; and pooping was no longer a religious experience.

Once we moved into the park, with the exception of mean old man with an oxygen tank, things were going well, until …

My dog walker, Mrs. M, adopted the most adorable beagle basset mix, we'll call Buddy because that is his name. Buddy, also a rescue, is two years old and has epilepsy. He loves Mrs. M, but he won't go near anyone else. He and Esmeralda are boyfriend and girlfriend — she, the older woman, he, the younger man.

Mrs. M soon discovered that Buddy found two spots where he loved to poop, Mary's yard and Madge's yard. Good citizen that she is, Mrs. M always cleans up after Buddy, but someone in the neighborhood was not doing his or her duty, and feces were discovered in both of their yards.

That is when the Poop War of 2012 began. Mary accused Mrs. M of leaving a present in her yard, which of course, Mrs. M denied. Then Madge declared that Mrs. M and Ms. K, who happens to have a beagle puppy, are not welcome to walk their dogs near her yard. Madge said she does not like dogs and as the first person to move into the community several years ago, she feels she has a right to establish her rented lot as off limits to dogs.

I have declared neutrality in the Poop War of 2012. Esmeralda pees in Mary's yard all the time, and Mary has not said a word. I think giving Mary some of my truckload of mulch didn't hurt. Madge's yard is not convenient for walking, so we have never had an issue.

But when the women folk get to arguing, beware of your alliances.

My being so young, charming and handsome does have its advantages.

One day, I was at the mailboxes, and Madge pulled up in her rather large and old SUV, stepped out and made nice, nice with Esmeralda. I thought this strange since Mrs. M and Ms. K both told me she doesn't like dogs. We chatted for a second about nothing in particular and went our separate ways.

As I was walking back to my house, Mrs. M and Ms. K approached, and both asked what she said to me. I said nothing really. She talked to Esmeralda, and that was it. Something told me neither was happy with that answer. I think they wanted me to declare war on Madge.

My being so young, charming and handsome can at times be a disadvantage.

Fortunately so far, no one is angry with Esmeralda or me.

I just hope I am not called in to mediate a truce. Getting into the middle of a poop war seems like a pretty shitty prospect to me.

I USED TO BE HOT

There was a time in my life when I marveled at the fact that I had friends going back ten years. Now, I have friends going back as long as forty years.

When you don't have kids, your sense of time is a bit off. For example, when my friend Johnise's daughter went to college and cashed in the matured savings bond I gave her mother when she was born, I was befuddled. I am rarely befuddled; dumbfounded, yes, but rarely befuddled. How could she be that old, and how could a savings bond I bought be mature? Where had the years gone?

The mirror is not a good indicator of aging — unless you've really let yourself go. In that case, I can't help you. You're done.

The first time I realized how much I had aged was when I had to renew my passport five years ago. After comparing the photo from my twenties to the one of me in my early … never mind which decade, I spent the next two days studying my face in the mirror and saying, "When did that happen? How did that get there?"

I have one thing going for me as far as aging, and one going against me — kind of a blessing and a curse. On my mother's side, we don't age drastically and tend to look younger than most people our age. On my biological father's side, the men have not lived past fifty-eight. So while we continue to look youthful, we make a beautiful corpse.

"Wow, look at him. He looks younger than I do, and he's dead!"

"He's better looking, too!"

Aging for average people is easier. For beautiful people, aging is hell. These are the people who keep plastic surgeons in business. Lately, I have observed a new trend in Hollywood facelifts. There is a surgeon out there who is making everyone look like Donald Duck. I was watching *Happily Divorced* last week, and Morgan Fairchild was a guest star, but I didn't know it was Morgan Fairchild until she spoke. Her cheeks were puffed out, her mouth had a permanent grin, and her eyes were slits. The same thing happened when Delta Burke was a guest on *Drop Dead Diva*. Barry Manilow has also taken a trip to the same doctor, but his results are the most drastic. He can no longer open his mouth! I am a huge fan of Barry Manilow's, but the last thing a man should do is get a facelift. They just come out looking like old Lesbians.

My how times have changed. In the 1970s, Aunt Dorothy's sister got a facelift, and they pulled her so tight that she couldn't close her eyes. Now, they pull someone so tight, they cannot open or close their mouths either.

The strange thing is none of these people look younger or even better. They look scary. What do they see in the mirror? Do they have an urge to go pantless in a sailor suit?

My friend Frank has a neighbor who is in her sixties. We were heading out one day, and he stopped to speak to her. I could tell she never had any work done. As he drove away, I remarked that she was a very attractive woman. He agreed. Sure she looked her age, but she looked fantastic. She had aged gracefully. We both commented on how she had obviously had no work done and shouldn't.

Now, all of us have that moment, as I mentioned above, when we realize we no longer look eighteen ... or twenty-nine.

Do you want to know how you'll look in ten years? Look at yourself first thing in the morning. You hate me now, don't you?

When I first came out, I must have looked good because every guy over forty would buy my drinks in a bar. Having a Jewish liver, it didn't cost them much. The first time I had to buy my own drink was the last time I think I went out to a bar. I figured I was no longer young and hot. In the Gay world, I was considered middle-aged. I had turned thirty!

Unlike many Gay men, I accepted my new status and moved on. The thirties are a difficult time for Gay men. You are no longer a boy toy or fresh meat or that term I hate more than any other — a twink. You also aren't old enough to be a daddy.

Then, your first gray hair comes in, then another and another, and all of a sudden, twenty-year-olds, who just a few birthdays ago wouldn't give you a second look want to be your boyfriend. Oy vay.

Strangely, I have never been attracted to twenty-year-olds, even when I was one. I always liked men in their forties. However, I am still attracted to men in their forties, which concerns me because I don't want to be the eighty-year-old troll who inappropriately grabs forty-year-old men. Elizabeth Taylor, *alev ha sholem*, remarked that she liked men of a certain age, who at one point were older than she and before she knew it, younger than she.

My genes say I'll be dead long before then, so I'm cool.

I asked my friend Danny what was the stage between Daddy and troll, and he said, "Last week." See, I told you I would repeat that joke. Feel free to steal it.

The forties are another strange time. This is the last decade when you can tell people your age, and they say, "You don't look that old."

Until ...

You hit forty-nine. That is when God plays a cruel trick. Until forty-nine, the aging process is quite subtle. A slight change here, a slight change there, then BAM!

You look in the mirror one day and scream, "What the fuck!"

That is what happened to me. Despite all the years of moisturizer, night creams, formaldehyde, and a hyperbolic chamber, in one year, I aged ten years. I knew I had aged rapidly when someone asked me how old I was and when I told him, he just nodded.

At first, it was difficult. I wore a veil whenever I had a social engagement, and I only used twenty-watt pink bulbs in my house. As a matter of fact, I avoided all situations with bad lighting, and I never, I mean NEVER, looked down. This is when you go from being versatile to being a strict bottom. Believe me, you'll look better. If not, then you will never have sex in the daytime again!

However, I soon learned to accept my aging face. But there are times ...

The other day, I ran into an old friend from more than twenty years ago at an event, and we were having lunch with a bunch of other people afterward. While we were catching up, someone asked him how we met. He relayed to them the story and said, "Milton was in his twenties then, and he was hot."

To which I replied, "Yes, I used to be hot."

Instead of smiles, I got looks of pity.

Then, I swigged my Geritol with a vodka chaser and ordered another — a double.

NOT A FAMOUS JEWISH ATHLETE

There is a television commercial I cannot stand about a once-a-year osteoporosis medicine called Reclast. A middle-aged woman in a garden shop pushes a wheelbarrow, goes swimming with her friend, buys a tacky lavender sequined dress, and wears the dress for dinner that evening. The part that annoys me more than anything is how it begins with the woman saying, "Hi, I'm Jane, and I'm an on-the-go woman. I've been active all my life."

The reason it annoys me is that I *am* Jane! I have even bought a tacky dress and worn it to dinner, but in my defense, I never wore lavender sequins.

Although I have been active all my life, I am hardly an athlete for two reasons. Guess what they are? Having trouble? What is the title of this book? Now, you get it.

When I was nine years old, Mrs. Kroskin, my friend Suzanne's mother (and I have known Suzanne since infancy), decided to produce a show for our Rodef Sholom Temple Hebrew School about famous Jews in show business. The first draft had the show going on for forty days and forty nights.

She and I butted heads over creative differences. I think Mrs. Kroskin was not used to such an opinionated and obnoxious child, who had a flair for the dramatic. I was such a diva. However, she did recognize talent and asked me to impersonate Al Jolsen singing "Rock-a-Bye Your Baby." I did sing it on one knee, but I refused to wear black face.

Her first inclination was to produce a show about famous Jewish athletes, but that program only lasted ten minutes.

Now, whenever anyone discussed the lack of famous Jewish athletes before 1972, someone was bound to mention Sandy Koufax, who refused to pitch the first game of the World Series in 1965 because it fell on Yom Kippur. My argument was you only mentioned one Jewish athlete, and although my first pet was a Repenomamus,* the esteemed Mr. Koufax was before my time.

Currently, Sandy Koufax serves as a member of the advisory board of the Baseball Assistance Team, a 501(c)(3) nonprofit organization dedicated to helping former Major League, Minor League, and Negro League players through financial and medical difficulties.

After 1972, we had Mark Spitz, a great athlete, who was also blessed with good looks and a pre-Tom Selleck, porn star mustache, who did more for Speedos than anyone else in history. But, he suffered the curse of all Jewish athletes — a Jewish mother. Although accepted to dental school, he decided to pursue other options after the Olympics. To this day, his mother says about her record-breaking son, who made Jews everywhere proud, "He could have been a dentist."

This reminds me of the joke my friend Bill told me years ago. The first Jewish President of the United States invites his mother to the White House for the weekend. His mother tells her friend about the invitation.

"My son invited me down for the weekend."

"Your son the doctor!?!"

"No, the other one."

I was born with a Jewish body. Jewish bodies are not designed for tossing balls, running laps or hitting things with sticks — except rocks if you are Moses and angry. They are designed for sitting in a room and studying. As Totie Fields, *alev ha sholem*, said, "All Jews have bad eyesight and bad feet."

Do you know the boy who hits puberty, fills out like Tarzan, and is blessed with natural athletic abilities? He isn't Jewish. And if he is; he's adopted.

I was born with the least athletic body God ever created. I know what you're thinking. But Milton, you are so sexy and hot and a vision of health and vigor, how can that be? Oh … you weren't thinking that?

By the time I reached puberty, I had a body like McLean Stevenson's, who is also dead, *alev ha sholem*, — narrow shoulders, droopy boobs and wide hips. A classmate said of me when we were getting weighed in ninth grade, "You are built like a girl." She wasn't lying. I was built like Nana, whom I have mentioned I look exactly like in drag … even as I age.

In spite of my Venus de Milo shape, I was determined from an early age to work with what I had. I played football, but due to poor eyesight and lack of coordination, I played center. All I had to do was hike the ball and mow down whoever was in front of me. Since I was a foot taller than everyone else, I excelled in this position. They tried making me a receiver, but I couldn't see the ball until it either smacked me in the face or flew over my head.

With the mention of football, I have to say something about little league football. Why is it every little league coach makes his son the quarterback of the team regardless of his abilities? My little league coach's son was named Dookey. I am not kidding; that was his name. And, you doubted my Southern roots. By the coach's own admission, Dookey had more penalties than any other player in the league, and he sucked at football! But in every game, he was the first-string quarterback. I cannot begin to estimate how many balls I hiked to him that he dropped. As a result, the South Morrison Vikings lost all but one game.

I liked football because my father was so far away from the action that you couldn't hear him criticizing me on the few occasions he was sober and came to a game. Basketball was another story.

Playing center in football is an easy way to hide one's lack of athletic ability. Unfortunately, in basketball, this is impossible. Hating basketball was also a factor. Buy me tickets to any sporting event, and I will go. I don't like to watch them on television, but I do like live sports. Buy me tickets to a basketball game, and I don't care if the seats are next to Jack Nicholson, I will pass.

When you're tall, everyone wants you to play basketball. Ucccchhhhhhh. I played two seasons for the Jewish Community Center team. I was forced to play the first season and tricked by my mother into playing the second. I forget what our mascot was — maybe a gefilte fish. What's worse is that on a church league, which this was, the basketball courts are only a few feet from the bleachers. My father, who was usually drunk, would sit courtside and scream at me to pay attention, go this way, go that way, do this, do that, the entire game. He was obnoxious and relentless. Other parents would tell him to calm down. Then, he would scream at me the entire ride home about how bad I was. I had to take a Milltown after each game. Did I chain smoke then?

I often wonder how I didn't turn out to be a serial killer.

Ironically, Grandma, his mother, would relay stories about how he couldn't even make a team because coaches would laugh at his lack of athletics or ability. But, my issues with Mr. Macho and my masculinity are between me and my pharmacist, bartender, and kick shield.

Interestingly, every team I ever made, not just the South Morrison Vikings, was always the worst in the league. Without fail, the season would end with our losing all but one game. I think we once lost to a school for the blind in a blowout. My high school football team had the worst record in the entire state.

At the age of fifteen, I began my quest to turn this Dodge Aspen of a body into an Imperial. I did what every Gay boy did back then. I bought a weight set after the Charles Atlas program didn't work.

I have never quite made it to Imperial, but I have managed Chrysler Newport a few times in my life.

With discipline and training, I transformed my pear shape into one that on Manhunt would be described as athletic and on Girlhunt would be called big boned. Unfortunately, what I ended up with were Gay muscles.

For those of you who prefer the opposite sex, Gay muscles are only for show. They look great in a tight T-shirt, but they are useless when it comes to sports and most day-to-day tasks. This is why Gay people never rent a U-Haul. We hire movers. Have you ever asked a Gay man to help you move a couch? If he says yes, film it. You will see a guy who can bench press two-hundred-fifty pounds for reps having trouble picking up one end of a sofa. It is a phenomenon that scientist cannot explain.

These shortcomings have not stopped me from pushing my body to do things it was never designed to do. In my twenties, in spite of Jewish bad feet, I took up powerlifting, and I joined a volleyball team. When I spiked a ball, people got hurt. In my thirties, in spite of my lack of coordination, I learned modern, ballet and tap dancing, and I became a long-distance runner, while starring in my own cable-access talk show — *The Milton Rose Show*, filmed in West Palm Beach, Florida. Did you catch it on Tuesday nights at 10:00 pm in the 1990s?

In my early- to mid-forties, I had more intellectual pursuits and wrote five books and more than four dozen short stories, all of which were published. I had to prove I was still Jewish and preserve my spot in the afterlife by avoiding athletics for a while.

When I first began any of the above activities, I wasn't just terrible, I was a disaster waiting for a place to happen. But I had a few things going for me, determination and a pushy personality, and even though I love being in charge and barking orders, whenever I am trying something new, especially something athletic, I assume I know nothing and listen and take directions very well. It's OK that it will take me longer than everyone else to get it. That is how I became a good center on the football team, an experience I always draw from when pushing this body that was made for drag to do something only a straight guy would do. Also, my previously mentioned demographic, straight men, love helping me succeed at sports — it is the strangest thing. They are never hesitant to touch me and correct my form.

As if Krav Maga wasn't enough punishment for me (and by the way, the instructor says I am doing really well — or he likes the fact that I pay my monthly dues on time; I don't know), I decided to do something I had not done in more than a quarter century, join a team.

It would have made sense for me to join a volleyball team or a swim team (I did that, too), or even a flag football team, but for some weird reason, I chose a sport I have never played — softball. I have not swung a bat since ... seriously, I can't remember.

So, I bought a glove, a bat, cleats, and batting gloves (Walmart has a great sporting goods department), and wearing a color coordinated outfit with my hair perfectly coiffed as usual, I showed up for my first practice. Was I good? No, I sucked lemons, but the coach, who is one of those guys you know was born with a naturally athletic body, worked with me, and I was able to hit the ball — twice! I actually caught it a few times, too.

After our first practice, we had lunch and a meeting to discuss the season and uniforms. The uniform discussion took up most of the meeting. Did I tell you it was a Gay softball team in a Gay softball league? Thank God! The uniforms will be both tasteful and flattering.

Being a Gay team means at least half of the players across the league, especially the ones with Gay muscles, will probably suck as much as I do!

* A three-foot long, thirty-pound dog-like prehistoric mammal that roamed the earth with dinosaurs and was known to attack them in packs and eat them. As a point of reference: Esmeralda weighs 26 pounds.

SUFFERING HAPPILY

Christian holidays are festive and filled with fun activities and sweet food like jelly beans, chocolate bunnies and fruit cake. Jewish holidays are filled with suffering and food that sits in your gut for days. Hanukah may be the exception, but then again, made correctly, latkes can constipate you halfway to Purim. Even though Purim is festive, there is a fast involved. With every Jewish holiday (and we have many; look at a Jewish calendar), there is always fasting.

"I can't make it to work today; it's the Fast of Gedaliah."

Do you know how many people have converted to Judaism just to get more days off? Jews for Jesus only work three weeks a year!

But, you gotta give it to the Goyim. They have two High Holy Days. Christmas and Easter. Both are marked by sales and pagan traditions. I will never get the Goyim. They celebrate the birth of the Messiah by waiting in line at Best Buy for twenty hours for an iPod XIV that they wrap and put under a tree they cut down and put inside the house.

When was the last time you went to a *Rosh ha Shana* sale?

They celebrate the resurrection by chasing colored eggs all over a lawn, while being chased by a giant bunny, then wear fancy hats in a parade down Fifth Avenue.

By the way, I love *Easter Parade* with Fred Astaire, Judy Garland and Ann Miller. Big surprise, huh?

Time to share a tradition in my family that brings shame to my brother and me: In the late 1960s, on Easter Sunday, we would go and park in front of a predominantly Black church and watch all the women going in with their new Easter hats and outfits and comment on them not unlike my friends on *Fashion Police*. In my defense, I was only seven or eight when our parents would do this.

The thing that drives me craziest is everyone wishing me a Happy Easter. This year, I responded with Happy Passover! I confused a few of my fellow Trailer Parkers.

When I lived in Mount Pleasant (which is neither a mount nor pleasant, discuss), we had a neighbor I called "Happy Holiday"; her real name was Chicken. I am not making that up. She would wish you a happy whatever until the next holiday. So, Merry Christmas through New Year's, Happy New Year through Martin Luther King Day,

Happy Martin Luther King Day through President's Day, you get it. I would wish her the Jewish holidays in the same manner, but with so many holidays, I would get mixed up.

Is it Happy *Tish B'Av* or Merry *Tu Bishvat*? Oy, this is giving me a headache.

The irony is many Jews celebrate Christmas and Easter — at least the gift giving and chomping ears off bunnies part, but when was the last time you heard Bubba say to Dookey, "What'cha doing for *Shavuot*?"

For almost five decades, I have been explaining Jewish holidays to my gentile friends. So, for the last time:

"They tried to kill us; they didn't; let's eat."

Of all the Jewish holidays, one makes you suffer for so long that you have to "count the *omer*" — until your next bowel movement, and it is my favorite holiday of all! Yes, Passover or *Pesach* to those of the Hebrew persuasion.

For eight days, we get to eat more tasteless constipating foods than at any other time on the Hebrew calendar, and I love it. Here's why. The holiday starts with a massive spring cleaning, and my inner Joan Crawford comes out in full force. "I am not mad at you; I'm mad at the *Chametz*!"

My mother loved Passover; my father hated it. Then again, he didn't like anything to do with Judaism, or Jews, or being Jewish. Yes, he was Jewish — very Jewish.

On Yom Kippur at around 10:00 am in the morning, he would start kvetching about going without food and being forced to suffer needlessly. Seriously? You are only skipping two meals. Oy Vay. On the second day of Passover, he would kvetch about how the matzah was tearing up his stomach. At my bar mitzvah, he complained that the rabbi's sermon was too long and that I should have stopped at one Torah portion and chanted an abbreviated version of my *Haftorah*.

And once, he complained that my name was too Jewish. I don't make this stuff up.

Our Passover Seders ranged from the drama filled small family affairs with just Grandma in attendance to the free-for-alls we would have at Aunt Devera's house. I love my Aunt Devera, but those services were so non-Sederlike. Uncle Seymour would scream at his sons, Aunt Anita would spill a glass of wine then have a meltdown, my father would make some off color joke that made no sense, Mother would compete for center of attention, and Aunt Flossie and I would roll our eyes at everyone else. The highlight was Rosalee's homemade gefilte fish. It was fried, and the fish was unidentifiable. Even Aunt Anita's cat turned up its nose at those smelly, crusted fish balls. To this day, I don't know what she put in her gefilte fish, and I don't want to know for fear of finding out I ate skate or viperfish.

My brother and I reached a point where we refused to go anymore because we found the whole evening to be sacrilegious. Can you imagine your children complaining because a Passover Seder is not traditional enough?

The last holiday I spent with my mother was Passover, and I led the service for the first time. I had to balance it between traditional and quick because Dad or "Arnold the Gentile-Wannabe" was there as well. It was the least drama-filled Passover of my life, and I think it was because we knew it would be my mother's last one.

What came next was the strangest Passover I ever led. I was dating Blond Frankenstein (as my friend Christian referred to him), and it turned out one of his Jewish friends had never been to a Passover Seder, so I invited him and six other people. I was one of two Jews at the table. The service and food, if I say so myself, were nice, but they drank seven bottles of Manischewitz Blackberry wine! The next day, all of them complained they had diarrhea. I responded, "We don't drink Manischewitz by the bottle!" I don't remember one full bottle being consumed at a Seder, let alone six.

Jackie Mason says gentile homes have no cockroaches because there is no food. How much gin can a cockroach drink?

Later, a new tradition started with rotating Passovers with my friend Ed with various friends and family, mostly his, rotating in and out. The part formerly played by Grandma was now being played by his sister Nancy. An entire treatise could be devoted to stories of Nancy's idiosyncrasies. I like Nancy, but then again, I am not related to her.

Our services were quick but covered all the important parts, and we always enjoyed ourselves. Last year, Ed moved to Palms Springs. Take all the overly tanned, wrinkled up Jews in Boca, transform them into overly-tanned, wrinkled up Gays, remove the humidity, and you have Palm Springs. He is going to kill me for that one. I couldn't help myself.

So, now I needed a new tradition. Do I host? Do I participate in the synagogue Seder-match (a system I created ten years ago that the Rabbi scoffed at but is still operational). But, I also longed for a more traditional Passover Seder rather than the abbreviated edition.

Then I received an invitation from my good friend, Allan. I accepted. He is one of my favorite people, and I knew it would be a good and traditional Passover Seder.

Not only was the service perfect, the company and the food were just as wonderful. But, the best part of all was that for perhaps the last time in my life, I was the youngest at the table, and I *wasn't* at a nursing home. I couldn't believe it. That meant I would get to read the four questions and open the door for Elijah.

I never felt so young and beautiful in my life! Thank you, Allan.

Happy Passover, Everyone!

THE GREAT RADISH INCIDENT OF 1974

Now that spring is here, aaaaa ...... choooooooo!

Give me a second.

I have to share something. When I sneeze, the windows rattle, car alarms go off, and the United States Geological Survey alerts the public. I don't sneeze once. I sneeze at least a dozen times. There are times when I check my Kleenex for gray matter. I once gave myself a concussion during a sneezing fit; seriously I had to go for a cat scan. They didn't find anything. Laugh amongst yourselves.

Here is the strange part: If I scream goddammit or even better, mumble it when I stub my toe, Esmeralda immediately stops what she is doing and hides under the bed. If I sneeze, she just looks at me. Maybe she doesn't care because she sneezes as much as I do, which as you know is why she got the name Esmeralda. I still check for unicorns and Mother Goose every time she sneezes. Only the Gays will get that one.

Where was I? Oh yes, spring.

Who knew that this lifelong apartment dweller would have a knack for landscape design? Or so, my neighbors tell me. I have put in a walkway on either side of my house and had a truckload of mulch delivered, which I had to share with my neighbors, for how much shit can one man shovel — apparently, a truckload. I have planted bushes and flowers, color coordinated my pots of various and lovely designs, made a brick platform for my grill, seeded and watered my lawn, and created a pebble garden around my deck.

I need an intervention because every time I see a garden shop, I have to stop and shop!

Now, the best part is that for the first time since Betty Ford was found passed out under a sofa in the Blue Room, I can grow my own vegetables and make Michelle Obama proud as I fight Gay Jewish Obesity. If you didn't know, Gay Jewish Obesity is quite the epidemic. Whitefish salad can take its toll on a girl's figure.

Due to a large groundhog population in my mobile home community, we are advised to grow vegetables on our decks with

243

screens around them or the ground hogs will be eating fresh tossed salads daily and farting nightly.

I did make one mistake, telling a member of my family that I had planted vegetables in my deck garden. If there is one thing my family loves to do it is remind you of every mistake you made from the time you pooped into your first Pampers to the second before the conversation started.

I was constantly reminded of how when I was five years old, I dented all my Matchbox cars, so they would look as if they had been in the Demolition Derby. Apparently, I am the reason we are not millionaires because the twenty or so cars I damaged would have been worth a fortune someday. For the record, I go to automotive swap meets all the time, and the most you will get for a Matchbox car is $15. So, considering I damaged maybe twenty cars, I owe my family $300.

Funny thing about my family. When I would point out their financial mistakes, they would get angry. For example, my mother used my penny collection to pay the newspaper boy when I was out playing football. There were over three-hundred coins in that collection. I had an Indian Head Penny that today is worth about $1,600. Somewhere there is a former newspaper boy driving a Cadillac on my dime … I mean penny. But God forbid, I ever reminded her of that. Somehow, I was portrayed as the bad guy for bringing it up.

So, I told my brother about my string beans and tomatoes that finally sprang up for spring, and being the Stern that he is, he asked if I was growing radishes. Leave it to my only living relative to remind me of the Great Radish Incident of 1974.

Oh my God.

Here is what happened. While my family was not known for having the best landscaped lawn. OK, that is putting it mildly. Our yard was designed by Lilly Munster, and my mother's indoor houseplants were from the Morticia Addams collection. For a couple of summers, we attempted gardening. I remember one snotty neighbor, obviously a gentile because he had one of those huge gardens, and the Goyim are really good at gardening (remember, God kicked us out of the garden to go to medical school — or Boca, I forget which), saying, "Oh look at your Victory Garden."

Anyway, we grew green peppers, which I hate, cherry tomatoes, which my brother would eat off the vine every time one ripened, and radishes. One day, while watering the garden, I decided that the radishes were too close together, so I transplanted them. I wanted them to be spaced properly. This might be when my OCD started. I had them perfectly spaced, but unfortunately, they died. Who knew you couldn't transplant radishes.

Well, you'd have thought I took the magic beans and bought a donkey or was it the other way around?

The entire family was on my case because we had no radishes. Radishes! Who the fuck needs radishes? They were goddamn radishes! I was eleven years old. Eleven-year-olds do stupid things, and in my case, try on his mother's wedding dress, too. Come to think of it, if I ever get to use a time machine, I am going back to the summer of 1974 and transplant the radishes again, but this time while wearing her wedding dress. Then at least it will be worth mentioning for the next thirty-eight years!

When you think about it, I went from football practice to my secret drag show? I just got a brilliant idea — Drag Football!

Back to the current story ...

One thing I always heard was, "You can dish it out, but you can't take it." For the record, no one in my family could take it, and I had to take it every time anyone mentioned gardening or a salad. When going out to eat with anyone in my family, I prayed there would be no radishes on the salad.

I decided at that point after the Great Radish Incident of 1974 never to attempt gardening in the presence of relatives again.

While we are pointing out gardening disasters, let me relay one from Dutch Village the summer my brother and I lived together. We had a small patch of grass behind our apartment that abutted the Monastery of the Poor Clares. Did you know they take a vow of silence and only talk for twenty minutes a year? I couldn't do that for an hour.

My brother decided to grow tomatoes. Our neighbor had planted elephant ears in her plot. I don't know who went crazy with the fertilizer, but somehow the elephant ears were actually the size of elephant ears, and my brother's tomato plants grew to more than seven feet tall! The tomatoes were the size of soccer balls. Every night I had a dream like the episode of *Lost in Space* when they landed on the planet where the plants had feelings and would scream if you picked an apple or a flower. I wouldn't go out the back door for fear of being attacked by either the elephant ears or one of my brother's steroid-laden tomato plants.

I think I did eat one of the tomatoes, which may explain why I was six-three at the beginning of that summer and two inches taller at the end, and I was twenty three years old at the time!

Of course, I have never mentioned the gargantuan tomatoes to my brother since then because I didn't see a reason to dwell on the past ... until now.

And for the record, I still love my brother, and I did not plant radishes. After all, I don't have time to transplant them into neat little rows perfectly spaced apart, and I know if I planted them, for some reason that only my therapist can explain, I would.

I CANNOT RUN IN FLATS

Have you ever watched a baby learning how to walk? They run first. Actually, they run, then fall, then get up, then run. It is easier to balance yourself when you are moving quickly, which babies figure out immediately.

Have you ever watched a man try to walk in heels for the first time? They go slowly. The take a step, they whine, take another step, they whine. Why does it take them so long to realize running in heels is much easier than walking in them? They call them high heel races for a reason! A race is a blast. A high heel walk would be annoying with all that whining — like watching a bunch of very slow cats.

You heard it here first. Walk quickly in your heels, and you will be ever so graceful, which brings me to the following.

In my ongoing quest to do crazy shit before I turn fifty, I decided to do one of those extreme obstacle courses that have become popular in the last few years. As a matter of fact, they are so popular that you need to sign up for one at least six months in advance.

A few of my Gay friends in other parts of the country have completed these, and they said they were a blast. Everyone was muddy and shirtless and looking all smoky and hot. However, I couldn't get one Gay friend around here to do one with me; they wouldn't even come and watch.

As I searched for an extreme obstacle course with any open slots, I came across a new one called Hero Rush, benefitting fallen firefighters. They had openings, so I signed up as a VIP (you get better parking), competing in the Men45+ category. The race was to take place on April 28, so I figured the temperature would be hot enough for good eye candy while I lay flat on my back after falling off a wall or something.

The day was approaching, and the weather was not looking too good. At the beginning of the week, they were calling for temperatures in the sixties, by the end, in the fifties, and the day of, cloudy and in the forties. Well, that discourage me from falling on my back and watching the hotties fly by.

With this being the first of the first for this particular event, I figured they would have some kinks to work out, but I decided to go with the flow. I arrived an hour early as instructed, and they had postponed the first wave as only ten people showed up, so they combined it with our wave (they call each group a wave), and at 9:00 am, the bell rang and we were off. It was actually a 911 call since this course was designed by insane firefighters, who moonlighted as serial killers.

The first obstacle was a flight of stairs with no railing then you grabbed onto and slid down a pole. I have done a lot of things with poles over the years, but I never slid down one. Once you did that and crossed a black rubber strip, your time began. All of us wore chips like runaway dogs, so our owners could find us, but for the record, even Esmeralda is not crazy enough to try something like this.

There were obstacles that involved hopping over walls, crawling through smoky mazes in the dark, dragging dummies through tunnels and pulling hoses over walls. Photographers were supposed to be stationed at each of the nineteen obstacles, but I found out later there were only six photographers. A girl needs her photo op. Jeez.

What I did not realize was the amount of running involved — and not on pavement, but through woods and fields and on rutted pathways. A third of the way in, I twisted my ankle.

Honey, I just can't run in flats!

Being the Neanderthal that I am, I just put some dirt on it and walked it off. The only problem I had was the zip line. Apparently, they had a weight limit and did not tell anyone. You can bet that whenever there is a weight limit, I am over it. I grabbed onto the zip line, and down I went — straight down! I didn't even zip! I thought, "That can't be good."

Then I twisted my ankle again. I put more dirt on it and walked it off.

Toward the end, you first wade waist-deep in a pool of green muck that is supposed to be like hazardous waste. Since when do firefighters wade through waist-deep green muck?

The last stunt was wading through ice cold water (did I tell you it was forty degrees outside) while a bunch of kids spray fire hoses on you. Do you know how much pressure comes out of a fire hose? I went under, and when I came up, my hair was a mess. I didn't even want to know how my face looked. I did take a mental picture of every one of those brats (a Sephardic curse would be in their futures).

Once extricated from the pool, you run some more then hop over three lines of fire — real fire, but you are soaking wet and freezing, so catching on fire would have been the least of my problems.

I finally saw a photographer at the end.

I actually enjoyed it, and believe it or not, would do another one, but next time in July!

After changing in the men's tent alongside a rather attractive Jewish straight man in his thirties who was behind me the whole time and who was a delightful conversationalist — so my demographic, I walked the grounds and went to the food pavilion. I ordered two hot dogs. I figured no one knew me here, so who was going to look down on my plate. It was 10:30 am.

While scarfing down my post-obstacle treat with a root beer, I heard the following from two guys at another table who had just finished the race:

"After Cobalt, we went to Nellie's for a drink, but no one was there."

"Were you able to get the Lady Ga Ga tickets?"

I found my Gays!

I walked over and introduced myself and noted that we may be the only three members of the family there.

Now that I had found my Gays and one straight Jewish man, all I needed was a middle-aged yenta, and my audience would have been complete!

Later that day, I found out the first place finisher in the race was a nice Jewish boy in his twenties. That makes three famous Jewish athletes.

In case you were wondering, or if you weren't, I am going to tell you anyway. My score was #1 in the Men45+ at Hero Rush (I think I was the only one over 45, but that is just between us girls). Official Finish: 00:48:03.4; Overall: 17; Men: 16; M45+: 1.

Not bad for an *alta cocker* Gay Jew living in a trailer park.

I didn't sprain my ankle. It turned out I broke it.

But, battle scars are hot.

WORLD'S GREATEST CHEST MODEL

No one, and I mean no one, has tried harder to get his picture in any publication more than I have, yet, I never appear anywhere. I am tempted to get a billboard that says, "Appearing Nightly in a Trailer Park in Jessup, the One, the Only ..."

I am beginning to feel like Jeannie. She could not be photographed, so a mannequin stood in for her when she married Major Anthony Nelson.

There are those people whose pictures appear all the time in the newspaper, magazines, local flyers, etc. No matter where they go, a photographer is always present. We have a local rag called *MW* (*Metropolitan Weekly*). Every week, they have a spread of pictures showing who was at this A-list event and that A-list event — with everyone dressed in tuxes and holding cocktails. Every week, I see the same goddamn faces. I can actually document how people have aged since I moved to the area fifteen years ago. Some, not so well. There is one person who has had a sex change, and I have watched the transformation totally in the pages of *MW*.

Since I don't go to or get invited to A-list events, I have no chance in hell of appearing in *MW*'s weekly spread.

Every year after Capital Pride, they have spreads in *MW*'s print and online versions of every picture they took during the parade and at the festival. Since moving here, I have participated in the Pride Parade on a float six times, and I walked between two antique cars handing out beads two years ago. I participated in the festival in one way or another for the first twelve years I lived here. Photographers would come around and take my picture, but get this: whatever pictures were taken of me were never posted or published!

No pictures of our entire Straight Eights Car Club contingent were published! I take full responsibility. Had I not participated in the parade ...

When I was in my twenties, I was constantly told I should be a model. I never pursued modeling because my portfolio would have been all blank pages. Maybe I could have been a ghost model?

My brother appears in the newspaper all the time in ads and in spreads about his business.

I must confess that I did appear in the newspaper a long, long time ago in a land far, far away. The summer of 1969, a reporter and photographer from *The Daily Press*, both of whom were friends of my mother's, came to our house to take pictures of me and interview my mother about my beginning first grade that fall. I appeared in a two-page spread with a girl who was also in my class. The first day of school, Mrs. Diggs (the greatest first grade teacher of all time) put the newspaper spreads on the bulletin board for everyone to see. I was so proud.

But, my mother must have made a deal with the devil because that would be the last time anyone would publish my picture.

Once when appearing in a musical revue, a photographer and reporter were sent to cover the rehearsals. The director decided that the three of us who were performing "Money" from *Cabaret* should be the subject of the photo spread. There I stood with these two women on either side of me. All of us were in long sleeve black tops with gold coins sewn onto our costumes. I was finally going to appear in the newspaper.

I was so excited when someone called to tell me that the article and picture were published the following day. I immediately opened my paper, and what did I see? The two women who were in the number with me; their faces were in front of a black backdrop with coins sewn onto the fabric. That backdrop was my chest. My head was cropped from the picture. Seriously?!?

I was so mad because those two women were the most annoying prima donnas I had ever met.

Whom does a Jew have to blow around here to get one goddamn picture in the newspaper?

A few years after I moved to Washington, DC, I was on the board of Bet Mishpachah, and with my good friend, Ellen, we planned the twenty-fifth anniversary celebration of the synagogue. A reporter and photographer from the *Washington Blade*, a gay newspaper, came to the event to interview us. They took quite a few pictures. The following week, the article was published with one picture of everyone doing the "Electric Slide." I was completely cropped out from the left side of the picture. Seriously?!?

As I have mentioned, I participated in the Hero Rush obstacle course benefitting fallen firefighters. Before the race, I bought a picture package from a professional sports photography company. I figured that since the pictures were for personal use and not publication, I would have a chance to have some photographs to share after the event. Five days after I took first place in Men 45+ (I cannot stop mentioning that), I was supposed to get an email telling me my package was ready for download.

On the Hero Rush Facebook page, I managed to find three pictures of me that random people had taken. I immediately downloaded them even though I looked terrible in all of them.

Five days went by, and I heard nothing. Two weeks later, I received the following email:

"Hi, what is your full name and bib number? We cannot seem to locate any pictures of you?"

My response:

"Look for the two snotty women running in front of a sweaty dark green backdrop. That backdrop would be my chest."

I clearly should have been a chest model.

HI, I'M FORTY-NINE AND BUTCH!

They say when a man gets older his testosterone level goes down, while for a woman, testosterone levels go up. That is why Grandpa has titties and Grandma has a beard. If they live long enough, they can shop in the same department. You can't afford a sex change operation? Wait a decade or two.

This also means that the fems become even more fey with age. Can you imagine? Ironically, all those butch lesbians get even more manly with age. What is scarier is that the bears end up with furry boobs, which brings us back to my Aunt Paula. Or, maybe we should just leave that one alone.

As I approach a certain mid-century milestone, I have noticed certain changes. The biggest change is that I make sure everyone knows how old I am, and I don't know why.

"How does this shirt look on me? I'm forty-nine years old." "You can't touch your toes? I can, and I'm forty-nine years old." "I'll take a pound of the kosher bologna and a half pound of macaroni salad. I'm forty-nine years old."

Now, I have always said that if a day went by that someone didn't mention my height that would be the day I died. I have yet to go for twenty-four hours without hearing anything similar to, or actually, the following:

"If someone Milton's size were to attack you, what would you do?"

"Wow, your head just missed the door frame."

And my favorite every time I get into a car: "That seat goes back further." My reply is always, "It is back all the way."

So, it isn't enough that I am a freak, I have this incredible need to point out that I am also an old freak. As I said, I cannot help but tell everyone my age. I am like Marie Osmond on *Dancing with the Stars*, a show, by the way, I hate. Every night, she would tell Tom Bergeron, "I am forty-eight." Finally, she said, "As a woman my age ..." and he interrupted, "You are seventy-three, right?" Even he was sick of it.

Like Tom Bergeron, I am sick of hearing myself mention my age. Sometimes, I feel as if I am on the outside observing myself and wondering who is this annoying age-obsessed moron?

Have you ever found yourself doing something annoying repeatedly, and you don't know why? Maybe all of us have a little bit of a split personality.

As I grow older, I am also obsessed with my aging body and especially my dropping testosterone levels. I read somewhere that peanut butter is good for maintaining good testosterone, which is why I can usually be found standing in front of the cupboard with an open jar of Skippy's and a soup spoon.

However, there are certain things you cannot stop. For example, my ass is a full three inches lower and much more jiggly than it was twenty years ago. If I go jogging, I think someone is tapping me on the shoulder, and I look as if I am smuggling sofa cushions. I have always had a big ass, and while it has been a curse at times, the blessing is that when I do turn eighty (and believe me, you will know when I turn eighty), my pants will still have a good shelf upon which to rest.

While women complain about falling boobs, men also experience the effects of gravity. Our balls drop. If I walk across a room naked, I get rug burns on my scrotum.

Then, there is the sex drive. That drops, too. The first sign that your sex drive has diminished is when you cannot answer the following question: "When was the last time you jerked off?" If you have to think about your masturbation schedule ...

In your teens, the answer was always within an hour. In your twenties, the answer was usually no more than twelve hours. In your thirties, a day, maybe two. In your late forties, you can't remember.

And although masturbation is good for prostate health, you still don't have the energy — or the time — to do something for your own well being.

While all the above has happened to me, I am experiencing a strange phenomenon since moving into my mobile home.

I got rid of all my old drag wear, except for one pair of stilettos and Nana's pearls (one never gives away the pearls). In addition, I now do a lot of physical and manly things.

Even though I have been a life-long fitness nut, in the past year, I have taken my physical activities to a whole new level. First, there was Krav Maga, which now I am so obsessed with that if I miss a class, I do everything possible to make it up, even driving thirty miles to the sister facility to take a Sunday class. While I had no intention of completing the six-hour belt testing when I first signed up, now I am training to test to the next level in September. If I am partnered with a young guy in class who is out of breath while I am still going strong, I always ask how old he is then tell him how old I am. I never miss an opportunity to say, "I am forty-nine years old, and I can do this. What is your problem?"

I competed in one of those extreme obstacle courses where I sprained and broke my ankle, and now I have signed up for another one. "She's a cool one; she's returning to the scene of the crime," said Ethel Mertz. The best part of these obstacle courses is that I get to compete in the Men 45+ category, which gives me another opportunity to tell everyone my age from the people assigning bibs and chips, to the woman with the walkie-talkie monitoring the race, to whoever is standing next to me at the starting line. None of them give a shit, but that doesn't stop me.

Next year, I will be like Sally O'Malley on *SNL* — "I'm fifty! I can kick and stretch and kick again. I'm fifty!"

This past week, I was asked to participate in an experimental boot camp at my gym. Six people were asked, and they signed up, but only three of us showed up for the class. Two women in their thirties and I. You guessed it. I made sure they all knew how old I was. "Hi, I'm Milton. I'm forty-nine."

Well, the class began with two trainers and three students. We did all this kettle ball stuff, and plank push-ups, and climbing stairs, and barbell push-ups with clean and jerks, and other things I never saw before. I was enjoying being pushed to my limits and on the verge of cardiac arrest, but I whined more than a grounded teenager.

After thirty minutes, they declared the class over. I said, "That's all you got?"

Me and my big mouth. The trainer, who couldn't get over how I could whine for thirty minutes then ask for more, pushed me and pushed me. Straight guys may love me, but they like to try to break me, too!

I finally said, "I'm doing the best I can; I'm almost fifty. I'm just an old drag queen trying to maintain his figure."

He said, "Who cares! Fifteen more!"

I did fifteen more. I was sweating so much he called me a puddle. He also congratulated me.

Afterward, I asked when the next class would be. He thought I was nuts but glad I wanted to come back.

I went home, took a shower in Irish Spring, put on some Old Spice, and drank a Pabst Blue Ribbon while sitting on my porch with my hound dog, Esmeralda.

The question though is when did I become so damn butch?

Is this mobile home emitting testosterone from the steel frame? Is my AMC station wagon not just a lesbian magnet but a lesbian maker? And, when did I buy a pack of wife beaters?

I think I need to go dress shopping. Any takers?

AN UNEXPECTED GOODBYE

Esmeralda's life was never an easy one — until she met me of course. She spent the first eight years in a cage being bred as much as three times a year in a puppy mill. Then, she ended up in a hording situation with aggressive dogs and an obese, chain smoking white woman with mental problems. Then, she was adopted by the Chatty Giant (guess who that is?), who thought it would be cool to move from a luxury apartment to a trailer park. Well, the last two years weren't so bad, were they?

One morning while walking and looking for just the right spot to pee, Esmeralda collapsed. She wouldn't get up and was breathing heavily. I thought she was having a heart attack. After a few minutes, she decided to get up and finish the walk. For the rest of the morning, everything seemed fine.

After lunch, she collapsed again and wouldn't get up, so I carried her back to the house and called the veterinarian.

Unfortunately, her regular doctor was not in, so the doctor on duty examined her and said everything seemed fine, so it must be her back. I argued and said she had developed a cough, and it looked like congestive heart failure. All my dogs have lived to old age, so I have seen all the illnesses and ailments associated with old dogs.

The doctor wouldn't hear of it, and she put her on Prednisone.

After five days, Esmeralda was miserable. She couldn't catch her breath, and she was getting bloated.

On Tuesday, July 3, I came home from work early, and this time, she wouldn't walk at all. I called Mrs. M to come over because I wanted to be sure I was not imagining her symptoms. As soon as she arrived, she confirmed that Esmeralda was not doing well even though she was fine during her two times outside. Then Esmeralda tried to stand up but couldn't and sort of flopped around the room. She let out a scream and pooped all over herself. I dreaded the worst.

I cleaned her up the best I could and drove her to the Baltimore Emergency Animal Hospital.

They were very good and took her back immediately. The veterinarian came out and said they put her in an oxygen crate. I immediately protested and told them she would scream if put in a cage, but they assured me there were no bars. It was a Plexiglas enclosure, and Esmeralda had nested immediately. She then offered to let me come back and see her.

Esmeralda didn't even react when I came back. She was just so uncomfortable and trying to catch her breath.

The doctor confirmed what I said all along. She was experiencing congestive heart failure. I asked if the Prednisone made it worse, and she said yes.

I was advised to go home and call back in a few hours to see if there was any improvement. Reluctantly, I did. For the first time, I was alone in the house.

At around 10:00 pm, I called back. There was no improvement, and they wanted to keep her overnight.

I prepared for bed, confused as to what to do, since I was used to walking Esmeralda first.

At 10:45 pm, the doctor called me and said she wanted to try another treatment, but I told her to wait, and I would be down in fifteen minutes.

I was dressed and in the car in five minutes, and yes, my hair was done, and my lipstick was on. I may have been distraught, but I was still me!

They immediately took me back, and Esmeralda looked worse. She didn't even react to my arrival. I asked if she was on a medication that was making her drowsy, but she wasn't. She was still struggling to breathe.

I then asked the doctor what the prognosis was. I was told that if she pulled out of this, she would no longer be able to walk outside on hot days. Her mobility would be limited, and she might have nine more months, but probably less. If the temperature was higher than seventy degrees, I would need to carry her outside, put her on the grass, and after she did her business, carry her back inside. She would also be on medication for the rest of her short life. In addition, since this had gone on for so long, her heart was becoming more damaged and weak with each passing hour. The doctor was also disappointed in the lack of any improvement in her condition. Esmeralda was not responding. She was clearly suffering.

The entire time I was petting her and the doctor was talking, Esmeralda had no emotional reaction. The look on her face said it all.

I told the doctor that I am a firm believer that if a dog cannot run, jump and play, she does not have a dog's life. I also am not one to over medicate or put a dog through painful and miserable treatments just to assuage my own guilt or prolong the inevitable and avoid a tough decision. I also know that I would not want a life where I had to be carried everywhere and could not go outside for more than five minutes.

I was the one who had to ask my mother if she wanted a DNR. No one else in my family could handle it. I also have a DNR.

For the second time in my life, I had to make a decision no one should have to make alone. I decided to put Esmeralda out of her misery. The doctor didn't even argue, and I could tell from her body language and speech that she agreed I was making the right decision.

They had me sign the papers and pay the bill, including the cremation arrangements. I guess it is easier to get money from someone who isn't hysterically crying.

Then, they carried Esmeralda into the room. She just lay there. No reaction. She was so uncomfortable and struggling so hard to breathe.

Before giving her the second shot, the doctor said to her, "I'm sorry." I felt more sorry for the doctor than for Esmeralda. My poor baby's heart was so weak that it took much longer than it did for Serena, two and half years earlier, for the medicine to do the deed.

Then, it was over.

I stayed with her for a few minutes, arranged for her to be picked up by the cremation company then left the room.

There were people in the waiting room who knew what just happened in that other room, so I avoided their eyes. While I enjoy being the center of attention and can be a drama queen when appropriate, I do not like pity. I left quickly, got into my car, and cried hysterically for ten minutes.

We had two years and two months together. Two crazy years while I tried my best to show a rescue beagle, I named Esmeralda because she sneezed, that humans can be nice and life can be good outside of a cage.

I never could convince her that window treatments are not the enemy or wall-to-wall carpet is not a lawn.

Ironically, it was on the anniversary of Esmeralda's first attempt to run away that she left me for good.

Who knew a trailer could be so quiet and lonely.

WHAT HAVE I LEARNED

Well, it has been a year since I put a deposit down on my first home with wheels! A couple of months later, I took possession of that home on wheels. After twenty-six years of living with people on the other side of my walls, I finally had four walls of my own, which were delivered on wheels.

I am now a proud member of the Poor Gay Jewish Trash or PGJT contingent, but after a year, I wish to remove one of my letters — the letter P. I am now Gay Jewish Trash or GJT. This brings us to our first lesson.

As an apartment dweller, I was paying an enormous amount of money for a small space and absorbing other people's marital problems. As a mobile home owner, I pay a small amount of money for almost double the space (if you include my yard and shed), and other people's marital problems are no longer mine, unless I want them to be.

I have discovered that trailer park, or shall I say mobile home people, are friendly and don't put on airs as Miss Daisy would say. They offer to let you borrow things, and they share. They also get angry if they offer you their ladders, and you go buy one instead. "Why did you buy one? You could have borrowed mine."

I have also discovered there are still a few racists left in the world. For example when Miss Linda had her deck replaced, she stated, "I tried to get those Vietnamese to put in the ramp for free, but you know how they are with money. I had already Jewed them down to $6,000 as it was, and now I have to deal with these Mexicans in and out of my house all day." Years ago, I would have said something, but I felt a giggle coming on at the absurdity of her remarks, and immediately went into my home and laughed. I didn't think people like that still existed. Ironically, she hired the man who did her nails to do her deck. I think she was most upset that it was acrylic with French tips.

Most dogs in a mobile home park are male, and the preferred breed is Bijon Frise. Seriously, we have five of them, and two are named Rocky! Esmeralda was the only girl out walking the streets and got all the attention.

Your neighbors will memorize the cars of every man who visits your house, so if you plan on being a slut, be proud or take this opportunity to tone down your extracurricular activities. Better yet, become a traveler rather than a host. Besides, if you host, you will inevitably get the following phone call, "Hi. I think I'm lost. I just pulled into a trailer park."

If a guy you just met says, "You live in a mobile home? I have always wanted to own one." Don't go out with him. He is treating you like Yoko Ono. Why did the Gay man date Yoko One? To see the apartment, of course. Once he sees your pre-manufactured walls, you will never hear from him again. You can trick with him, but don't date him.

Dogs love trailers. OK, not at first. Mine ran away the first time she saw it. "I'm not living in that bloody hovel," she said as she leapt out the back door. Beagles are British. But, after a week, she grew to like living in a home. She could finally sleep through the night without hearing, "Go ahead; hit me; I dare you; hit me; go ahead <THUMP>."

What they do like more than anything is being able to sit outside while you wax your car or do yard work. Beagles love to bake in the sun, and from what I have witnessed, Bijon Frise love the sun as well.

Carrying groceries from your car, which is parked in your own driveway, into your house is so much easier than carrying them through two security doors and a two-block long hallway, while you say hello to people who avert their eyes.

The men who go to the gym at 5:00 am in a city that allows mobile homes are more manly than those who go to a swank gym in the city at that hour, but then again, who doesn't love rough trade?

Mobile homes emit testosterone, and you will be more butch.

Mobile home communities are usually located off the beaten path, so running errands during rush hour does not require a helicopter rental.

As a home-owner, you will find that you have a flair for landscaping or interior decorating, or any number of home-owner skills you couldn't tap into while renting other people's spaces. You will also find yourself in a garden shop more often than you ever expected. As a matter of fact, even when you go into Walmart or Weis, you will stop when you see a rack of house plants or bushes or flowers and say to yourself, "I wonder how these will look on my deck?"

You will no longer walk around naked in your home with the blinds open … unless you want.

If you can let go of any preconceived notions you have about owning a mobile home, you will discover how buying a brand new home does not mean being house poor for ten years.

The most important thing I learned is that I can truly be happy living as a Gay Jew in a Trailer Park, and I wish I had done this twenty years ago.

HAVE YOUR HEARD THE ONE ABOUT THE GAY JEW IN THE TRAILER PARK?

For a year, I have been wracking my brain trying to come up with a joke or a punch line. For a guy who is usually quick with a joke or witticism, this one stumped me, and I have lived the life!

So here goes:

Have you heard the one about the Gay Jew in the Trailer Park?

After moving in, his dog tried to run away, he discovered his inner landscaper, and he spent a lot of time explaining what a *Mezuzah* was to his neighbors.

MILTON STERN

Milton Stern actually lives in a mobile home community in Jessup, Maryland. An author of biographies, novels and short stories, a humorist and a crazy magnet, he is available for public appearances or consultations for trailer park landscaping. Contact him at miltonstern@miltonstern.com or on Facebook.

aring any underwear. "Excuse me," I said, having a hard time loc
inded by that bulge in his crotch. "but don't I know you?" "Mayb
nd of t

with Ray

loser?

id. "Lik

ce body

lly, he l

up to t

staking

, I coul

ood raci

ng with

we go c

ill see u

ed?" he

rivacy.

hard. I

k, traci

ed it, ha

with my

bbing, I

about

God,

in?"

s stro

e on

I ev

any i

ie sa

ery le

ne sv

e in

behi

in p

vent

grab

t, so

bing

n cor

ie sound of unzipping filled the small space. I don't know who's

, but before I knew it, I had his rod in my hand, and mine was in h

it to do?" he asked, his tone challenging. I knew exactly, and sank